Managing Performing Living

W0009561

Fredmund Malik

Managing
Performing
Living

Effective Management for a New Era

Translation, Coordination, and Review
Peter Franklin and Sebastian Hetzler

Campus Verlag
Frankfurt / New York

Bibliographic information published by the Deutsche Nationalbibliothek:
The Deutsche Nationalbibliothek lists this publication in the Deutsche Nationalbiblio-
grafie; detailed bibliografic data is available in the internet at http:/dnb.d-nb.de.
ISBN 978-3-593-38278-4

Cover design: Gundula Hißmann and Andreas Heilmann, Hamburg
Typesetting: Publikations Atelier, Dreieich
Printing: Druckhaus "Thomas Müntzer", Bad Langensalza
Printed in Germany

www.campus.de

Contents

Part II
The Principles of Effective Management 63

Preface to the English Edition

On its publication in March 2000, the German edition of *Managing Performing Living* attracted great interest and has continued to do so ever since. People obviously find it useful that – and how – this book describes what all managers require always and everywhere in their capacity as managers. I have been particularly pleased about the numerous positive reactions from the not-for-profit area, from public service, the education and health services, and numerous other non-profit organizations.

The publication of the English edition offers the opportunity to make some additional remarks and clarifications. These clarifications refer to obviously prevalent misunderstandings on the topic of management, which have emerged in a small number of reviews and letters I have received.

One reviewer was of the opinion that the "new era" mentioned in the sub-title receives too little attention in the book – and with it the much-discussed "New Economy" and the new types of company arising in it which, it is believed, require completely new and different management. I consider this opinion to be a misconception and not just since – in the wake of the first bankruptcies of "New Economy" firms – the unshakable truths of business and management have asserted themselves. If this has demonstrated one thing in all clarity, then it is that these companies need exactly what I deal with in this book: correct, competent and effective management – much more so than those companies which are somewhat condescendingly assigned to the "Old Economy" – more often than necessary as a result of a lack of knowledge about the business world. Rarely has something been so universally so misjudged as what is known as the "New Economy". It would be easy to avoid: a minimum knowledge of economic history and a minimum of management expertise would suffice.

My reservations about the romantic ideas and the alleged blessings of the "New Economy" do not mean that I attach no importance to change.

On the contrary. In my book about corporate governance[1], I described in a long chapter on the "great transformation" the changes in progress and their probable significance. They have been recognizable for a long time, at any rate since the beginning of the nineties. I have discussed the problems and the opportunities connected to them with thousands of managers in seminars. As a result of my many years of work on the systems sciences and cybernetics, and on the phenomena of complexity, self-organization, information and communication, I have been fully aware of the significance of the new technologies. It is precisely from cybernetics that the new technologies arose. That this is unknown to most people who try to impress others with the term "cyber" is one of the countless ironies of history.

If one knows one's way around these areas a little, it quickly becomes clear what demands are to be placed on management in the "Cyber Age". This applies firstly to the management of the technologies themselves. That is to say, to their development and use. But, in particular, it applies to the management of organizations which use the information and communication technologies or whose products these technologies are, and it applies to the management of the people who have to work with them. High tech requires an abundant amount of management precision; and what is needed least of all are romantically sentimental or even quite simply naïve ideas, such as unfortunately prevail in much of the literature and in many training seminars. At least half – and probably many more – of the failed "New Economy" companies failed because of unprofessional, sometimes dreadful management.

But high tech and e-business are by no means the most important aspects of the "new era" although most people see it that way. The subject of this book is of greatest significance for the truly constitutive elements of the "new era" – knowledge work and the knowledge worker – that is, for all those people for whom knowledge is their main raw material and who for this reason in reality cannot be managed in any reasonable sense but who must manage themselves. This goes for people within organizations, but also for those who have to cooperate from the outside with organizations. For knowledge workers, management is – as I show in this book – not only decisive for success but for existence.

But the "new era" of the subtitle possesses a second meaning. I believe there is a good chance that we are moving towards an era in which one of

---

1   *Die Neue Corporate Governance – Richtiges Top-Management – Wirksame Unternehmensaufsicht*, Frankfurt 1997, third edition 2002.

the key thoughts of the book – namely professionalism in management – will have the same status as in any other profession – an era in which management knowledge and management practice are relatively free of fads, charlatanism, empty promises, misunderstandings, false doctrines, and extreme stupidity. Quite rightly, we expect from professionals such as doctors, lawyers, auditors, judges, public prosecutors, teachers, and professors professional competence and responsibility. So why not from managers?

It is scarcely imaginable, at any rate it is not desirable, that in a modern society the management of its institutions, their design, control and development should be conducted with less seriousness, soundness, and conscientiousness than has long been taken for granted in other professions and functions of society. This book is intended to accelerate this process and to contribute to the creation of a situation in which nonsense can be revealed as such and is more difficult to propagate.

It is occasionally said that the third part of the title of the book – *Living* – receives too little attention in the book itself. In a certain way, this is correct. In explicit terms, I have written less about this word than its position in the title would suggest. Implicitly, however, the whole book refers to *Living*. Summarized in one sentence, my opinion is that those who by and large keep to the suggestions made in this book have a good chance not only of being an effective manager but also of having a life in addition to their occupation – perhaps precisely because of success in their occupation. The art of reconciling working and living in a sensible fashion is less widespread than is desirable. Instead, the misconception is all the more rife that the one must be sacrificed for the other, that working and living are irreconcilably contradictory, and that it is therefore necessary to decide in favor of one of the two. It is possible to learn precisely from effective people that this is not correct.

Readers familiar with the work of Peter F. Drucker will recognize the influence which, through his books and through a few personal encounters, Drucker has exerted on my thinking about management, and a number of people have detected a reordering and further development of Drucker's insights in my book. Greater praise is hardly possible. After more than 30 years of working on management my opinions naturally result from many sources. However, one of the most decisive is, without doubt, Drucker and I am proud to have a profound knowledge of his work. His contribution to management – in a widely understood sense –

cannot be overestimated. Wherever I have the opportunity – in seminars, lectures, and in my writings – I have pointed out to managers for years, how fruitful it is to read Drucker. How important such advice is I experience practically every day, because far too few have studied him sufficiently.

There are a number of others to mention: for example, Hans Ulrich and Stafford Beer, to mention only two to whom I owe much, and on whose work I have built. In contrast to the widespread fashion in management literature of continually reinventing the wheel, I consider it more important, whenever possible, to build on and extend what has already been achieved. I believe that knowledge can progress and that this can happen cumulatively. It is true that this is disputed in philosophy and in some of the social sciences of a particular school of thought which believes it to be better always to start at the beginning again. I do not think much of this approach. As far as possible, I have therefore adopted existing fruitful findings and insights. It is precisely there that I see a contribution to the progress of management and to the establishment of standards for the managerial profession – which incidentally has absolutely nothing to do with its standardization, as one reader insinuated.

Fredmund Malik

St. Gallen, New Year's Day 2003

Foreword and Introduction

This book answers the question of what people should know and be able to do if they wish to be *effective* and *successful*, in their *profession* primarily, but also in their *lives*, as *managers* as well as *specialists*. This book is the "equipment" required by *every* person in an organization *always* and *everywhere*. It is a book about the *effectiveness of people in the organizations of the future*.

Managing Performing Living contains the knowledge and tools that should always be available and ready for use in *all* organizations – of companies as well as in the various other institutions and organizations of society. This book shows what is required in *every* position, if a person has to *manage* and *perform* and also *live* as a human being would like to.

Managing Performing Living is a book about *correct* and *good* management. Whether people consider themselves to be managers and describe themselves as such is secondary; what is important is what the profession, activity, function, and position within an organization demands. Though this book is written for managers in the business world, it is by no means intended only for them. Management extends beyond the business world to all areas of society.

Senior physicians, directors of scientific institutions, theater managers, civil servants, rectors and deans, directors and secondary school teachers, program managers in science, and museum curators are also faced with management tasks. In modern society, almost everyone spends their professional life within organizations. Never before in history have so many people, both in absolute and relative terms, had to carry out de facto management tasks. This is set to increase dramatically in the future, with the advent of the service, information and knowledge society, and the requirements will also visibly *increase*. Most of us will have to manage, whether we want to or not; whether we are aware of it or not; whether we have to manage other people such as staff, colleagues or superiors, or "just" ourselves. However, only a few of us are adequately prepared for this.

We are all, without exception, *affected* by management. And we should have an interest in the *quality* of management whether we like it or not. It is useful and in many cases critical for success to be able to differentiate between good and bad, correct and incorrect management. This will determine the *efficiency* of every social organization, their *competitiveness* in the business world as well as the *quality of life* of most people.

Management is the most important function in society. This is true for developed countries and perhaps even more so for the less developed. Many facts indicate that the actual cause of the predicament of the so-called underdeveloped countries is underdeveloped management – the fact that management cannot function in that society or that it has developed in an undesirable way. This alone makes the question of good and bad management important, because management is the organizing and driving element of a society and its institutions. Whether this is something positive or desirable or even representative of progress can be decided by the individual alone. What is undisputed, is that management is a *reality* that can no longer be wished away. We must come to terms with it.

However, we need not resign ourselves to the way social organizations are managed, to the existing quality of management, to its effectiveness and efficiency. These can be improved and I believe they must be improved, radically in some cases. Similarly, we do not have to put up with the ever increasing amount of rubbish that is disseminated under the guise of "management".

From a historical perspective, management is still very young, not even a hundred years old, and most of its development has ensued since the Second World War. That is why more tolerance is called for here than in the well-established areas of science that have a very long history of development. However, even with great tolerance we cannot close our eyes to the fact that there is no other field in which so much rubbish can be advocated without opposition and in which fads, charlatanism, superficiality, and pseudo-scientific nonsense lacking any logic are disseminated arbitrarily at will and accepted without criticism. This would be unimaginable in any science or in any of the practical professions based on the sciences, be they those of doctors, engineers, lawyers, or specialists in finance and accountancy. In view of the importance of management as a social function, this is at the very least noteworthy. In reality it is dangerous.

With this book, I wish to contribute to the creation of professional standards. Management is a social function which, to date, has no such standards. In the absence of standards, it is little wonder that everything seems to be "somehow" acceptable, valid, and right. However, this only adds to the confusion and is harmful.

In over 25 years as a management teacher, consultant, and as an independent entrepreneur and manager, I have got to know thousands of managers from practically every age group and organizational position, and from various cultural backgrounds. I have held discussions with them, observed them and above all, worked with them on vastly differing problems and in diverse situations. I have come to know how they think and feel, what they consider important and unimportant, what they can and cannot do, what is easy for them and what is difficult, what they are happy about and what they have to suffer, and how they react to all of this. They were and are managers of large corporations and small family-owned companies. Others were managers in governmental and non-governmental organizations, in the business world and the non-profit sector. They included the successful, those used to success and those spoiled by success, as well as those who were denied success, be it due to personal failure or due to circumstances over which they had no control but for which they had to take responsibility. I have had the opportunity to get to know good and bad managers, those who managed properly and those who did not.

Such differences do exist. We can observe them and learn from them; they are of enormous practical value. Once they are recognized, we become aware of the numerous misconceptions, errors and erroneous theories that exist in management and management education. To expose them and offer better solutions is one of the intentions of this book.

These errors relate to such important subjects as motivation and management style, corporate and organizational culture, international and multicultural management. The question of the role psychology can play in management and where it is misplaced is answered here. The book is also about the consequences of certain motivation theories as they are generally and constantly propounded in books and seminars which, to a certain extent, lead to a tragic dependence on these theories instead of achieving what they profess to, which is enabling people to behave in an autonomous and emancipated way. And it is about a few largely disregarded or underestimated things, such as the importance of trust and the utilization of individual strengths. Related to such errors is the fact that certain systems, including human resources systems, show systematic defects in their structures such as in performance appraisal, the design of tasks and jobs, as well as the training and development of people. In my opinion, most of the attempts to achieve the generally undisputed objective of bringing humaneness into management are cursed by major mistakes. Despite the best of intentions, the opposite of this goal is very often achieved which is why I am suggesting alternatives. Management, performance *and* life can certainly go hand in hand but the path that leads to this is different from the one usually taken.

In the new society that is emerging its economy and all its organizations will require more and better management than many people can yet conceive. Our previous organizations could weather all kinds of errors. They had patient employees, good-natured customers, and either no competitors or those who adhered to the rules of the game. These organizations could tolerate and compensate for mistakes in management. In essence they were relatively simple to manage because, among other reasons, they were brick and mortar organizations, because all that was important could be experienced through the sensual organs. We could see, hear, and touch them.

In new organizations and in the future, information and knowledge are and will be the most important resources. Little will be experienced directly through the sensual organs in the usual way. These organizations will have very highly trained employees who will have high expectations in terms of the quality of their tasks and their management. At the same time, however, they will easily make mistakes as they are amateurs, when it comes to management. "Old virtues" such as loyalty will have a lower value particularly because many more people than ever before will have more alternatives and options. Customers will be anything but good-natured, and competition will be merciless.

Such organizations cannot tolerate management mistakes and they will not forgive dilettantism. Their management will have to be high performance, high precision management. It will need to meet the highest standards of professionalism achieved so far and may even have to surpass them. The guiding principle will be the level of training and professionalism of neurosurgeons, pilots, and conductors of major orchestras. This is the second intention of *Management Performance Life*.

I wish to thank everyone who has contributed to the creation of this book, knowingly or unknowingly:

- The infinite number of managers, many of whom became my friends, with whom I worked, discussed, observed, and from whom I learnt a lot;
- The participants in my management seminars who always forced me to re-examine my opinions, reflect on critical issues, and become more precise;
- The students in my lectures who helped me to forge links between the managers of today and the managers of tomorrow;
- My colleagues at the St. Gallen Management Center who with the expert competence of an interdisciplinary team, ensured that theories were scrutinized over and over again and who were not always be convinced even by what I thought were very good arguments;
- The industrial psychologist Prof. Linda Pelzman for our many friendly professional discussions, her critical review of the manuscript, and the numerous improvements she suggested;
- Prof. Hans Siegwart who, as a business administration expert with a lifetime of studying management practice, gave me his professional opinion on the manuscript and went far beyond the limits of friendship to make it clearer and more understandable;
- Dr. Dana Schuppert, who with her experience as a top management coach, untiringly refuted doubts about the concepts published in this book.

I thank my wife and children, who are studying totally different subjects, for helping me to articulate my thoughts better and making my arguments more incisive. Finally, I wish to thank my long-time office manager and secretary Ms. Ruth Blumer, who once again prepared the various drafts of this manuscript with professionalism, perseverance and commitment. I also thank Jürgen Horbach and Dr. Stefan Bollman of the Deutsche Verlags-Anstalt for their support and help.

Fredmund Malik

St. Gallen, 29 December 1999

Part I
Professionalism

The Ideal Manager –
the Wrong Question

There is hardly a discussion on management that does not mention the *requirements of managers*. If we get to the root of the matter, a particular concept almost always seems to dominate, sometimes expressed but more often tacit in nature, and that is the image of the *ideal* manager. As soon as the word "management" is heard, most people instinctively focus on this aspect by asking the question: Who is an ideal manager? This question also dominates the literature on management. The training of management staff is based on this concept, and it is *wrong*.

The Universal Genius

After decades of empirical research in this field, it is easy to answer this question today, and this makes it the focus of interest to the exclusion of everything else. Everything that could be researched in this field has been researched. In 40 years of empirical social research, every possible questionnaire has been answered, every interview taken, and every test conducted. As a result, we know the profile of an ideal manager in great detail.

It is for this reason that personnel managers, who think that they have attained some level of competence, have a list of some size in their "toolbox" which they consult for personnel-related matters such as staffing decisions, creating profiles of requirements, establishing criteria for performance appraisals, writing job advertisements, and also devising training programs and presenting papers.

This list enumerates all the qualities which, according to common opinion, are expected from a person being considered for a management level position: the skills, the knowledge, the personality and character traits, the experience, qualities, and qualifications. It all sounds so plausible that we hardly think of questioning it. After all, it is also supported by countless research projects. How can it be doubted?

Let us take a few examples. In a recent study, 600 of the largest companies in Germany were questioned on the management qualities they look for. The result was striking: *team-builder, visionary, communicative, charismatic, committed to the company, with an international perspective, ecological and social focus, integrity, multicultural skills, and intuitive decision-making.* Typically, the characteristic *customer-focused* came last with the least number of votes.

In the bulletin of a large Swiss bank that operates globally, there was an article by one of its top managers on the "Twelve I's of the Ideal Profile". It told us that, apart from possessing other qualities, the manager of the future must be *interrogative-integral*, an *integrating intermediary* as well as *inter-communicative-instructive* – perhaps not quite what we learn in school.

In a recent issue of the most widely distributed management magazine in a German-speaking country "The ABC of New Requirements" was published which listed a total of 45 "key qualities for the future manager". These were divided into "personal qualities, management qualities and organizational factors" – a compendium of desirable skills. To impart some practical utility the piece was presented in the form of a test which could be taken and evaluated immediately. The fact that certain terms in the test lists, such as *communicative competence, empathy, and future-orientation* or *system integration,* are open to widely differing interpretations is magnanimously overlooked. If a score of between 1.0 and 2.5 is achieved, it can be assumed that "you or the person taking the test meets all the requirements in the new profile of a business virtuoso". Aha...

These examples are not exceptions, nor are they compiled out of an obsessive desire to support my outlandish opinion. They are *typical* and *representative* of a universal way of thinking that has gained ground not only in business but also in other social spheres. 90 percent of all job advertisements mention these kinds of peculiar requirements. Furthermore, many common management tools are based on these things: performance appraisal systems, potential analyses, personnel selection procedures, salary fixing systems, etc.

I too learnt all of this in my studies and I accepted it for the reasons stated previously. However, as time went by, the more I came into contact with real people in the course of my work, and the more experience I gained, the more I began to have my doubts. Plausibility, or the fact that it is taught in universities or is the prevalent opinion, is no guarantee for the correctness of a concept. In our history many things were taught – even in universities – and believed, even by experts, which were nevertheless absolutely wrong. Plausibility has often also proved to be misleading, as we can learn from theories advanced through the ages from Copernicus to Darwin.

What type of idea is spread by these lists and catalogues of requirements? What is the basic type of manager that emerges here? It would not be unfair to say that the list of requirements essentially portrays a *universal genius*. In some strange way, the idea has taken root that a manager, especially a top manager, should be a cross between a general from a bygone era, a Nobel Prize winner for physics, and a TV show host.

Although this ideal type can be *described* and descriptions indeed abound, we cannot find such people in the real world. In my opinion it is this that constitutes one of the most significant problems encountered today in management education as well as management practice.

My comments so far are not meant as a criticism of the science. It renders what is demanded and expected of it: It answers the question by providing the characteristics and skills of the *ideal manager*. And the answers are right. The ideal managers could well be as they are presented in the studies. *It is not the answers that are wrong; it is the question.*

The Effective Person

My suggestion, therefore, is to *drop* the question. Although it can be answered, neither the question nor the answers have much practical relevance. Even if we were to temporarily accept, for the sake of argument, that universal geniuses do exist, we would be forced to conclude – on the basis of statistics alone – that they are rare. Too rare to allow any hope that their numbers could occupy even a fraction of the management positions available in a modern society. I will explain this in more detail in one of the following chapters.

I suggest another question. Instead of: *Who is an ideal manager?*, the question should be: *Who is an effective manager?* The formulation of this latter question is very different from the former. Its starting point is not geniuses but *ordinary* people, because there are no others, even though there may be some who find it difficult to concede this point.

Based on this alternative question, the basic problem of management is not: *How can geniuses give a brilliant performance?* That requires no explanation. The basic problem is: *How do we enable ordinary people* – because we have no others – *to turn in extraordinary performances?*

In this case, I am not talking about the oft-quoted *excellent performance* which is routinely mentioned in any discussion ever since the book by Peters and Waterman[2] hit the stands. No one, not even the "topmost" top manager, can consistently turn in star performances. Even the thought is absurd. To base our requirements on such a premise is not only theory in the worst sense of the word. I consider it to be, above all, inhuman.

Neither, however, is standard performance any longer adequate today. We need more than that. This is at the *core of the paradox* of management today or, to formulate it in a less pompous manner, this is the reason why management is required at all. Only ordinary people are available in sufficiently large numbers. However, what is demanded by customers, and by the pressure of competition, is extraordinary performance.

Who are effective managers or how are they effective? Whenever we observe people with these questions in mind, we can only come to the conclusion that these people are totally different.

No Common Ground

From this background I started years ago to find out more about people who had achieved something in the course of their lives, people who could be called *performers*. What do these people have in common? The simple and eternally surprising answer, which does not fit into the predominant view of management, is: *absolutely nothing.*

Effective people are as different as human beings can be. What is being sought, namely *common features*, simply does not exist. Attempts to do so can be likened to the search for the Holy Grail. What – on the other hand – does exist is the *individuality* of human beings.

---

2   Thomas J. Peters/Robert H. Waterman Jr., *In Search of Excellence*, New York 1982.

No two persons are alike. This observation gains more relevance the higher the positions people hold. A person does not ascend to the higher positions and even the top of an organization by virtue of the fact that he or she is an indistinguishable copy of another person, a genetic clone almost. Their rise is more due to the fact that they are *different* from the others.

In my long personal experience as a management consultant, I have met managers who were highly intelligent. They were the brains who had not only one degree but two or even three which may have helped them to get to the top of their profession. However, I have met many more managers with normal, rather average intelligence who may never have been lucky enough to go to university and they were equally good managers. Some managers conformed to the required ideal image of being a communicator; they were extroverts who could easily make contacts, and this had probably made much in life easier for them. On the other hand, a larger number of managers were introverted, some even shy in nature. These were people who would break into a sweat if they had to give a talk in front of more than three people, but they were no less competent. Some had the almost universally required charisma, they were what one might call personalities; their presence could be physically felt as soon as they entered a room – this may have contributed to their success. Others did not possess this quality; they were inconspicuous people who did not attract the attention of anyone outside their organizational environment, but their accomplishments were at least equal to those of others from the first group. Some were concerned about appearance, possessing great style – this could be important in certain branches of industry and certain positions; others did not place any importance on this aspect and they were equally successful. Some were interesting people, others boring; some exuded charm, others had, at best, the charm of a dead mouse.

Being or Doing

There is no end to the list. The conclusion, however, is this: Effective people share *no* common features apart from the fact that they are *effective*. The "secret" of their effectiveness does not lie in the answer to the question: *What should a person be like in order to be considered for a management post?* It is not the personality or character, education or social origin that matters. Neither does the key to their effectiveness lie in their virtues, as is so often supposed. Desirable as these are, and as little as I would advise against being virtuous, I would, in the same measure, not invest all my faith in virtues when it comes to discussing management qualities. Naturally, there are effective people with outstanding virtues, and those may make things easier for them. However, this aspect is not crucial.

The key to the achievements of effective people – the performers – lies in the *way they act*. It was *how* these people behaved that was significant, not who they were. As human beings, as a type of person, as personalities they are as different as human beings can be. They do not conform to any profile of requirements and certainly do not have any likeness to the academic ideal type. However, there is a common thread that runs through all their actions.

It took me some time to determine what this common thread might be. *Firstly*, because it took a great deal of effort to free myself from the learnt perceptions and conventional opinions; and *secondly*, it had taken even more time to determine what, contrary to common thinking, was really important.

The peculiar fixation on the question of what a person should be like is only encountered in management. In the case of surgeons, we want to know whether they can operate; little else counts. Musicians for an orchestra are selected and evaluated on the basis of how proficiently they play their instrument. High jumpers must be able to jump high, and long jumpers must be able to jump a long way; a coach would be very puzzled by the question: What are high jumpers like? A similar question in the case of managers, then, cannot be justified under any circumstances. Naturally, there may be certain characteristic traits which play a significant role in deciding that a person *cannot* be considered for a *certain* post. However, this is due to the individuality of the person and the particular position and is not a general ideal concept.

The only characteristics effective people have in common are a few elements in their working methods. *Firstly*, there are a few *rules* which they follow, consciously or unconsciously, in whatever they do and wherever they do it, rules by which they discipline their behavior. In this book, I will explain these rules in the form of *principles*. *Secondly*, we can observe that effective people perform certain *tasks* with special care and thoroughness. *Thirdly*, we discover that there is a striking *methodical-systematic* element that permeates their method of working: the element of craftsmanlike *pro-*

fessionalism, and certain *tools* required to attain it, which they know how to use competently and at times even like virtuosos. Basically, they are the same elements as can be found in every other profession.

However, these elements are very different from current lists of requirements. I regard the search for profiles of *ideal* requirements, and also their application in actual practice, to be of little use. In fact, I consider them to be *misleading.* I would even go as far as to say that they are basically *inhuman.* To demand from people what they cannot ever achieve is the perfect example of inhuman behavior.

If anything, the justification for such lists would be that the ideal profile defines the benchmark to which a person can aspire, despite not being able to attain it. However, these lists of requirements are so far removed from reality that, in my opinion, they are not even suitable as a vision. I am not exactly known for advocating low performance standards. However, it is a well-known fact in motivation theory that standards which are virtually impossible to achieve do not only fail to motivate people, they can actually discourage them.

Perhaps speakers at seminars and congresses, and authors of relevant books and papers should occasionally question themselves as to how far *they* meet the requirements they call for. It is one thing to expound on requirements but quite another to at least furnish some evidence that they can be met. If this criterion were to be applied, more than 80 percent of the literature on management would be rendered irrelevant and many lectures would not be given, though this would prove to be very beneficial for the quality of management and the credibility of its representatives.

Recently, a speaker at an important congress expressed his opinion in all seriousness: "The global manager of the twenty-first century is knowledgeable about the people of this world and can speak at least five languages well enough to engage in negotiations." In a conversation I managed to have with him later, I found out that he – well over 45 years of age – had visited the USA four times and Hong Kong once, could speak passable German (his presentation was by no means a linguistic masterpiece), English for everyday use, and a little French. This is not a unique case; unfortunately it is typical. Nevertheless he had the temerity to stand in front of the audience and pompously expound on his particular bugbear without – and this is unfortunate to note, too – any one of the managers present contradicting him.

We should not question whether someone conforms to an ideal profile but whether he or she has learnt to be *effective.*

Interviews Are Useless

What is striking is that only a few effective people can *describe* the way they act. Many are not even aware of the way they function. *Firstly*, they have not explicitly learnt it and *secondly*, their first and foremost concern is the *substance* of their work, therefore they do not pay attention to the actual way they work. They cannot put into words much of what they do correctly, perhaps even perfectly.

The most problematic thing for them is the element I call principles, the rules that govern their actions. This is nothing extraordinary. Only a few people who manage to achieve something are in a position to describe this element. To be able to do something and to be able to describe it are two totally different things. This is not only true in management but also in other fields such as art and sports. I have never heard of a violin soloist who could describe how he or she played the violin. They can demonstrate but seldom describe it – neither is this required of them. Football players cannot – as a rule – describe how they score goals nor can tennis champions explain how they serve.

For this reason, I have long since given up *questioning* managers about their practices. Interviews, and other forms of questioning too, are hopelessly unproductive. People either do not give a useful answer at all, or they give an answer they think others want to hear – the usual answer. Some of them even instruct their assistants just before the appointed date of the interview to look up literature for what is *in vogue* at the moment. This seldom addresses the issue.

It seems to me quite remarkable that empirical research in this area is so starkly dominated by questioning methods. In particular, the description of managers in the *media* is almost exclusively based on questioning. Although these methods are hardly on a par with the methodical standards of academic research, they exert a far greater influence over a wider audience with their image – or, more correctly, their caricature – of a manager.

The best method is *observation*. Unfortunately, it is also the most difficult one, inasmuch as it is the most time-consuming, and it is not easy to approach the people we would like to observe. What is significant is not what people *say* but what they *do* and how they do it, and this can only be determined by observing them. Over time, a pattern emerges and gradually we also learn how to describe it.

The study of biographies is of great value, which is why they have become one of my important sources. Apart from a few exceptions, the amount of worthless literature on management is so voluminous that it is not worth the effort to work through it. It is perfectly obvious that biographies have their own set of problems. *Firstly*, reading them is very time-consuming. There are hardly any biographies which have less than 500 pages. *Secondly*, there are fewer biographies, on performers in the field of business than those in politics, the armed forces and, to some extent, art. *Thirdly*, the working practices adopted by these people are usually only a side issue for the biographers. Good biographers, however, can be identified, among other things, by the fact that they also pay attention to this aspect. *Fourthly,* judgment must always be exercised to qualify the sometimes excessive and idealized portrayal in biographies.

In short, people must be *studied* and not only questioned if we want to know something about them, especially if we want to ascertain why they are effective and what makes them effective. It is not enough to be satisfied with a few brief impressions, a bit of hearsay and hasty allocation to a type, as is only too often the case.

Whatever may be understood by knowledge of human nature, one thing is certain: There is no easy way to attain it. Yet, it is precisely this which is sought, expected, and even promised. A human being is too complex a creature to simply be placed into one of a few pre-determined categories. However, this is exactly what so many people want to do. To possess a knowledge of human nature, to be able to slot people into compartments and evaluate them is not only expedient, it also betrays a certain fascination that could be attributed to the fact that it promises to confer power and influence over others. This is why charlatanism thrives in this field. Ten questions here, seven basic types there, supplemented with multiple-choice personality tests and always garnished with some psychoanalysis and astrology. Unfortunately, it is not so simple.

Professionalism Can Be Learnt

If, according to the conclusions drawn from this chapter, the effectiveness and professionalism of people do not depend on what they are but on how they act, a certain optimism can be justified with regard to the purpose of this book. Indeed, a person cannot learn to *be* like another person; but to a certain extent, they can learn to *act* like that person. The common features of the way effective people act can be passed on but not their nature, characteristics, or personality. It is possible to identify the principles and rules which govern them, the tasks that they consider important to carry out, and the tools they usually use; and it is also possible to learn this. This provides a foundation upon which management can be made into a profession which will be able to satisfy the same standards as any other profession.

Erroneous Theories and Misconceptions

The question about the ideal manager is not the only error that distorts our understanding of sound management. There are certain other misconceptions and distinctly erroneous theories which contribute to confusion and undesirable developments; in particular, they provide fertile ground for the spread of fashionable trends and charlatanism which regularly make an appearance.

Erroneous Theories

I have selected *two* ways of thinking which, in my opinion, illustrate the misleading and harmful views of management particularly well. To some extent, these are extremes of a continuous spectrum. Basically, their most important elements are to be found today in numerous variations and shades across the entire spectrum of management and its study. The first manifestation, in its most common form, can at best be called the *"Pursuit-of-Happiness" approach*; the second is the idea of the *"Great Leader Personality"*.

The Pursuit-of-Happiness Approach

In its most extreme form, this approach asserts that the *main purpose* of organizations, particularly commercial establishments, lies in making the people working in them *content* and, if possible, even happy. In any case, it lies in showing them the path to happiness, whatever that means and however that can be accomplished. In watered down versions this is considered one of the significant *secondary purposes* of an organization. This approach seldom finds expression in its extreme form. However, moderate versions of the Pursuit-of-Happiness approach have infiltrated *most* management areas and influenced them to a considerable extent.

This way of thinking has many roots. The strongest is a consequence of the view that the state or society is responsible for the people's well-being. This was one of the predominant ideas of the twentieth century and an erroneous one as – even if this is always disputed – it led to either a lack of desire to perform and a decline in motivation, or it led to improper control of performance which was difficult to correct. This approach merged at several points with the "feeling of well-being", "situational", "involvement" and "self-realization" streams of the "psycho scene" in its entire variety of apparently inexhaustible and incomprehensible forms, be it shamanism, or esoteric, or New Age methods. Far Eastern philosophies, which fitted the bill, also entered the picture.

In management, pursuit-of-happiness ideas can be found in the human relations movement; they appear in various forms as part of the participation and democratization requirements as well as motivation theories. They are a part of the discussion on management style and the requirement for enabling and empowerment. The clearest, if not the most "modern" expression, is the work satisfaction theory, which has influenced personnel management since the fifties. The basic premise is this: *Make people happy, and they will perform.*

The incorrectness of the theory does not lie in the premise that people should be content. Who could possibly take exception to such an objective? The error lies in the idea that it is not the individuals themselves but *another party* who is responsible for this – be it organizations, companies, or, as mentioned earlier, the state and society. Furthermore, it is based on the view that contentment must *first* be created and only *then* can performance be expected.

Firstly, this theory ignores the fact that probably no change or progress, in whichever way we may define it, has resulted from *contentment*. If people in any past era had been content with the status quo, they would probably not have changed it. At least the *impetus* for change must have originated from some form of discontentment with the existing situation and this discontentment, for whatever reasons, led to changed performance.

Secondly, this approach overlooks the fact that our organizations would be clearly overstretched, if they wanted to make people content and happy.

They just cannot do it. Every organization is established for a *specific* purpose for which it is then organized and structured. The purpose of a commercial enterprise could be the manufacture of cars, toothpaste, or clothing, or to offer banking services or insurance. The purpose of a hospital is to cure people, and that of a school is to educate them. It cannot even be said with any certainty that organizations are, to some extent, competently fulfilling their particular purpose. Beyond fulfilling the purpose for which they were established, social organizations are remarkably *incompetent*. There are no good multi-purpose or all-round organizations, and it is very doubtful whether there ever will be any. This is equally true of a commercial establishment, a school, a hospital, or a public administration body. Every attempt to convert *single-purpose* organizations into *multi-purpose* ones has *failed*.

This idea is usually met with incomprehension. The prevalent way of thinking, apparently plausible to many, is this: If large companies can manufacture cars or produce toothpaste, develop medicine or build skyscrapers so well, they should be capable of much more. Unfortunately they are not; they are good in their own specialist areas because they do nothing else. This is sometimes difficult for even experienced managers to accept and has always led to the spread of undesirable strategic developments in the economy as well as in politics. This can be seen in the constant recurrence of periods of conglomerate formation with their typically euphoric belief in unlimited possibilities, and is also apparent in the failure of the welfare state with its repeated attempts to fulfill an ever-growing number of purposes. In each case, the consequence was and is an almost total loss of productivity due to excessive demands and wastage, leading in turn to a financial and identity crisis.

Even the performance of those organizations in which perhaps the most hope is invested that they will fulfill the purpose of making people happy, namely the churches, is questionable. All too often in the past, the consequence of these endeavors has not been heaven on earth but a *totalitarian hell*.

We may complain, but we cannot simply ignore the fact that our organizations are very one-sided "creatures". Established solely to fulfill specific, very limited purposes, they in no way provide the most congenial or pleasant conditions for living and working. What we may hope for is to make them *effective* and to gradually improve the working and living conditions in them to some degree.

The *third* aspect is that if we are fixated on the theory of work satisfaction, we are in danger of overlooking the fact that there could be an alternative, namely the reverse: *Give people the chance to perform and many – not all – will achieve a remarkable degree of satisfaction.* This is the maxim I prefer. It seems to be the best way in which the interests of both the organization and the people can be served.

The Pursuit-of-Happiness approach can assume a particularly well-camouflaged form, which is therefore particularly dangerous for organizations, where we would least expect to find it: in a certain type of manager who appears to be very focused on achievement. Such people are given to boasting about how they always "need new challenges". Not all, but a large number are nothing more than egocentric people on a particular type of self-realization trip. It is what *they* need that interests them, not what the organization needs. They are not usually concerned about whether they can meet the challenges or whether they can get the results. They need the "kick", if possible one in which the media is interested. In all too many cases, they leave behind a mess for their successors to clear up, while they themselves move on to the "new shores" of other challenges.

Naturally there are cases – which shall be dealt with in this book – in which people need challenges, especially those set for them by their organization. However, I would recommend a healthy dose of skepticism and a closer look when employees, and particularly managers, speak with great fervor of the challenges they seek. No objection can be made to "challenges" people set themselves privately, whatever they may be. Organizations, on the other hand, do not need *excitement*, they need *results*.

The Great Leader Personality

The second incorrect theory is the view that organizations do not, in reality, require *management*, they require *leadership*; it is *leaders* and not *managers* that are needed. Though this approach – the "Great Man Theory" – is not identical to the ideal manager type, the demarcation between the two is so indistinct that it is often difficult to differentiate between them. A combination of the two portrays a character from an ancient heroic epic rather than a person who can be taken even the slightest bit seriously in the context of the reality in our organizations.

The study of *personality traits* and *characteristics* of so-called great leader figures has always aroused fascination. People have always believed that we can learn something from the uniqueness of historical situations and people.

In the eighties in particular, the demand for leaders once again came to the fore. Until then, this requirement had usually been restricted to the upper echelons of political and military organizations. Now, people began to generalize the requirements and apply them to the most common and unspectacular management positions in all types of organization. Suddenly, local savings banks, DIY stores, sausage skin factories, shaving cream manufacturers and, last but not least, even large industrial groups wanted not only good managers, they also wanted *leaders*. There were calls for a "new manager" with very special qualities and skills, "rules for winners" were devised and there were loud demands for forceful, dynamic, visionary and charismatic leaders who were to determine the purpose and direction of the organizations, appeal to people and evoke inspiration, identification and loyalty.

Even the call for such leader figures is dangerous, as can be seen time and again from the annals of history. The chances of the right people thinking that the call is meant for them are infinitesimal. The few that have been found who were not only *great* – whatever that may be[3] – but also *good* are unique and exceptional cases. The demand for this type of leader has met with little success due to a "lack of numbers", so to speak. Based on statistics alone, today's society requires a great many more people capable of carrying out management tasks than the number of the desired type of leader it can ever hope to mobilize.

Due to various other factors, discussions about the concept of a "leader" tend to be misleading in a manner that is partly naïve and partly dangerous. I do not wish to go into detail here but will merely outline three of the most important points.

Firstly, in the German-speaking world the constant use of the English word "leader", even though it can be translated simply and clearly in German as "Führer", is very significant. Obviously, people do not have the courage to do this, as they would then have to deal with the issue of whether the term also indicates the fascist-totalitarian idea of "Führer" and of how they can convincingly distinguish their ideas from this connotation. Most authors on leadership do not possess an adequate knowledge of history or level of intellect for this task, and others skirt around this sensitive problem deliberately.

---

3   Refer to Johannes Gross, "Größe des Staatmanns" in: *Von Geschichte umgeben. Festschrift für Joachim Fest*, Berlin 1986, pages 75 and 88; and Wolf Schneider, "Die Sieger", Hamburg 1992, page 42 and following pages.

Secondly, the discussion also tends to be misleading, because it once again places more emphasis on characteristics and personality traits than on action and practices; the stress is laid on what people *are* instead of what they *do*. The potential to perform is judged by attributes. However, there is no proof that such a connection exists, and it has been clearly refuted throughout history. In this book I will show that a better alternative exists.

Thirdly, a peculiar, tactical pattern can be discerned clearly and almost constantly, though the degree of deliberateness cannot always be clearly determined. Management and leadership are defined in such a way that they render the entire discussion futile, as neither theoretical nor practical progress is possible with such definitions. Everything the authors consider inferior and unacceptable, in the sense of being bureaucratic, non-innovative, non-dynamic, backward looking and so on, is allocated to the category of "management". Everything else that is considered to be good and desirable comes under the category of "leadership". Therefore, they are comparing *bad* management with *good* leadership. This is either incompetence or mischief, perhaps even intentional stultification under the assumption that no one will notice it. No sensible discussion on either management or leadership is possible if it is based on such a premise.

A completely different method is required here. Bad management must be compared with bad leadership – of which there are numerous examples available in history – and good management with good leadership. Therefore, the difference between good and bad management must first be identified. Only then can a meaningful discussion ensue on where and in what respect leadership transcends good management. If, in this way, it can be shown that leadership clearly means something more and is qualitatively better than good, correct and professional management, there can be said to be some progress.

Even if certain things appear to be plausible, the trend in the eighties and nineties, when extraordinary demands were once again made with regard to an individual's personality, is therefore useless and it is basically just a waste of time. Furthermore, it is remarkably naïve and superficial; it seems to overlook the Führer disaster of the twentieth century – otherwise we would have to suspect plain cynicism.

To avoid any confusion: I do *not* dispute that good leadership *can* exist, *has* existed in the past, and is *required* in certain situations. I maintain, however, that the way of thinking criticized here is misleading, rather than being an approximation of a practical, justifiable leadership concept.

Misconceptions and Errors

Apart from the two fundamental theories discussed, there are a few errors about management which are so widespread that I wish to eliminate them right at the start of this book. Quite a few other misconceptions and errors will also be dealt with in the relevant context.

The View that only Top Managers are Managers

Top managers are managers; that is clear. The mistake lies in the small word "only" which misleadingly limits the view to the most senior managers who function as agents for large companies and, as such, are very visible. This mistake is relatively widespread and it is harmful. It strengthens the illusion that whatever this small group of people does is typical or representative of management as a whole.

There is no doubt that top management is management, but it is only a *part* of it and quite possibly not the most important part. Instead of this misleading limitation to the very top managers, I suggest that we should assume that anyone who manages is a manager, regardless of the designation he or his position has, regardless of status symbols, rank within the organization, etc. Whoever carries out *de facto* management tasks is a manager. *Firstly*, this broadens the perspective to include more than just top management; and *secondly*, it takes into account the large number of managers which will be discussed later.

The View that only a Person Who Has Subordinates is a Manager

This view incorrectly equates management with *people management*. Here too, it is true that a person who manages other people is a manager. However, management cannot be restricted to this group of people and this element alone without overlooking crucial factors in the functioning of organizations.

This belief excludes all those people who are important to an organization for the *contribution* they make and not because of their subordinates. For an ever-increasing number of *specialists*, almost all of them knowledge workers, the fact that they may or may not have employees under them is of secondary importance. Very often they do not have any. They are important not because of the subordinates and their management, but because of their personal expertise, their *special knowledge.*

The importance of the chief foreign exchange broker in a bank is not due to the number of employees under him. The same holds true for a tax expert in an international enterprise or the chief designer in a fashion house. Their importance is defined by their contribution. Management is important for this type of people, not because they have to manage *other people* but because they have to manage *themselves.*

Few organizations would be able to function without such people; they play a *crucial* role in the success of an ever-growing number of organizations. Therefore, they must be included in our definition of managers. These people are very aware of their contribution to the success of the company, a fact that does not always make them the most pleasant of people. They are often reluctant to accept that they are managers, and convincing them of this is a very difficult task. They must think and act as managers – in relation to themselves and their knowledge. The consequences of excluding them would, in most cases, be serious, perhaps even catastrophic.

The View that only Subordinates Need to Be Managed

This error is directly related to what we have just discussed. The source of this misconception is by now an almost outmoded idea of organization, work and performance.

Management includes, but does not primarily consist of the management of subordinates. This was the case in the past and, though the world has changed radically in this respect, this view continues to persist. Managing subordinates is, of course, important but it is not the most difficult task for a manager. That is why it is all the more astonishing that the old model, almost without exception, still holds sway. What we think of is a supervisor with subordinates, and the question which results from this picture, namely what does he or she need to do to be an even better supervisor.

I always question managers on *what is their most important or difficult problem.* In all these many years, only a few have replied that it is the management of their subordinates, as one might expect according to the traditional model. Almost without exception, the answer is: *My boss!* Or: *My boss's boss.* Or: *My colleagues.*

The reasons for these replies are perfectly obvious – making it all the more surprising that the actual situation is given so little attention in literature and training. Management, in the case of subordinates, is less problematic as every manager can, as a last resort, use the instrument of *instruction* – the command. Not that I recommend this. It should be the *ultimate ratio* and seldom actually be used. However, this hardly needs to be emphasized as instructions are seldom issued because employees are not stupid. They do not let things come to a point where the boss needs to give a command. People sort things out for themselves long before this.

However, the instrument of instruction cannot be used on colleagues or the boss. At least, it *is* available to be used with subordinates, even if it is seldom actually used. In the case of colleagues or the boss, however, managers do not have it *a priori*. The entire demanding management arsenal which is incessantly propagated – communication, cooperation, powers of persuasion, assertiveness, etc. – is not required primarily in the area for which it is recommended and for which training is given, namely the management of employees. It is required for the management of other parts of the organizational network to which a manager belongs; for the management of relationships that extend sideways and upwards in the organization's hierarchy.

The View that Management Is a Commercial Issue

This error has a detrimental effect on *non-commercial* organizations on account of two points of view. *Firstly*, it leads to the assumption that whatever works in business must work in *every* organization. *Secondly*, this error also leads to the opposite assumption: Organizations in the commercial sector are completely different from those in other sectors. As a result of this reasoning, features which could perhaps be incorporated to great advantage in these other sectors are ignored.

Management is not typically "commercial". Neither does it have its origins in business. Other – much older – organizations were managed long before the advent of companies. Nevertheless, one thing is brought to prominence particularly well in business and that is the fact that a systematic application of management leads to success and results. The *effect* of management can be observed most easily and clearly in business.

Even though there are certain things that all organizations can learn and adopt from companies, this should not tempt us to believe that whatever the business sector does is correct and can be used for other multiform organizations. A hospital, a public administration body, or a research institute is so fundamentally *different* from a commercial organization that they must develop their own solutions.

On the other hand, there are things which the business sector could learn from non-profit organizations – this too is unfortunately overlooked as a result of the prevailing misconceptions. For example, nowhere can better personnel management be found than in well-managed non-profit organizations.

The View that Management Is a Matter of Psychology

The importance of psychology in management scarcely needs to be emphasized. On the other hand, the *"psychologizing"* of management, as one might call it, is harmful. *Firstly*, it is related to the *reduction* of management to direct interpersonal relationships, that is to say the limitation of management to *people management.* The management of people is, as has already been mentioned, a part of management but management encompasses far more, such as the structure, development and control of an institution in its entirety. If taken out of this context, the people management aspect cannot be understood.

Secondly, "psychologizing" surfaces wherever any difficulty, problem or conflict is perceived or interpreted only in the context of psychological categories, usually due to inadequate knowledge of both management *and* psychology. Without analyzing them, it is assumed that these types of problems must have psychological causes, and consequently the solutions are also sought in psychology. In my opinion, most of the apparently psychological difficulties result from a lack of craftsmanlike professionalism, as discussed in this book, and are due to the fact that elementary management tasks are either not carried out or are carried out badly. In this case, even properly applied psychology does not help.

Thirdly, a large portion of the psychology recommended for management practice is derived from the field of therapy. This in itself is disputed by expert psychologists. There are approximately 600 different psychotherapeutic procedures, and they are largely considered to be questionable with regard to their theoretical quality and also their practical effectiveness.[4]

However, what is more important for management than internal psychological problems is that this brings with it the *dominance of the pathological case*, as I have termed it elsewhere[5], into organizations. The psychotherapist is not primarily interested in usual but in unusual cases, not in healthy but in sick people. From his point of view, this is completely legitimate, but for management it is more or less useless.

Although there are always *difficult* people in every organization – the behavior of some may border on the pathological – most employees are normal, healthy people. Or to put it more precisely, since no one can define normality properly, perhaps we are all abnormal but only to a normal extent.

The fixation on difficulties, problems, conflicts, discord in relations and communication, which can be observed so often in management training, either dulls the minds of men to the really important psychological issues, or they are turned into neuroses. If anything, we would require a psychology for *healthy* and not *sick* people in management.

Fourthly, it is particularly bad, if psychology which can be taken seriously is replaced by a strange mixture of psychoanalysis, esoteric thought, New Age metaphysics and astrology, frequently enriched by some odd nuggets from ideologically colored ecology and remnants of leftist tendencies from the 1968 movement. This quagmire of thought and its unique irrationality holds a tremendous appeal for an astonishingly large number of people. A remarkably large number is unable to resist the spell of this way of thinking and succumbs to it. This is one of the main ways through which charlatanism and all kinds of other mischief gain entry. Generous doses of these are to be found not only in management literature but also in company training programs.

I am not talking about definite deviationism which, as such, is usually desired, if it occurs at all. What I mean is the confused "soup" of half-truths, superstition, unverified statements, and meaningless formula which

---

4   For example, refer to Dieter E. Zimmer, *Tiefenschwindel*, Hamburg 1986, page 375 and following pages.

5   Refer to my book, *Strategie des Managements komplexer Systeme*, Bern/Stuttgart/Vienna 1984, fifth revised edition 1996, appendix page 543 and following pages.

can creep into organizations without the knowledge or consent of top management as a consequence of naïve trust in the competence of those in charge of training and of seminar organizers, or as a result of carelessness and ignorance. Due, in part, to a lack of clear standards, everything seems to have some validity *somehow* and therefore seems permissible.

It is precisely this that makes the issue of good and correct management so important. Once this amalgam of superficial knowledge, metaphysics and superstition takes root, it is very difficult to correct.

The View that Management Is Dependent on Culture

This error is a consequence of the increasing focus on corporate culture which dates back to the early eighties. It gained impetus through the globalization debate. The idea of cultural dependence is obvious and understandable, but it is *incorrect*. It shows a confusion between the "what" and "how" of management. *What* effective managers do is the same, or very similar, in all cultures. *How* they do it depends to a significant extent, but by no means exclusively, on the relevant culture.

For example, every well-managed organization has clearly defined objectives and a functioning control system, irrespective whether it is an Italian, Spanish, Mexican, or Chinese organization. On the other hand, how objectives are decided, which objectives are set, how it is checked whether and to what extent these objectives have been achieved can appear to be vastly different, as far as external appearances are concerned in the individual cultures.

Even if we do not define culture as ethnic or national and geographical, as in this example, the same holds true even according to other criteria. Whether high or low tech companies, knowledge or labor intensive organizations, fashion or technology industries, capital goods or consumer goods – the "what" of good management is always the same. The "how" can – even in the same country – be very different, and it *is*. For instance, the external appearance of the management of an Italian machine tool company is very different from that of an Italian fashion enterprise.

This circumstance encourages the postulation of different culture-dependent types of management. In reality, this only adds to the confusion. It is simply bad science when form is confused with substance.

Therefore, there is little reason to make a lot of fuss about intercultural management if we disregard the self-evident fact that there are certain customs and conventions[6] in every country, which must *firstly* be learnt as a matter of politeness and *secondly* respected. However, this has nothing to do with management and everything to do with the minimum of manners, decency and refinement, resulting from an upbringing worthy of the name. I accept that this can no longer be taken for granted – perhaps to a great extent due to the very large number of managers required by a modern society. However, to speak of other *types* of management because there are badly brought up and therefore, badly behaved people even in higher positions is absolutely wrong.

It is the same for "international" management. This type of management has never existed, neither has its opposite, namely national management. What does exist are *organizations* that operate at national, international or multinational levels; incidentally these are not only commercial enterprises. Organizations, which are designed for and operate only at a national level, may well, and probably will, have considerable and perhaps insoluble problems if they want or are forced to operate at an international level. However, this has less to do with *management* and more to do with a lack of *knowledge* about other countries such as not knowing foreign languages, an inability to master foreign currency risks, or simply to respect the customs and conventions of other people and countries.

Management can be right or wrong, good or bad, capable or incapable but not national or international, monocultural or multicultural. It is as little country or culture specific as are sports. Golf is played in the same way everywhere, just as is tennis or chess. Certain types of sports may not be very popular in some countries, and this could be attributed to culture. Thus, skiing is certainly not a traditional sport in the USA as it is in Austria or Switzerland. However, when skiing – particularly when skiing well – the Americans follow the same principles as the Europeans. Similarly, the rules for management effectiveness are the same everywhere, such as the rules of language for instance. Good English is evaluated according to the same standards all over the world, even in the many countries where it is spoken incorrectly and with an accent.

---

6 Relevant literature is for example, Paul Watzlawick, *Gebrauchsanweisung für Amerika*, Munich/Zurich 1978, 1984 and Max Otte, *Amerika für Geschäftsleute*, Frankfurt 1996, revised edition 1998.

Management as a Profession

In my opinion, the only way in which we can, to a satisfactory degree, answer the management questions of modern society with its manifold organizations from companies to non-profit organizations, is with what, in political science and law, is known as the "constitutional approach" or "constitutionalism"[7]. This book and the suggestions in it are based on a few fundamental concepts of this approach which are particularly relevant for management issues.

Constitutional Thought

The *first* principle of constitutional thought is that the fate of an organization should not basically rest on *individual people*, even though there have been important and influential individuals in the history of probably every organization, and there will be in the future. The true yardstick for a top manager is not the success achieved during his period of service, but the organization's situation *after* he leaves. Does it continue to be successful, does it have enduring strength in spite of the change at the top, or does it collapse because everything revolved around this one person?

The *second* basic thought is that *everyone*, even the top level managers in an organization, must adhere to *rules* which are not subject to their influence. It is the principle of the "Rule of Law" as opposed to the "Rule of

---

7   For more information: Friedrich August von Hayek, *Die Verfassung der Freiheit*, Tübingen 1971, page 221 and following pages, and his three-volume work *Law, Legislation and Liberty*, London 1973-1979.

Man" that delineates this thought.[8] An organization should not be subject to the arbitrary decisions of the people managing it, irrespective of their importance, their abilities and the successes they have achieved.

The *third* significant element, and perhaps the most important for this book, is the principle that it is not the peak of performance, the single prominent achievement that overshadows everything else, but *continuity* of a high but generally achievable level of performance that counts in the long run. Related to this is the perception that continuous improvement is more important than striving to achieve overwhelming, brilliant success; that continuity is indispensable, and that constant change of policy even in a very dynamic environment can ruin even the best of organizations.

It took a very long time for the constitutional approach to gain recognition. Previously, the problem of state and government leadership was tackled with the question: *Who should lead us?* The answers varied greatly depending on the era and philosophy: the strongest, the best, the one ordained by God, the cleverest, the people, the majority… They were and are all wrong, although this insight is still not one of the self-evident facts of general education today.

What is far more important, however, is that it is not only the answers that are wrong but also the question itself. The question should be: *How do we organize our political institutions so that even bad and incompetent leaders can wreak little damage, and how can we rid ourselves of such leaders in as simple and bloodless a manner as possible?*[9]

Whatever was valid for the political institutions of a relatively simple society is valid today on a much bigger scale for the organizations in our far more complex modern society. *How must our organizations be structured, and how must management function so that the organization does not only fulfill its purposes in the best possible way, but also so that bad and incompetent managers are prevented from causing too much damage, their incompetence can quickly be detected, and they can easily be replaced?* The questions are clear even though the answers are not simple. Up to now, most of the questions were incorrectly framed, and it is no wonder that little progress has been made.

---

8   Refer to Friedrich August von Hayek, *Die Verfassung der Freiheit*, Tübingen 1971, page 195 and following pages

9   Confer Karl R. Popper, "On the Sources of Knowledge and Ignorance" in: *Conjectures and Refutation*, London 1963, fourth edition 1972, page 25.

Even when the constitutional approach is used as a basis, everything possible is done to find the most suitable people to carry out management tasks. This remains a core task. However, all selection criteria and methods are questionable and unreliable. This is the crucial weakness of every personal and characteristic-oriented management theory.

The conclusion derived from this is that it is not the *selection* of managers that should be given more emphasis but their *training*; managers are not *found*, managers are *made, trained,* and *molded*; and an organizational context – a constitutional framework – is created in which correct action is promoted, rewarded and – if all else fails – enforced. The key question of the constitutional approach is not *Who should manage?*, it is *What is correct management?*

One of the very few managers of this century who not only understood this but also acted accordingly is the man under whose guidance the US company General Motors grew, from a hopeless start to be the world's largest manufacturing company and, more importantly, remains so today – 80 years after he took charge and 40 years after he retired from the same company. That was Alfred P. Sloan, who assumed the position of Chief Executive Officer at General Motors in 1920 and retired as Chairman of the Board in 1956. I do not wish to ignore the difficulties faced by General Motors in the last several years but they cannot be attributed to a president who ended his term of office in 1956.

One of the equally-few authors on management who have understood the constitutional approach and advocated it is Peter Drucker. He has, not without reason, called Alfred Sloan the "true professional"[10].

Alfred Sloan was possibly the first man who, based on constitutionalism, clearly saw that management should be understood and practiced as a *profession* in order to solve two problems. *On the one hand*, to manage organizations *well* and, in relation to their purpose, achieve performance and success and, *on the other hand*, to *legitimize* management in society. At a time when the image of the capitalistic tycoon dominated the economy of America as well as Europe, this was very farsighted and unusual. And Drucker is without doubt the first who *formulated* it in a comprehensible manner.

---

10 Peter F. Drucker, *Zaungast der Zeit*, Düsseldorf/Vienna 1979, page 227 and following pages.

Management as a Profession

Against this background, I would suggest that management be considered a *profession*; in principle a profession like any other. From the outset, I wish to make a clear distinction between management and *vocation* and any form of mystification, glorification, and idealization.

The myth of the extraordinary, naturally talented person with special abilities and characteristics is widespread and is clearly a source of fascination in management education and practice. This is not at all healthy for the issue. It hampers a practical understanding of one of the most important functions in modern society. Above all, it hinders sound training. In principle, I do not wish to dispute that there are people who have a special talent for management – perhaps even a vocation for it. However, it is of little use to focus on these people and take them as examples. We cannot learn anything from them; one can only admire, marvel at, and perhaps revere them.

Therefore, I have – as a start at least – a more modest concept which nevertheless goes a step further than the glorification and idealization schools of thought. If management is understood to be a *profession*, more importance is given to what can be learned and, to a certain extent, *taught* – the craftsmanlike side, the *professionalism*. As I will show in this book, there is more evidence available on what can be learnt than is generally assumed. Most managers are satisfied with just a little of what can be learnt and, therefore, they work well below the performance level that could be achieved.

This is a problem in all societies even today, a problem not well understood because, to a great extent, management itself is still not considered a social function. Anomalies, difficulties and undesirable developments, be they economic or in society as a whole, result from management weaknesses much more frequently than is recognized or expressed. Up to now, we have lived with these undesirable developments, and that is why there has been little pressure on managers to improve, even in the business world where they are most prominent. In the future, however, society will not be able to tolerate deficiencies in management. Without professional and particularly *precise* management all areas of society will, to a great extent, no longer be able to function.

Management *can* be learnt; but it *must* also be learnt. A manager does not automatically do everything a manager should be capable of doing, nor is this ability inborn. Hence, I make a distinction not only between management and vocation but also between management and another, equally widely held viewpoint; management as a so-called secondary or amateur activity, a hobby as it were. This perception is never clearly expressed but it is apparent from the actual behavior of a large percentage of managers and from their training. Up to now, we could afford to take this attitude.

Management must be learnt just like any other profession, a foreign language or a type of sport. Management is not simpler or easier than these and it must therefore be practiced. However, neither is it more difficult and anyone can achieve a certain degree of competence, higher than that of an amateur, and many can become highly professional. The fact that there are people who have more of a talent for management than others does not alter the *possibility* or the *necessity* of learning management. Related to this is the need for criteria and standards, such as have been developed by every profession. However, in management these are practically non-existent to date.

On the one hand, I have, therefore, a more modest concept of management that does not presume to be applicable to those lofty beings that imagine they are destined for greater heights. On the other hand, much heavier demands are to be made than those that can be met at an amateur level or by a large percentage of the people practicing management today.

However, can we in principle be content with management as a profession – something that *can be learnt*? Do we not require something *more* for certain tasks and positions – an inborn talent? Can we be content with *management* at all? Do we not need something more – at least sometimes, namely *leadership*? To begin with I will leave these questions open, because the answers depend on what we understand by management. This book is my answer to that question.

According to my suggestion, management *is* not only a profession but it is a part of almost every profession. This is related to the fact that almost every profession today, in clear contrast to earlier times, is practiced within an *organization* or depends on organizations. Management is the profession that renders the *institutions* of a modern society effective, and it is the management part of every profession that makes the *people within* institutions effective.

Very few people have problems with their effectiveness outside an organization. Organizations have created the problem of how to progress from plain work to performance, from effort to results and from efficiency to effectiveness.

Since this is almost always overlooked or ignored in management litera-ture and in management training, it is one of the main reasons that they are irrelevant. We talk about either people or organizations. However, the actual issue is quite different: Management is about *people in organiza-tions* and vice versa, *organizations with people*. The two cannot be sepa-rated, unless it is at the expense of the practice losing all meaning.

If we look at the reasons why managers consider management training programs to be interesting but "purely theoretical", this error always comes to light. Their working conditions, which are an integral part of the reality of their situation, are not taken into account. If we ignore the con-text within which management is practiced, we almost automatically de-velop absurd ideas.

The Most Important Profession in a Modern Society

I have said that management is, *in principle,* a profession like any other. However, there are a few aspects that differentiate it from other profes-sions and which, therefore, justify taking it particularly seriously.

In society, there are more important and less important professions. If there were no mountain guides tomorrow, the lack would not be felt by most peo-ple. As a passionate mountain climber, I would have a problem; but only a few others would take any notice. If there were no ski instructors, the problem would be somewhat more serious but still not a tragedy. It is an entirely differ-ent matter when it comes to pilots, lawyers or doctors as well as managers.

Almost everything, which should be important to us in our society, de-pends on management, on the *professionalism* and *quality* with which this profession is practiced. This is by no means laudable but it is the reality. Management – the *organizing, controlling,* and *guiding* function of a soci-ety – also determines economic *value creation* and thus our *level of pros-perity*. Management mobilizes the resources of a society or lets them lie fallow. It converts raw materials into resources, and then transforms these resources into economic value.

The *productivity* and *innovativeness* of a society depend on manage-ment. Resources can be used productively or unproductively. They can be used for old, outdated purposes or for new, promising ones. What is done with them depends on management.

Whether a society and its economy are *competitive,* depends on management. It is customary to speak of interesting and uninteresting, good and bad sectors. However, this makes little sense when examined more closely. In every industry there are companies which are doing well and others that are experiencing difficulties. The general conditions could be different in each sector, but they are generally similar within the same sector. If the terms of competition are similar, but the results very different, there can only be *one* factor influencing the outcome: the way in which the companies are managed. The best evidence of this is provided by Switzerland and Japan, whose competitiveness and economic success can be attributed almost exclusively to their management competences. In their entire history they have never had what is usually considered to be a location advantage. Cases in Japan also clearly illustrate how *management mistakes* can lead to a loss of competitiveness and how this happens.

I believe it is necessary to expand upon this thought. It is true that I primarily talk about developed countries in the western world; above all, I take my examples from there. However, management is not a characteristic of these countries alone nor is its importance restricted to them. The opposite is more likely the case: that management is of even greater importance for the underdeveloped and emerging countries. Setting aside the ideological, socio-romantic explanations for the condition of underdeveloped countries, we come to the conclusion that the development of a country is linked, above all, to the quality of its management. Hence, there are no underdeveloped *countries,* there is only underdeveloped or inappropriately developed *management* in these countries, which includes nepotism and corruption. Wherever it has been possible to introduce and organize management, the economic and social conditions have quickly improved.

This can even be observed in developed countries, especially in their non-economic sectors. If we expand our view to include management in sectors other than just the business world and if we are not distracted by superficial designations and titles, then management also determines our *level of health and education.* Both depend on people who carry out de facto management functions, even if they themselves do not or are reluctant to call themselves managers. They have other *designations* – medical superintendent, stationmaster, director, dean, head of the institute, or whatever it may be. Their *work,* however, consists to a considerable extent of management functions similar to those of a marketing manager in business, a financial manager, or a plant supervisor. This fact can be generalized. Strictly speaking, there is no social sphere today that can do without organization and therefore management.

Finally, even most people's *contentment,* and perhaps even the issue of whether they can be happy in life, is affected by the actions of managers. Not that I consider making people happy to be the responsibility of social organizations, and especially not the business sector. I have already justified this in the previous chapter. However, everyone who has a job has experienced the joy that comes from working with a competent boss and the hell that it is to work with a boss who is an incompetent failure, perhaps even a dubious character. When all said and done, the day's experiences and incidents are not left behind at the workplace, they are an inseparable part of the persons when they go home. According to statistics, every person employed is linked to approximately 2.5 other people, their spouse and children, who are affected by their experiences, moods and feelings and are thus indirectly affected by management.

These few observations alone demonstrate the importance of management. Therefore, there is every reason to take it seriously. This is why high, in fact the highest, standards are necessary. Management cannot be left to amateurs nor should easy, simple-to-solve problems in a favorable economic situation be set as standards. The *difficult* problems should set the standard by which the professionalism of management is measured. Management is an "all-weather" profession, or better still, it should be seen as a *"bad-weather" profession.* When everything is going well, when the organization is functioning and the economy is booming, management is not really required. It is required in difficult situations. The training and preparation for the manager's profession must be designed for these situations. This is a self-evident fact in every other profession. Pilots are not only trained for flights in fine weather but also for demanding and difficult operations and situations.

A Mass Profession

One special feature of management is that it has become a mass profession. More people than ever before are carrying out de facto management functions today. This fact will be significant in several parts of this book.

Formerly, management was a *privilege*, perhaps even the *burden*, of a *few* people. The number of leaders, managers, commanders, and rulers was small; the few management positions available could only be attained in certain specific ways. People were either *born* to the position as a nobleman or had the *calling* as in the case of the church.

A society did not require much management – it had no organizations. To be more precise, it had only a few, mainly small and, above all, simply structured organizations. The administration, the church, the army – there were no others. Even the largest of them were *small* and *simple* in comparison to modern organizations. Therefore, management was hardly necessary.

Today, the situation is totally different. The modern society is what Peter Drucker has long been calling "organized society", or better still, "the society of organizations".[11] Whatever we do, we do not do it as an individual but as a user of an organization, as its customer or employee. Management is an inevitable consequence of the formation of organizations. All organizations, not only those in the business world such as companies, require management. Management is required for the organizations in the health and education systems, for public administration as well as non-government and non-profit organizations. Therefore, in every country today, many people, a hundred thousand or even millions, must carry out management tasks within organizations – irrespective of whatever else they may be doing.

It would be a crass error within this context to view as managers only those people who are *visible* as mouthpieces for their organizations or those that appear in the media. As I have already stated: *Anyone who manages is a manager.* Even the foreman in a factory carries out management tasks and is, in this respect, a manager. He is perhaps not as important as the board of directors but important enough for *his* management skills to be taken seriously.

If we apply the narrowest criteria, at least 5 percent of the employed population of a developed country consist of managers in the narrow sense of the word. This percentage is comprised of managers in normal industrial companies, the basically outmoded sectors, and typical public administration agencies. If we analyze modern sectors such as computers, infor-

---

11 The expression "society of organizations" is mentioned explicitly and in all clarity by Peter F. Drucker in his book *The Age of Discontinuity*, London 1969, second edition 1994. He had conceived this thought at least ten years earlier.

mation technology, software engineering, biotechnology, consultancy services, finance, service organizations in general, or organizations in the fields of science, art and culture, the percentage is considerably higher, as much as 20 to 25 percent – and growing steadily.

This is why I call it a *mass profession*. For instance, Germany has approximately 30 million people who are employed. Even 5 percent is a remarkable figure, to say nothing of 20 or 25 percent. A country such as Germany, therefore, has several million people who – irrespective of what they call themselves and whatever their self-perception is – must carry out de facto management tasks and are therefore managers.

Just a short time ago, we would automatically have thought of management in terms of an *industrial society*. It is obvious that management plays an important role here. But now and in the foreseeable future, we will need to talk about a *knowledge society*, even though it is likely that no one can yet state exactly what that is, what it will look like, and how it will function.

This much can be said: In a knowledge society, management will play a much more important role than it does in an industrial society. There will be more de facto managers, even if they will probably have very impressive designations, which are not yet known to us, and their tasks will be more difficult than those of today. Regardless of whether the information or service aspect is given precedence and in whatever way the knowledge society develops, it will require *more* and *better* management than any other earlier form of society. This factor takes us directly to the next peculiarity of the management profession.

A Profession without Training

It is striking that only a few managers have *systematic* training in management. Management is the most important mass profession in modern society, and it is – and unfortunately we cannot ignore this unpleasant truth – a profession without training. I do *not* wish to state that all managers are bad or incompetent. There are good and very good managers, those who have mastered their craft. However, they did not achieve this through training but in some other way, which I shall explain in detail.

In no other profession is the training in such a bad state as in management. No one would step into an airplane if the pilots had as in ˙

training as do managers. Similarly, very few people would go into hospital for an operation if this were true of doctors. Considering the *number* of managers, the *importance* of management, and the *risks* involved in management mistakes, this is an astonishing state of affairs.

It is true that a large percentage of managers today, if not the majority, has a degree. However, universities do not train people to be a *manager*. They learn an *academic subject* – be it in the field of science, technology, economics, or perhaps law, psychology, or something similar. And because they are experts, they gain employment in an organization, get to the top of the profession, and one day, while occupying a high position, discover that *management skills* are required along with *technical* competence. Hardly anyone is prepared for this in a systematic way – as is the case for pilots who are trained to assume command of larger aircraft as a matter of course.

Strictly speaking, there have always been only *two* organizations which actually systematically prepare their future managers for their management tasks in the narrow sense and not only for their practical and technical tasks: the army and the church. "Systematic" means, for example, attending the military academies for a period of four years, and that on a *full time* basis. The same holds true for the pontifical academy of the Catholic Church. Even the best training programs in large companies do not come anywhere near to these standards in terms of *duration* and *intensity*. However, it is the content that we should analyze in particular detail and, in this respect, the verdict is discouraging even for the most progressive training programs.

With the exception of business administration, management is not taught to any appreciable degree in any other academic course of study. If any lectures are offered, they are optional subjects. Furthermore, since the main subjects of every course of study demand full application, the students have hardly any time to devote to management.

95 percent of all university graduates practice their occupation in a place where they can hardly be effective without some knowledge of management – *in an organization*, in precisely the environment in which it is anything but easy to *apply* the learnt abilities and knowledge and achieve *results*.

Privately, and in places where people have spent their lives through the ages and where habits and practices have been formed – in the family, on the farm, in small handicraft companies – hardly anyone had, as has already been mentioned, any difficulties with their effectiveness. When they did, they were corrected automatically and quickly because people could immediately *see* the results and also the mistakes. However, results and mistakes are much more difficult to determine in a modern society's organizations, and nothing is corrected automatically.

It could be argued that in the course of their career, a certain number of managers undergo further training such as a MBA course, for example. This is true, but it brings about no appreciable change in the situation described here. The MBA program does precisely what its name suggests: It teaches business *administration* but hardly any *management*. These two fields are by no means identical; in fact they have very little in common.

MBA programs are, without doubt, very suitable for those people who have received no training in business administration. They can acquire a knowledge of business administration relatively quickly. For those who have already studied business administration, they provide the opportunity to catch up on whatever they may have missed in their course of study. Apart from a few exceptions, they cannot be considered to be training for managers.[12]

It is also possible to raise the objection that much can be learnt about management from *internal training programs,* particularly in large companies or from seminars offered commercially. There are companies which have exemplary training programs but they are an exception. The seminar market, too, does offer opportunities to fill in the gaps in knowledge, though this is usually fragmentary and disjointed.

Therefore, it can hardly be expected that anything resembling a complete whole will result from such stopgap measures, which are merely an approximation of the systematic training, which is a matter of course in every profession and is universally expected from a university course. Nor can we hope to attain comprehensive competence or even knowledge from the occasional two-day or three-day seminars, usually attended years apart. Apart from this, there is also the problem of making a selection from the completely impenetrable range of seminars in a market where high quality exists side by side with pompous declarations, empty promises, and quite a lot of rubbish.

---

12 This is also confirmed in one of the most recent studies on the content of MBA programs in which the word "management" is indeed used very often, but other subjects dominate the material. Refer to *Mastering Management – Das MBA-Buch*, Edited by IMD Lausanne/LBS London/The Wharton School of the University of Pennsylvania, 1997.

However, I have emphasized that there are also *good* managers who carry out not only their technical but also their management tasks with great competence. Where they have learnt their craft is the subject matter of one of the following chapters.

Elements of the Management Profession

Every profession is essentially characterized by *four* elements. If management is to be understood as a profession, and if there is the same requirement as in every other profession, namely professionalism, then these same elements must also exist here. As they do in reality.

Tasks

Firstly, a profession is characterized by specific *tasks* which must be carried out. Every profession's tasks can be described and analyzed – be it the profession of a joiner or locksmith, a surgeon or a pilot – and the competent performance of these tasks can be learnt and taught. This is also true of the profession of a manager. Great consummate talent or aptitude is certainly not required to learn a profession's tasks. The learning of tasks requires, above all, the acquisition of some *knowledge*.

Learning tasks is much easier if talent is present. However, even people with an aptitude for surgery must *learn* the tasks of a surgeon. This does *not* mean that *anyone* can become a surgeon. Neither do I maintain that anyone can become a manager. However, a considerable number of people can become decent surgeons, a greater number than was considered possible 100 years ago. Before the introduction of systematic medical training surgery was an exalted skill practiced by only a few, very talented and perhaps particularly courageous men. Today it is possible to make approximately one-third of all medical students – as earlier mentioned – *competent* surgeons. Please note, not international geniuses. To play a decisive role in the latest advances made in surgery, for instance in neurosurgery or organ transplantation, something more than just "being a decent surgeon" is required. What is required is something different and much more than what the best training can impart. However, a third of the medical students can learn to competently perform surgical operations of an average degree of difficulty. And potential geniuses require training to be able to fully deploy their aptitude later.

Tools

The *second* element of every profession consists of the *tools* which are used to carry out tasks. The mastery of tools can be learnt, too. At first – for standard professionalism –, this requires no special aptitude. The mastery of tools requires one thing above all else, namely *training*, indefatigable, continuous training. In principle, the same is true as in the case of tasks: Even those who are talented must be trained in the use of tools. No surgeon is born with the innate ability to work with a bone saw or a laser scalpel. Even people with great talent must be trained to handle a tennis racket or golf club. What is remarkable is that it is the greatest talents who usually undergo the most rigorous training – and this is the case not only in sports but in all walks of life. We can observe this particularly in the field of music. Why then is this concept lacking in management?

Principles

The *third* element of professions comprises *principles* which are followed in carrying out tasks and the application of tools. They govern the *quality* of the work carried out and the use of tools. As in the case of the second element, no talent is required to know and observe principles. Instead what is required could be termed *insight*. Insight in two things in particular: in the importance of a profession and in the risks involved with mistakes. Even this can be taught and learnt. Apart from insight, a certain amount of *discipline* is also necessary for adherence to the principles.

Responsibility

The *fourth* element of every profession is the responsibility that comes with the profession. The degree of responsibility increases or must increase with the importance of the profession and the greater the risks attached to its practice. Even responsibility is not a matter of talent or aptitude, and it is certainly not a matter of some sublime element. What is necessary for responsibility is something for which I use the word *"ethics"*. I do not mean the ethics of the great Occidental philosophy. It is not necessary for a person to have studied the works of Immanuel Kant in order to act in accordance with professional ethics. I mean something more modest, simpler – a certain kind of *everyday ethics*. This involves *taking responsibility* for what we do and occasionally for what we have failed to do.

The first three elements can be taught and learnt. This is not the case with responsibility. Even after 20 years of teaching, I do not know of any way in which responsibility can be taught. We can *appeal*; we can demand *responsibility*; we can sometimes *enforce* it, by legal means, for example. However, these are essentially all secondary mechanisms. What seems to be essential is something totally different – a *decision*, and indeed a highly personal one, which everyone must take at some point in his or her life.

Apart from cases settled through the courts, it is impossible to force another person to take responsibility. However, there are people, and fortunately they can also be found in management and in high positions, who in the course of their lives have made the *personal decision* to take responsibility for whatever they do. Unfortunately, there are others, whose numbers seem to be increasing, who have made the opposite decision of *not* taking responsibility but avoiding it by using every available escape route. There are people who live their lives according to the motto: *I may have committed a mistake but I would be really stupid to take responsibility for it, too.* Regrettably, there are usually many and sometimes even very refined escape routes from responsibility in our society's organizations. Their elimination would be one of the tasks of a modern system and organizational architecture.

Everyone must make the decision for *themselves*, and only the person himself *can* make the decision. However, one thing is clear: A person who does not take responsibility for his actions or lack of them is *not a manager* – not even if he were to occupy one of the highest positions in society – and he can never be a leader. Such a person would be a *careerist*. People will have to bow to the *power* associated with the person's *position*, particularly those who have no option. However, they will not owe that person any *allegiance*. They will work for the sake of the income but not for the *sake of the cause*.

Sound Training Is Possible for Everyone

Based on the first three elements – the tasks, tools and principles, sound training can be developed for the most important mass profession. Most people of average intelligence can acquire the requisite knowledge. This knowledge is the subject matter of the next sections of this book. I will begin with the principles of effective management because these, as mentioned earlier, determine the quality of the practice of management as a profession.

I do not claim that these alone can create the conditions for *peak performance* in management. To carry out the most difficult management tasks competently, something *more* than can be learnt within the framework of training is undoubtedly required. This something more is talent, aptitude, probably some luck, too, and, above all, experience. However, anyone who concerns himself seriously with the craftsmanlike elements of management and works on himself and his competence will be substantially *better* than if he were not to do so.

However, what is more important and frequently overlooked is: *Without* a mastery of these professional elements, any talent is useless. The case of a clearly unsuitable person who is unsuccessful for this very reason is not remarkable. This is only to be expected.

There are two other types of cases which are worthy of note and which are directly linked to the elements of professionalism in management: the case of an untalented person who often achieves astonishing successes through consistent self-improvement; and the tragic case of the talented, often highly intelligent person working with great application, for whom success is elusive due to a lack of effectiveness.

Part II
The Principles of Effective Management

Introduction

The principles I shall be covering in this section lay the foundation for professionalism in management. They are a guide for carrying out management tasks and the application of management tools. They form the core of management effectiveness. I suggest that they also be considered as the essential part of every practical corporate culture. I have never considered the term "corporate culture" to be particularly useful, though I do think what it refers to is useful. Organizations require "the spirit of an organization"; they require *values* such as the value of effectiveness among others. I think these values can be most usefully and clearly expressed in the form of principles. Principles govern people's actions.

Before I explain the principles individually, a few preliminary notes are necessary to prevent misconceptions.

1. Simple but not Easy

The pattern of behavior, which I will explain in the form of principles, is not easy to recognize unless we have *learnt* to perceive it. Neither is it very easy to explain in words. However, once these principles are clearly formulated, they are easily *understood*. No academic study is required for their understanding.

Their simplicity, from an intellectual point of view, is perhaps also the reason why these principles are seldom, if ever, taught. This is true particularly in the academic field. Teachers are not very interested in them and, among the students, only those who already have considerable practical experience are interested. The others are not in a position to relate them to practice, as they have no experience of practice. Therefore, they do not realize the relevance of the principles suggested here.

In this sense, they are *simple* to understand; but acting in accordance with them is difficult for many. Why? There are three reasons for this; of which the last one is to be taken particularly seriously. *Firstly,* the application of principles requires discipline; we must overcome our natural inclinations – something not many people like to do. *Secondly,* many believe that principles cause them to lose flexibility. This is almost always an error; flexibility is often confused with opportunism.

However, there is a *third* reason, a genuine one that makes the application of principles difficult. Though the principles as such, and this is my theory, are the *same* for all organizations and *applicable* to the same extent, they are always applied in a specific *individual case*, which can be quite unlike previous cases, has probably never occurred before, or has never been experienced by a particular manager. A principle can be simple, but the individual case and its specific circumstances are usually very complex. Therefore, understanding principles is something very different from their application, because it is not only the principle that has to be understood. More important for the application of principles is what I know and understand about the actual details of the specific situation. Even the issue of deciding which, if any, principles are to be applied in a particular case can create difficulties.

All of this may sound complicated but most people are familiar with the essence of it. Lawyers are entirely familiar with this idea; it governs a substantial part of their profession. It is one thing to know the laws, it is quite another to apply them. However, everyone has already experienced this kind of situation to some degree. Before we can get our driving license, we have to first learn the traffic rules in theory; even if we have learnt them very well, it does not mean that we are good drivers who can drive confidently and with experience – I will use this word often – in accordance with the provisions of the Road Traffic Act. The key to the application of principles is *training and experience.*

2. Useful in Difficult Situations

As long as we have to deal with situations that are easy to cope with, we do not require principles either in management or anywhere else. The principles to be discussed here are useful, or even necessary, only in a *difficult* situation, when we are confronted with *complex* issues for which there are no obvious solutions. We need principles when we are still sitting in the office late on a Friday evening, working on a difficult problem, when everyone else has already begun their weekend and we ask this question: *What should I do in this situation?*

The situation must be portrayed in such graphic detail because one school of thought in management emphasizes the *complexity* of organizations and consequently the situation faced by managers. With regard to this perception, it disputes or doubts the utility of simple principles. I agree with this in so far as I accept the basic assumption of great complexity and consider this to be one of the main problems of management. Beyond this point, opinions differ significantly with regard to the solutions to this problem, or to express it in a better way, with regard to suitable, sensible or correct behavior within a highly complex environment.

I am of the opinion that the formation and functioning of complex structures, systems and organizations can, above all, be explained by rules, and that successful behavior within them should also be guided by rules. I have explained this in detail in another of my books.[13] In the final analysis, principles are nothing more than rules. It is precisely this perception that made me search for rules of behavior for managers in organizations which would help them deal with complexity – to seek *principles of effective management.* The principles can be very simple, though the outcome of applying and observing them can be highly complex. Or vice versa: Highly complex systems can result from the observance of very simple principles.[14]

3. Not Inborn – Must Be Learnt by Everyone

No one I know of was born with these principles or with behavior that conformed to these principles. Everyone has had to learn them. Not everyone has immediately or readily admitted this. However, whenever I have

---

13 Fredmund Malik, *Strategie des Managements komplexer Systeme*, fifth enlarged edition, Bern/Stuttgart/Vienna 1996. These issues are best addressed in the writings of Friedrich von Hayek.

14 This is essentially the substance of mathematical theory or one of its basic insights at any rate which as such is by no means new. It is the most important element of the social theory developed by the Scottish moral philosophers of the 18th century.

had the chance to look behind the scenes, I have found that even those who, for some reason, did not want to agree with this view, did not have natural talent but had had to learn management just as everyone else did. Why they were inclined to portray themselves as naturally talented has never been clear to me.

If everyone had to learn management, *where did they learn it?* Time and again, the same three ways crop up: The vast majority learnt management, and this is the *first* way, simply through *trial and error*, by trying out all sorts of solutions. This is a lengthy and laborious way, many mistakes are made, and the manager is relatively old by the time the lessons have been learnt. At the age of 20 we do not know what is important in management. Most were well into their late thirties and many way past 40 when they realized, to some extent, what was essential in management.

A small majority, and this is the *second* way, was very lucky to have had a *competent* boss in their first or second job, that is to say quite early in their career. Please note that I am not talking about a cooperative, pleasant or modern supervisor but a competent one. There are people who are both pleasant and competent, but most are not. Neither are they cooperative on principle or because it is considered modern. They are cooperative when it is sensible and effective to be so.

Therefore, the people who belong to the second group have, at the start of their professional life, had a supervisor from whom they can learn something. In the case of a few, the drive and sometimes even the passion to learn something about management, and be better at it, stems from the opposite experience, namely an *incompetent boss*, from the trouble they had with their bosses, or because they suffered under them. However, only the impulse was born here; they then learnt in the first or second way.

The *third* group comprises those people who were able to gain their first experiences of management very early in life, usually in their childhood. Typical examples are people who were heavily involved in youth organizations, those who were actively involved in certain types of sports, or others who were always, not just once, selected in school to be the class representative by their schoolmates. It is easy to see that this third way is a variant of the first; it is learning through trial and error. However, since these people started early, they gained experience much earlier.

These three ways in which management is typically learnt are not characterized by any particular system.[15] It is a lengthy process of learning through experience. At some point in time, we learn enough to be able to carry out our tasks to some degree. I do not hold the opinion that our organizations are filled with bad managers. However, the ways in which people assume or rather stumble into important and sometimes top positions are often highly problematic. It is inconceivable that people in other professions would rely on this type of learning.

4. Ideal and Compromise

If something is formulated as a principle, it sometimes has the appearance of being an ideal. Anyone with any experience would not be naïve enough to believe that an ideal could ever be implemented in management. Compromises must always be made. It is precisely *because of this* that principles or ideals are required, not in order to implement them but to gain the ability to differentiate between *two types* of compromises. Banal though it may sound to some, these are right and wrong compromises. Reaching the right compromise more often than the wrong one is one of the elements that differentiate good management from bad and responsibility from irresponsibility.

Every organization requires a few people in key positions who can differentiate between opportunism and clever behavior. Managers are required who, in difficult situations, not only ask the question mentioned above, *What should I do?*, but also the more important and more difficult question: *What would be right in this situation?*

There are such people, even though some people who are very attached to clichés may find it hard to believe. There are managers who do not look for the easiest or most pleasant option, who are not concerned with what the media or the unions expect, with what would best serve their careers or income, but who are sincere and honest in searching for what is right.

This does not guarantee that they will always find an answer. Even these managers strike a wrong compromise sometimes. However, the occasional

---

15 Only in a few countries is there a fourth way that is highly systematic and thorough. This is training received in the army. Traditionally, it has been very important in Switzerland, though it is losing much of its significance even here.

incorrect compromise does not cause any lasting damage. It is damaging and dangerous when wrong compromises *accumulate,* and this usually happens when the ideal is no longer set as the standard and the principles are forgotten or ignored.

5. What Type Should Be a Model?

What type of manager do I mean when I talk about good or competent managers? This book is the answer to that question and, by the end, I think the answer will be clear to the reader. I first want to mention the type I do *not* mean. I am not thinking of what could be called the "three-year wonder". In three years, a short time, almost anyone can be successful. This is relatively easy. However, this does not prove anything and is not evidence of success. Previously, such people fascinated me because they shot into the limelight. However, short-term success is meaningless. What counts is being successful in the *long* run, for a period of not three but 30 years, always making fresh starts, despite all the setbacks encountered by everyone at some time.

I have long since given up taking the media wonders seriously and studying them. These people either disappear into oblivion just as quickly as they emerged from it, or there is a very different, much more dangerous species: the *multiple* three-year wonder. These are people who apparently have a brilliant career and sometimes occupy the top positions in the business world and society. If their curricula vitae are properly examined, however, it turns out that they have only *one* skill, which they have mastered to perfection and that is that they know exactly when they should leave, and they always leave exactly six months before any sniff of the mess they have created starts to get around. Outwardly, they have brilliant careers; in reality they leave behind a mess everywhere and often even a "trail of blood". They are not managers, especially not good ones, nor are they leaders, they are *careerists.*

Managers must meet a minimum of two criteria before they are or, for the sake of good management, should be of interest to me as potential examples. *Firstly,* they should have occupied the same position for a sufficiently long period that they realize the mistakes they have made. Every manager has made serious mistakes. It is just that there are those who do not admit to them. However, of course this alone is not enough. Anyone can make mistakes. What is important, *secondly*, is how the person has corrected the mistake. This is far more important. Has the person not only committed a mistake but also admitted to it, or has he tried to escape responsibility?

What is also important to me are those people of whom their subordinates and colleagues say, often years after they have left the organization, "*We have learnt a lot from him*". It does not matter if they also add: "*He was difficult; it was not easy to work with him; he could be a bastard...*" as long as they qualify it by saying: "*...but we learnt a lot from him...*". When I hear such statements about someone, I know this person probably provided an example of good management.

Finally, I would like to draw attention to the following aspects, which are sometimes difficult to understand. *Firstly*, each individual principle may, at first glance, appear to be somewhat limited when taken by itself and in isolation. It must be considered in its entirety and, above all, thought must be given to its wider ramifications . To some extent, the consequences resulting from applying these principles may be diametrically opposed to prevailing thought. Therefore, contradictions will become apparent.

Secondly, for those who think that contradictions should, if possible, be eliminated, the question arises which of the two contradicting opinions is better, more correct and practical. I consider this to be one of the most important effects of principles. They provide an opportunity for a critical debate on the issue and, in certain circumstances, this leads to the elimination of wrong ideas and opinions. Compared to other disciplines there is hardly any critical discussion on management issues. In my opinion this is one of the most significant reasons for the fact that there are many fads in this field but little progress.

The application of these principles restricts charlatanism to a great extent. This is because they function as regulatory ideas, standards and criteria that separate right from wrong, practical from impractical, good from bad, and acceptable from unacceptable.

First Principle

Focusing on Results

Only the Results Are Important in Management

The thoughts and actions of competent managers reflect a general pattern which is their focus on *results*. They are primarily, sometimes exclusively, interested in results. Everything else is of secondary importance to them or does not interest them in the least. The fact should not be concealed that their focus on results can sometimes assume even pathological proportions which I do not consider good nor do I recommend it as, to some extent, it is difficult to tolerate. Nevertheless, it is the results that count for them.

A basic assertion of this book is that management is a profession. With regard to this first principle, it may be said that: *Management is the profession of achieving results or obtaining results.* The yardstick is the achievement of objectives and carrying out tasks.

This principle is not always important to the same degree. As long as results are relatively easy to achieve, perhaps due to a particularly favorable economic situation, management is not really under pressure and, in certain circumstances, management may not even be necessary. Under such conditions, this first principle is hardly used. Its application becomes necessary, useful, and even urgent when results are not achieved automatically; when real effort is required.

Of course, adherence to this principle does not mean that all targets will be achieved. To expect or presume such a thing would be naïve. Even managers who have made the principle of focusing on results the foremost maxim for their actions suffer setbacks and must accept failures. However, they do not give up because of this, they do not resign, and, above all, they are not satisfied with explanations and justifications.

A Self-Evident Fact?

It may occur to us to believe that this principle is a self-evident fact that managers act according to this principle in any case, and that it therefore hardly needs to be mentioned. Unfortunately, this is not the case. *Firstly*, this can be observed; we need only look for it. *Secondly*, every experienced manager will confirm it. *Thirdly*, this statement is confirmed by a small test, which I like to conduct occasionally. When I am with managers, and there is occasionally time to have a drink together, I like to ask the question: *What do you do in the company?* All of those questioned describe their actual work. This is only to be expected. Then comes the interesting part. About 80 percent then start to describe how hard they work, how much effort they put in, the amount of stress they are under, and how much trouble they go to. Only 20 percent talk about *results* after they have described their work.

I think this should be given some thought. Some are perhaps too modest to talk about their achievements; they think it would be interpreted as self-praise, bragging or presumptuousness. Even if we were to take that into consideration, the type of answers coupled with other observations would indicate that most people are more focused on *input* rather than *output* in their thinking and perception, and perhaps, therefore, also in their actions. Working hard, making an effort, withstanding stress, etc. are all important, of course. Without this, management would not work. However, this is all *input*. These are exactly the things that do not matter. What counts is the *output*.

Input focus can be recognized by another, very typical symptom. Eight out of ten curricula vitae that I receive when recruiting usually contain quite a long list of *positions* or *jobs* held by the applicant. However, only one out of the ten mentions what he or she *accomplished* in these positions, what his or her achievements were, and finally the extent to which targets were achieved.

Hence, it should not be assumed that people are, naturally of their own accord, focused on output. A human being is, by nature, not focused on output but, to a certain extent, focused on input. A baby asks: *What does the world owe me now that I am here?* It is justified in asking this question because, after we have brought it into the world, we owe it a few things – nourishment, education, love, etc. It is alright for a baby to have this attitude. However, at some point in time, let us say between the ages of 15 and 25, a person has to learn to turn the question around radically. It should no longer be: *What does the world owe me?* but the opposite: *What do I owe this world at this point, after I have been brought up for these 25 years, had the privilege of getting an education and training and having obtained a degree at university?*

Some may think that a question framed in this manner sounds pathetic. But this change in viewpoint and attitude is crucial for managers and their effectiveness. It is one of the keys to their success.

Once the principle of focusing on results is taken seriously, and the world is viewed from this standpoint, it is remarkable how many people are always in a position to say – and also to justify very well – exactly what will *not* work, what is *not* possible, what is *not* functioning. I would suggest that too much time is spent on this. Managers should direct their strength, energy, and attention to things that *do* work. If these people are young, we must give them the chance to retrain and show them some patience. However, if we are dealing with people from an older age group, we cannot stand by and watch for very long.

Misconceptions

This principle is often plagued by inappropriate application and misconceptions which frequently trigger very emotional reactions. *Firstly*, it is to be noted that I expressly call this principle a *management principle* and *not* a general *life principle*. Very often management and life principles get mixed up, confused or equated with each other. However, we must be able to separate them. What is right for management does not necessarily have to apply to life, and vice versa.

If one wants to apply the principle of focusing on results in their lives, one must make that decision on a very personal level. For my part, much of what I do in my life is not because of the results but for totally different reasons – because it gives me pleasure, because it is fun, because I think it is beautiful, etc. I am a passionate skier; however, I do not ski to win races but because I enjoy skiing. On the other hand, management cannot be practiced for the sake of fun or enjoyment. Management must be focused on results and its effectiveness measured according to those results.

Secondly, this principle in itself, as with all the other principles, has nothing to do with *style*. From experience we can say that many managers find it astonishingly difficult to understand and accept this. The discussion on management style, which has dominated literature and training for decades, has made it almost impossible for many to differentiate between form and substance, outward characteristics and content. What could perhaps be a question of style is how we apply or express a principle. This can be done harshly, roughly or loudly; but this is probably not a very helpful style. We can also apply it quietly, kindly, and in a friendly manner. This is another style, probably the better one. The principle itself, its substance, its assertion, and its validity, however, are not affected by the style.

A focus on results has nothing to do with brutality, backbreaking work or anything like that. Therefore, the principle of focusing on results is not only to be found, as many believe, in organizations in the *business world* to which harshness, and occasionally even inhumanity, are imputed time and again. This principle is found in *every* organization that is *well managed*, in every one that *achieves results*. Schools have to aim for results in the same way as business enterprises; the results are only different in their nature. Even hospitals have to achieve results; this is the sole purpose for which they are established. The same holds true for the Salvation Army, a military organization, or a society for the promotion of world peace. Even an association that sets as its objective the combating of harshness in management has to achieve results.

Inevitably the question arises: *What* results are actually meant when focusing on results? This question, as important as it is, is also independent of the principle. What I discount, for obvious reasons, is the sophistic opinion expressed occasionally that failure to achieve an objective is a result in itself. In purely formalistic terms, that may be true, but that is not what is meant here. However, a practical, positive answer can *only* be given when we are talking about a particular, specific organization. It is obvious that the results important to companies are different from those in the case of public administration bodies or cultural and arts organizations.

There are two categories of results that are always to be found in every organization. *Firstly*, there are results related to *people*, to their selection, promotion, development, and deployment; and *secondly*, results related to *money*, to the procurement and utilization of financial resources. In other words, every organization needs money and it needs people. Apart from this, it is difficult to generalize. Even within these two categories, there are vast differences between organizations. For example, even if money is important for every organization, its role in companies is totally different from the one in non-commercial or non-profit organizations.

Results must, by no means, be always and exclusively *economic* results, as is assumed only too quickly. Hence, management does not inevitably lead to a purely materialistic, economic viewpoint that people who do not work in the business world, and sometimes are not well acquainted with it, are quick to assume. They occasionally confuse results as a whole with a particular type of result that is given prominence in the business sector. As soon as this misconception is cleared, it is evident that, as has already been mentioned several times, *every* organization needs results. Organizations are established precisely because of this and for this purpose.

Therefore, the principle that results are what matters and, in the final analysis, nothing else, is applicable to all organizations. In complete contrast to widely held assumptions, this principle is much more important and also more difficult to apply in organizations which aspire to non-commercial, non-material and, above all, non-financial results. The principle is of particular importance in areas where quantification is not possible, something that is almost always possible, to a great extent at any rate, in the case of economic results.

Effective people do not question how much or how hard they work; they ask about the results. They care little, if at all, about their motivation, but are very interested in the results. After working hard, they are just as tired and exhausted as the others are, but that does not satisfy them; they also want to know if anything has been achieved.

And what about Those Who Cannot Accept This?

This gives rise to an important question: *What do we do about people who cannot live according to this principle despite all the explanations, distinctions and clarifications?* There are people, perhaps a majority, who say something to the effect that: *I understand what you mean but this is not my world; I cannot (or will not) accept this.* Are these incompetent people? Are they bad employees? Are they unsuitable? Though these possibilities cannot be ruled out, it is seldom the case. Many of them are sensitive, cultured people, who are, however, a little "detached from the realities of management".

The consequence is that these people should, *firstly*, not be given responsibility for other people, and, *secondly*, that they should not be responsible for an organization and its divisions. The attitude should be somewhat as follows: *You say that you cannot accept this principle. I am glad you told me this. It takes a lot of courage to admit to something like this in today's society. However, now that I know, it is my duty as your boss to ensure that you never get a management position in this organization...*

This certainly does not mean, and this must be emphasized, that the person has to leave. It could be that the person is a highly qualified specialist whose expertise and factual knowledge is crucial to the organization. However, such people must be kept away from this type of *management* position, in the interests of the organization and the people who would have to suffer under their incompetent management and, above all, in their own interests because they themselves very often suffer under the constraints of a management role. These types of people become ill in a management position, they cannot sleep, they are stressed, they become nervous, and it is not rare for them to lose their value as experts because they cannot perform under these circumstances. Such a burden should not be placed on people and, if it is, the mistake should be quickly rectified.

In order to avoid this type of error, I consider it important to ask, starting with ourselves, more often than is usual: *Do you really want to be a manager? Do you actually want that – and are you very clear about what that means? Above all, do you know that under certain circumstances you have to adhere to principles and make decisions, which you may feel are hard and painful?*

These questions are not asked often enough. Too many people aspire to attain management positions in complete ignorance of what they entail. These are not well thought out, deliberate decisions but people who stumble into situations which they do not understand. Most are seduced by status symbols, a better income, and the prospect of importance and influence.

I do not wish to present a case for the incorporation of clear and strict self-testing obstacles, similar to those that existed, and continue to exist, in religious orders, for example. That would perhaps be taking things too far. However, aptitude test criteria modified in an appropriate and sensible way would also be advisable for management.

The principle of focusing on results deeply affects a few convictions which are widely held and indiscriminately accepted. They are to be found in company mission statements, they are standard statements in lectures, are championed with the deep conviction of religious belief, and are usually defended emotionally, sometimes even aggressively. If these convictions are questioned, it is taken as an affront.

One of these religious tenets is: *Work should be pleasurable, it should be enjoyable.* It appears in various forms – as a demand, as an expectation, as a postulate of modern personnel management.

Pleasure or Result?

It would be easy to say that the best option would be both. However, it is not so simple. I wish to engender *skepticism* and encourage managers not to rashly accept this statement. Without doubt it sounds very *plausible* and also *humane* that work should be enjoyable. It is precisely because of this that I want to ask people to examine the issue *critically* and, above all, to think it through to its logical conclusion. This is not only applicable to *this* statement but in general to everything that sounds plausible and humane. Quite often there are serious errors and misconceptions associated with such statements, and they sometimes lead to consequences, which are the *exact opposite* of what a manager should or does want.

For these reasons, I want to submit a few thoughts for discussion. First of all, I naturally concede that it is wonderful when work is enjoyed. It would be ridiculous to demand anything else, the opposite for example, that work should be the cause of suffering. Despite and actually due to my skepticism, I do not wish to raise any doubt that wherever it is possible to make working a pleasure, *significant progress* has been made. It is a great *privilege* when someone has a job that gives him pleasure. Therefore, as a manager, we should also do something to ensure that as many people as possible enjoy their work in the organization. This is the *sensible* interpretation of this statement.

However, the issue becomes problematic when a desirable objective becomes an alleged *claim*, a demand, when people begin to believe that they have a "right" to work that is enjoyable.

I suggest that the following elements be reflected on and that subordinates be made aware of them clearly and unequivocally:

No job is enjoyable at all times: Some people seem to believe and expect that their work should be enjoyable the whole day, every day of the year.

This is, of course, a naïve illusion, and disappointment is therefore inevitable when someone has this expectation.

We should be happy, and it is certainly a privilege, when work in general and for most of the time is interesting and is able to confer a certain degree of satisfaction. To expect more is completely unrealistic. Therefore, we must be able to get through every stage, including those where we enjoy work to a lesser extent or not at all; this is the crucial test. We cannot hope to pass this test if our mind is set on the wrong expectations.

Every job has elements that can never be enjoyed by anyone: Even the most interesting tasks and activities have unpleasant aspects. All work has facets that are boring and troublesome but are a part of it. Even when efforts are made to reduce the arduousness to a minimum through careful job design, enough remains to occasionally make employees "grit their teeth".

Even those jobs which many people think are the most interesting, such as the conductor of an orchestra, a pilot, or something similar, have their boring aspects. Many conductors do not enjoy the endless orchestra practices or tour-related travel and hotel stays that are simply a part of the profession. Moreover, when the same Mozart symphony is performed for the 125th time, it becomes routine for the orchestra and the conductor; I know of people who, with all due respect, can no longer listen to Mozart for this very reason. In the same way, the 864th gall bladder surgery is an irksome routine for a surgeon; it is always the same and hardly ever enjoyable. In practicing their profession, pilots spend a substantial portion of their time carrying out tasks that are pure routine, which is not a source of pleasure to anyone. Even the chairman of a group of companies does not derive pleasure from every aspect of his work nor does he enjoy it every single day.

There are certain jobs that have to be done and are not pleasurable for anyone: Even though there is tremendous improvement in working conditions and in the automation of degrading work, with the best intentions in the world there will, in all forms of society irrespective of their stage of development, still (perhaps always) be activities that are not enjoyed by *anyone*. There are toilets to be cleaned, dustmen are required, and there are many jobs for unskilled workers that are not enjoyed even by those people who are satisfied with the lowest of standards.

The maxim that work should be enjoyable is even more questionable for people who, in the course of their work, are faced with misery every day: refugee helpers who cannot really help; social workers who cannot overcome drug addiction, prostitution, or homelessness; teachers and priests in the slums of large cities; doctors and nurses who all too often fight a losing battle in the intensive care units or cancer wards.

What are these people to make of the hedonistic demand which constantly surfaces especially in business management that work should be fun or enjoyable? In many cases it would be nothing short of hardened cynicism if a person could enjoy such work.

There may be several motives which drive people to take up such work; perhaps out of compassion or for humanitarian reasons but certainly not for pleasure or fun. They do not do their work for fun but because it has to be done. They do it out of a *sense of duty* even though this may sound pathetic or old-fashioned to many people.

Doing one's duty is an expression that has fallen into increasing disuse in the last 20 years. It is as good as never mentioned in management and motivation literature. In its place have come self-actualization, the hedonistic principle and self-pity, one of the legacies of the "sixties generation" to which I belong. Although I was witness to the movement at university and was fascinated by it for a (short) time, I now consider it to be one of the greatest evils of the second half of the twentieth century.

Performance of one's duty and a sense of duty are terms that do not form a part of the vocabulary of so-called intellectuals. They are, however, indispensable for the managers in society, and equally essential is the courage required to demand them, especially when they are not so popular.

There are things that must be done simply because they must be done and for no other reason, completely irrespective of whether they give joy or pleasure; in fact, especially when they are not enjoyable.

These considerations show that we must be careful in generalizing the statement that work should be enjoyable. What is more, when and as long as work is a joy, we are not really taxed as managers, and management is hardly required. Management is put to the test when the situation is difficult, when we can find little or no pleasure in work but the tasks have to be carried out all the same. As much as it is possible to agree with the essence of this demand and its sensible interpretation, uncritical generalization is equally dangerous. It produces expectations, and their consequences are demands that can never be fulfilled. Therefore, not only do I personally have reservations about this statement, I never actually use it.

The demand that work should be enjoyable does not take at least three other important points into account.

Firstly, it is a commonly held opinion that we cannot do something well if we do not enjoy doing it, that enjoyment is a necessary condition for good performance. We only have to take the example of doctors to doubt the veracity of this opinion. If it were true, we would hardly ever undergo an operation. However, in my discussion of the fourth principle, I will show that this opinion is absolutely wrong and why it is so in two ways: It does not correspond with the facts, and it is totally unacceptable in an organization; it is empirically and normatively wrong.

Secondly, the demand for enjoyment directs attention to precisely the *wrong* element. The assertion makes people concentrate on the work itself instead of something completely different, and more important, the actual topic of this chapter, namely, the *results* of work, performance.

My suggestion is as follows. Wherever work can be enjoyed, that is all well and good. However, even where this is not always or is never possible, what is occasionally possible is that pleasure can be derived from the *results*. Our thinking and motivation should focus on this. This is possible even when the work itself is dull, hard or bordering on humanely intolerable. Cleaning the toilets at airports, emptying the same rubbish bins day after day, and cleaning excrement and vomit from patients cannot be pleasurable even for illiterate unskilled workers. They know that they are at the lowest level of our society. They have no illusions on this score.

Nevertheless, even these activities can be linked to results, to a performance that can kindle a little pride. We should not fool ourselves that it will be a lot, but a woman who cleans the toilets can feel a certain amount of pride when her toilets are the cleanest in the hotel, and when this is acknowledged by a guest or the hotel manager from time to time. An auxiliary nurse can derive a certain amount of satisfaction from the fact that in doing his work he improved, to some extent, the condition of the people most desperately in need of care.

I would recommend that the sentence "Work should be enjoyable" be deleted from managers' vocabulary and that it should be replaced, if at all, with the statement: *The results should give pleasure.*

There are managers who say to me that this is one and the same thing. I simply do not agree. Even if the statements sound similar, there is a substantial difference between them. The *first* demand cannot be realized to any great extent even in our modern and developed world. The *second* demand can be realized to a far greater extent. The *first* statement produces expectations that cannot be fulfilled. The expectations associated with the *second* statement can almost always be fulfilled. The *first* sentence directs attention to the input, the *second* to the output, the results.

Directly related to this is the third point where the demand "Work should be enjoyable" does not take everything into account. To first fix the attention on results leads to a concentration on *effectiveness*, the effectiveness of the work. The work as such is not what is important. It could even be said that it is an unfortunately unavoidable, often irksome distraction from or a precondition for what is really important: what is *achieved* – and it is precisely this which relates to effectiveness.

Instead of concentrating on enjoyment in work, we should focus on effectiveness. In this I see a very important and grossly neglected task for managers. Giving people a sense of pleasure in their effectiveness, and pointing out that effectiveness can be enjoyable.

The interesting thing about effectiveness is that it can, on its own, be a source of happiness and thus become a source of motivation. The following facts can always be seen:

- The more effectively someone deals with something and the more thoroughly and seriously he does this, the more *interesting* this thing becomes. A major cause of boredom and frustration is the superficiality with which people approach something.
- The more effective someone is, the *easier* the work becomes. What previously could only be done with effort and exertion, can be done quickly and easily once effectiveness improves. The person decides to do something and then does it competently and effectively instead of constantly struggling and making a great effort with it. Supported by his effectiveness that person does not have constant struggle with himself.
- It is possible to experience the pleasure of *success itself* and the pride in it when looking back. The work as such may not have changed but this is not what counts and is no longer a fixation. Instead, it is the effectiveness with which the work is done that brings a feeling of satisfaction.
- The more effective a person is, the *greater* are the tasks that person can be entrusted with, and it is this that leads to better career prospects even in difficult times.

In summary, if work can be enjoyed, that is all well and good. However, what is more important is that the results of work and the effectiveness with which it is done should give pleasure and pride. Average managers are satisfied with the first; good managers aim for the second. They thus help their subordinates and themselves to achieve a much higher degree of motivation and achievement. They contribute towards helping the people they are responsible for to find what is perhaps the most important thing in life – meaning. Meaning, as we can learn from Viktor Frankl[16], is seldom found in an activity as such. Meaning is to be found in the results of an activity and in the effectiveness with which it is done, even when the activity itself has no meaning nor, with the best will in the world, does it make sense to anyone else.

Thus, it is clear that the first principle of effective management has many important effects. Its *first* effect is that it guides the people in the organization, their attitudes, their thinking, and their actions towards what the organization needs because it has been established for that particular purpose. The *second* effect is that, if properly understood and thought through to its logical conclusion, it contradicts widespread convictions and ideas on management. I indicated this at the beginning, and this will also be a characteristic feature of the other principles as well.

---

16 Viktor Frankl, *Der Mensch vor der Frage nach dem Sinn*, Munich/Zurich, third edition 1982.

Second Principle

Contribution to the Whole

What Matters Is Making a Contribution to The Whole

I find the second principle the most difficult to explain to people in lectures and seminars. Among the principles it is the most abstract, but it is important. The application of this principle brings about a radical change in the attitude of managers. It is one of the factors that reduces the impact of the greatest obstacles in the way of performance in organizations, and it lays the foundation for solutions to a whole range of notorious management problems:

- It is the essence of what we can call *holistic* thinking.
- It is one of the requirements for *entrepreneurial* behavior.
- It is the only way in which specialists can be converted into the *right type* of generalists.
- It is one of the few ways to create *flat* organizations with *little hierarchy*, or, at least, it ensures that the existing hierarchies do not have a disruptive effect.
- It is one of the elements that ensure an *enduring* state of motivation.

These provide sufficient grounds to take this principle seriously and to deal with it here.

The basic idea of the second principle is best expressed in the "story of the three bricklayers". Some may find this parable a bit pathetic but it serves the purpose. A man goes to a building site where three bricklayers are hard at work. There is no apparent difference between them. The man goes to the first and asks: *What are you doing?* The man looks at him, puzzled and says: *I am earning my living.* He goes to the second and asks him the same question. This bricklayer looks at him with bright eyes, visibly proud, and says: *I am the best bricklayer in the world.* Then the man goes to the third bricklayer and asks him the question. The bricklayer thinks for a brief moment and then says: *I am helping to build a cathedral...* Which of the three is a manager in the best sense of the word? Of course, this is a rhetorical question; it is obvious to anyone who, from personal experience, is familiar with the way organizations function.

A person is not a manager by virtue of his position and status, income and privileges, powers and authority. A manager is someone who perceives the whole or at least strives to perceive it and who then sees his task, irrespective of his position and specialization, as making a contribution to this whole. He envisions the cathedral and helps to build it.

Position or Contribution?

The crucial element of the second principle is that effective managers do not understand their tasks from the point of view of their *position* but from the point of view of what they can *contribute* from this position with their knowledge, abilities and experience. Position, status and privileges are not important to them as such; they are only important to them in so far as they help them to make a certain contribution. The position, and all that is related to it, is a prerequisite for doing something, achieving something.

It is positions that establish an organization's hierarchy. However, what is important is not the hierarchy itself but the issue of whether it is *obstructive*. Managers who are guided by their contribution render the hierarchy meaningless. It is still there, it has not been removed, but it has no impact.

You may suspect that I am far too idealistic and that managers are much more attached to material things, privileges and status symbols than is assumed here. It would, of course, be wrong to deny that there are such people, probably a clear majority, in organizations in the business world, at any rate. However, there are two things which should be noted. *Firstly*, not every manager is a materialistic person, as portrayed in the media. The popular public image of the manager, cultivated with the active help of at least a part of the media, corresponds to the reality in only a very limited way. Unfortunately, many elements of questionable attempts at in-depth psychology, interpretations of conspiracy theories, and also plain ignorance play their part in this. However, the *second* and much more important aspect is the line I draw between managers and *good* managers, between mere jobholders and managers interested in effectiveness.

I am by no means idealizing managers in general and attributing noble motives to them. I know too many far too well to do so. Nonetheless, I do not wish to thoughtlessly make the common mistake of assuming the opposite, of starting with negative assumptions. Even though it may be difficult for some people to believe, there *are* managers who actually want to make a contribution, either exclusively or primarily. *They are the ones* from whom we can and should learn. It is precisely this type of people that I have in mind for this book, and they were and are predominantly the type of people who interest me and who I have studied more thoroughly.

This does not necessarily mean that they do not bear in mind their own interests, their income, and their position of power. If *both* can be achieved, so much the better. However, what is important is that there are managers who, in times of doubt and given a choice, give priority to the *contribution*. In my experience, as pointed out earlier, they are not the majority; but neither are they as rare as certain zeitgeist commentators would have us believe. Whether many or few, this is a superficial criterion. What is important is that it is the *good* people who perform the real work, who really do something. They are not always those who are in the spotlight. For the media, or at least certain sections of the media, they are uninteresting; which is why we hear little of them, and also why many believe that such people just do not exist.

These distinctions need to be made in order to distinguish between genuine quality and mere PR glamour, to separate media events from real performance. These are the things that establish not only whether someone is a genuine manager but also whether a lecturer or consultant in this field is conversant with issues relating to management. This is exactly what is required if management is ever to achieve the same professional standards that have been established over time in other professions.

Hence, in the example given at the beginning, the third bricklayer is a genuine manager in the best sense of the word, even if he is only a bricklayer and will never be given power of attorney for the company, a nice office, or a higher income. The first bricklayer is not a problem. There are many such people, there always will be, and we will always need them. There are people who live their lives according to the motto: *I do good work for good wages, for more money, I will do more work, and for less money, I will do less work.* This type of person seldom presents any difficulties; once it is known how they think, they are easy to manage. We should not try to change them, unless they are still very young. The young people should certainly be asked whether this is really all they want from life. If the answer is yes, there is little we can do.

Specialist or Generalist?

The *second* bricklayer is a big problem. He belongs to the type known as *specialists*. A specialist is not only a person with special knowledge or special training but, and herein lies the problem, also one whose *self-perception* and *view of life* are based on and result from his ability. He is the type who is deeply convinced that the universe has been created for him to indulge in his special field. He is fervently, even passionately, interested in everything that happens in *his* subject; this is all well and good, it is the *professional ethos*. However, nothing *else* interests him, and this is *indifference*. He is proud of his expertise, and rightly so; however, he is equally proud of the fact that he does *not* understand anything else, and this is *arrogance*. Arrogance and indifference are the typical shortcomings of the specialist and create serious problems for every organization. They belong to a list of deadly sins, which go against the spirit of a good organization.

In this sense, *incorrectly* understood specialism is one of the causes, if not the most important cause, of frequently lamented *communication problems,* and of the problem of *losing touch with reality* encountered in so many organizations, which is mentioned less frequently but is equally important. Specialists know their own reality but the reality of the *organization* is a matter of indifference to them. Therefore, they can, with the self-assurance of the ignorant, operate unperturbed and oblivious of this reality.

Of course, I am not in any way against specialists or specialization. In fact, the complete opposite is true. I consider disdain for specialization as dangerous for all manners of progress and achievement, just as I usually consider the idea of generalists to be naïve and romantic. The view that we can create generalists by making a specialist study not one but two, three or four subject areas is particularly unrealistic. This method is totally unsuitable; it is impractical from the point of view of time and also with regard to what people can achieve.

Specialization is important and necessary. On the one hand, a modern society has only specialists; there are practically no other people because everyone is, in his own way, a specialist. On the other hand, society *needs* highly trained specialists in every field. Otherwise, little would be achieved today and, most importantly, without specialization, there would be little chance of becoming better than others, of becoming or remaining competitive.

What is being proposed here is a specialist who *integrates into the whole*, and this is only possible in practical terms when the second principle of effective management is given prominence. There is no other choice. We must make specialists, since they are the only people available, *productive* and *effective*. The specialist-only is useless; in fact he is dangerous. On the other hand, a specialist able to contribute to the whole is perhaps the most *important* resource in a modern society.

To return to the parable of the three bricklayers, the third bricklayer is as specialized as the second one. The difference between them is not in their competence *as bricklayers* or in their degree of specialization. They differ *fundamentally* in their *attitude to the whole*, in what they look at, what they take notice of, and what they consider relevant. They differ greatly in their behavior, which is governed by completely different principles.

Holistic Thinking

I said earlier that the principle of focusing on contributions is the real essence of holistic thinking. Today, there is a demand everywhere for a holistic and interrelated way of thinking. I, too, was for several years very active in introducing and promoting this concept. Now, I no longer do this. *What is holistic thinking? What is demanded of people in this context?*

A person thinks the way he does; he cannot do otherwise. We should be thankful if they occasionally think *correctly*, in the sense of *logically correct*. But holistic? This demand *cannot be met*. What is possible is *another* demand, namely to think *of* the whole. Admittedly, this is not always easy but it is possible. An employee can learn to do this; one of the first tasks for a manager is to make subordinates aware of the whole, to make it easy for them to perceive the whole.

This can probably be observed best in good orchestra conductors. Each musician is an exquisite instrumentalist and, as such, a high-grade specialist. This they remain for a lifetime. A clarinetist will never become a violinist; and the horn-player will never devote himself to the oboe. The musicians will not take up another instrument even within their *group* of instruments – which is why all talk of "wind instruments" or "string instruments" holds no practical significance for the musicians themselves. Other than as abstract categories, they do not exist for them. A trombonist cannot coax a useful note out of a trumpet. Even if they could eventually do so after practicing for a long time, they would be ruined as trombonists and, what is more, they would be bad trumpeters.

This does not actually pose a problem for conductors. They will never require a generalist; they only need these specialists and they would, therefore, never demand of a violinist that he also plays the trumpet. However, there is one thing they would do. The great conductors take great pains to make the musicians understand the piece of music, the symphony, *as a whole*, and what they ask of each instrumentalist is that he or she should *integrate* with the orchestra keeping the symphony in mind. Even a solo is a part of the whole and insignificant by itself. Virtuosity lies not in playing the instrument well but placing this talent at the disposal of the music.

Please note that I am not talking about integration in general, I am taking care to talk about integration only with regard to the piece to be played. Integration as such does not exist, something that is not understood by many who constantly demand it. What does exist, even in orchestras of course, is "interpersonal relations", so often talked about in the business world and something that is always thought of as positive, but this is a fallacy. There are friendships but there are also enmities; there is camaraderie but also cool distance; envy, jealousy, pleasure and admiration, almost every emotion that exists amongst people who work together. However, these are not elements of the integration necessary to create music. Whether the first trumpeter likes the second trumpeter or not is just about the most insignificant thing I can think of. It is the task which is important; it could be "Bruckner's Seventh" or, in the case of jazz, *Take Five*; the task defines what has to be done.

Contribution and Motivation

Contributing to the greater whole also affects the type of motivation required in an organization, a motivation that is independent of any incentives or motivational methods adopted by the supervisor. Knowledge of the whole, serving the whole, awareness of contributing something important to its creation, maintenance and success are largely independent of the interplay of everyday motivational strategies. On such a foundation, a much more stable and better state of motivation can be created than is possible with most of the other so-called motivators.

Now, I do not in any way maintain that *everyone* can be made to perceive the whole in the way that is discussed here. Neither is there such a requirement in the principle of focusing on contribution, something that is frequently misunderstood. The assertion is that this principle has been deduced from the thoughts and actions of good, *effective* managers, and that it is this way of thinking and acting that *makes* them effective. Knowledge and ability are not ends in themselves for these people, nor is their position or power. These are means and conditions for achieving something for the organization, company, orchestra, hospital, faculty, or department.

It is precisely this attitude, in other words, the application of this principle, or to use an even better phrase, the self-imposed obligation to be disciplined which, to give an example, makes managers use simple, understandable language instead of the technical jargon which they as specialists are so well-versed in. They do not want to prove to others, especially their subordinates, how clever they are but rather want to make themselves understood and thus have an effect on something. As specialists, they are in a position to impress their colleagues, perhaps with a lecture at a conference, if that is absolutely necessary. However, as managers, they refrain from this within their organizations.

As managers and as people who wish to be effective, they sometimes lift their heads from their files, let their gaze wander to the view outside their window and ask themselves: *What does my area of specialty mean to the world and to this organization? Who benefits from what I am doing here? What should I do to ensure that it is worthwhile?* They are aware that the benefits will not accrue in their own backyard but will be enjoyed outside the organization, by those in the market and the recipients of its services. Focusing on contribution is the foundation of customer orientation; it is a requirement for creating customer benefit, and is therefore also a basic condition for professional marketing. These are important elements of entrepreneurial thinking.

The principle that the contribution is what matters is also a requirement for being open, innovative, and always capable of learning. The tunnel vision found in the specialist-only is much more dangerous than actual blindness, because the specialist *believes* he can see, and he is proud that he does not look beyond his areas of expertise. The specialist sees the diseased liver, not the patient; they see the profit, not the company; they see the address to the jury, not the defendant; they see the product, not the customer.

Contribution instead of Title

It is obvious that this attitude cannot be demanded from everyone. However, it must be demanded from *managers* and they must be educated and trained for it. Most managers are not clear about, familiar with, or aware of this attitude. I have already mentioned that, whenever possible, I always ask managers the question of what they do in their company. And I also revealed that they all talk about their work in reply. But *how* do they do this?

The first says he is the manager of market research in such and such a company. The second reports that he is the director of so and so a bank. The third is the quality assurance manager and the fourth says that he is the shop floor supervisor in the ABC company. All four answer with the post contained in their job descriptions or their contracts; they answer with their titles. However, this is not what is important, and this is not what is being asked either. The question is not: *Who are you?* but *What do you do?* It goes without saying that a person can state the designation of his position. However, this does not in any way guarantee that he knows what it means, knows what the whole is and what he has to contribute to it.

If we are interested in management effectiveness, we cannot be content with this. We must ensure that as many employees as possible in the organization, first and foremost the managers, see the "cathedral", that they see the whole, their purpose, and their role with as much *clarity* as possible.

How is this done? Essentially, it is very simple. The manager asks his subordinates at regular intervals: *What is your contribution?* Or better still, to be more precise, slightly less polite, and thus more effective: *Why are you on the payroll of this company?* It is astonishing how rarely this elicits a proper answer. Most people do not know how to answer this question, not least due to the fact that they have never been asked such a question. We must then discuss this with them in detail. We should work towards enabling them to give a certain type of answer. Their answer should not begin with: *I am...*, but with *In this organization, I am responsible for...*

For instance, what is the role of a market researcher, if his work is to be a contribution to the whole, to the success of the company? Should they collect data? Should they conduct interviews? Should they commission the services of market research institutes? All this may well have to be done but it is certainly not the most important thing. The complete answer in the case of the head of market research would be something along these lines: *It is my duty to ensure that my company knows exactly what our customers want...* This is a useful start, at any rate. A market researcher who has understood this does not need to be shown the way; they know it themselves. They can *independently* place themselves and their contribution in the service of the whole; they do not require any further guidance.

This is another way in which hierarchies are perhaps not removed but are rendered irrelevant *in reality*; they do not disappear but they become insignificant. And, more importantly, the market researcher who has understood all this and acts accordingly should actually be seen as a net-worker. Unfortunately, this concept is seldom clear in our own mind. We talk a lot about *networks* but what exactly does this mean? Very often, it is taken to mean "People who sit at computers". Under certain circumstances, such people could be a risk and extremely costly if, and for as long as they are unaware of the whole, and do not place themselves at its disposal – in the same way as the bassoonist in the orchestra does.

In my opinion, we should never assume that an organization's employees are aware of these things. We *think* that these things are obvious, or should be obvious. They are not, and this should be our guiding premise. Accordingly, one of the tasks of management is to ensure that all these things are made clear.

The Consequence of Organization

Formerly, organization was not a problem. There was a very simple reason for this: *The job organized the people*. Whether it was a hundred years ago or in the present days, a farmer has never had to be told what he has to do, when he has to get up in the morning, and what he has to contribute. When the cows get restless around five o'clock in the morning, it is clear what has to be done.

The world was *tangible*; it could be perceived using the *five senses*; it was understandable because we could *touch* it. The world could be felt, heard, and seen. What is the situation like in our modern organizations and not only in large ones? Almost all of them have reached such a degree of abstraction that comprehending them using the senses is completely impossible. Modern people in the modern organization literally suffer from what is known in technical terms as *sensory deprivation*. They suffer from withdrawal and, we can honestly say, from progressive withdrawal of sensory experience. They cannot see the whole, as we can see a cathedral or at least its plan; we cannot smell a modern organization, neither can we hear it or touch it. Actually, it can only be (re)constructed in our head. This, however, is something out of the ordinary, and only a few people have ever learnt to do it. Therefore, people withdraw to their small areas of expertise which they know and understand.

While in days gone by, the job organized the people, the reverse is true today: *People must organize the job.* However, people have not learnt to do this either. Therefore, one of the management tasks is to train people to do this. As mentioned earlier, in essence it is simple. We discuss with them the contribution they are to make. This automatically forces us to think about the "cathedral", and to find ways to make it as visible, clear and understandable as possible. The discussion continues until the people spontaneously begin their answers with: *I am responsible for…*

It is my suggestion that this should be done once a year for a whole day, and the discussion should only be on this topic, without a dozen other items crowding the agenda, as is unfortunately the case on so many occasions. We should do this once a year with younger, new or inexperienced employees and approximately once every three years with older and more experienced employees. For the latter, the issue needs not be overstated, but it should not be abandoned completely either. The reason for this is simple. Within approximately three years, every job changes because the economy and the world change. Today there is a lot of talk about *change*; people philosophize about it. However, the practical consequences are seldom given any attention. One of them is that jobs change, usually unnoticed and insidiously, but after a time they undergo such a change, cumulatively, that we are faced with a totally new situation.

In conclusion, I would like to return to the core issue. If we ask a musician after a concert: *What did you play?*, and in reply he just shrugs his shoulders and says: *...no idea, I blew the trumpet...*, then something is wrong with this orchestra. We must ensure, and good conductors do exactly this, that the trumpeter says: *Today? Today we performed Beethoven's Third as we never have before, and I played the part of first trumpet.* Naturally, the man can and should be proud of being a first-class first trumpeter. However, if he is *only* that, then he is what, outside the field of music, we call a *technocrat*. He is a wind player but by no means a *musician*. He is one of those people who are proud of banging out the *Minute Waltz* in 54 seconds flat because they have never understood the difference between a speed record and music.

The principle of focusing on the whole and on your own contribution to it is, as I said at the beginning, perhaps the most difficult of all principles to explain and understand. As I have also mentioned, it strikes at the root of a series of chronic management problems. It helps in pointing out the right direction at a few important crossroads, and it prevents us from falling into the pitfalls of the most widespread incorrect beliefs.

Third Principle

Concentration on a Few Things

What Matters Is Concentrating on a Few Very Important Things

Many managers and a sizeable portion of management literature seem to be devoted to the unending search for the "Holy Grail", for a miraculous and secret recipe. This is a useless venture. However, if it did exist, one of the first candidates would be *concentration*. Needless to say, there is nothing mysterious about it, just as there are no secrets in management, though some people will never give up their obsession with mystification.

The Key to Results

The principle of concentrating on what is essential is of great importance *everywhere*. However, it is particularly, even overwhelmingly, significant in management because no other profession and no other work is so greatly and systematically subject to the menace of dissipating and squandering energy.

These hazards lurk in other occupations, too. However, it is only in management that they are so *institutionalized*, so commonly accepted and so misunderstood as signs of particular dynamism and job efficiency. Conversely, there is nothing so *typical of effectiveness* as the ability, the art or, even better, the discipline of concentration.

However, the word "concentration" alone is not enough; it can still be misunderstood. The essential point is to limit ourselves to *a few things*, to a *small number* of carefully selected focal points if we are interested in the result and achieving success.

At times, there is an objection that this principle cannot be applied to complex and interrelated situations and that, to some extent, it stems from an outmoded idea of management. In fact, *precisely the opposite is true*. It is because so much has become complex, interrelated and interactive that this principle is so essential. It was never so important previously for the simple reason that it is just not *required* in *simple* situations. In simple situations, there are fewer distractions, and thus the principle is followed automatically. When plowing a field, a farmer can only be disturbed by mosquitoes or a rapidly approaching thunderstorm. Otherwise, he concentrates completely on his work – totally and exclusively on this one activity until it is finished.

The situation is very clear; we can *deal with* many different things, even simultaneously. However, we cannot be *successful* in many different areas. Once again, the difference between input and output, work and achievement, activity and success is important here.

Wherever effects, success and results are observed, we can also observe that the principle of concentration on a few things has been followed. Almost everyone, who has become well known or even famous as a result of his achievements, has concentrated on *one* thing, *one* task, *one* problem. This was and is often taken to the point of obsession, sometimes verging on the pathological which, of course, I do not recommend. However, what is always valid is that *concentration is the key to results*.

Different people from different walks of life are reported to have followed this principle, people such as Albert Einstein and Martin Luther, Bertolt Brecht and Pierre Auguste Renoir, Johann Strauß and Ludwig Wittgenstein. Particularly informative are the examples of people who were effective and successful despite working under difficult conditions such as illness, handicap or overwork. Without exception, the reason for their success lay in concentrating on their work, which they did due to the pressure of circumstances. One of the most remarkable cases is that of Harry Hopkins[17], who was the eminence grise in Washington during the Second World War as the closest personal advisor and representative of US president Franklin D. Roosevelt. Despite suffering from an awful disease and being close to death towards the end – he could only work every other day and then for only a few hours – he achieved much more than perhaps any other person by concentrating strictly on the really important issues and by disregarding everything of secondary importance, so much so that Churchill named him "The Lord of the Heart of the Matter".

---

17 See Robert E. Sherwood, *Roosevelt and Hopkins. An Intimate History*, New York 1948.

Equally informative are the cases of people without any outstanding talent, who achieved the extraordinary because they laid particular emphasis on concentration. One such case is that of the American president Harry Truman. Seldom have the American newspapers been so united as in their opinion that Truman had not a shred of talent. Nonetheless, no one has achieved as much as he did from such an unfavorable position, and that, too, during possibly one of the most difficult times the world has ever gone through. Likewise, the talent of Herbert von Karajan is by no means undisputed amongst experts. Several people, and not only those who envied him or were his rivals, were of the opinion that his talent was rather limited. That he, despite this drawback, changed the music world like hardly anyone else before him is due to the fact that Karajan was a prime example of systematic, concentrated work. He focused completely on a particular objective. To some, he was the "Virtuoso of Self-discipline"[18].

In modern times, which are, to some extent, well documented, there are two people who tackled many different things, sometimes simultaneously, and were nevertheless successful or considered successful. They are Leonardo da Vinci and Goethe. In both cases, many facts indicate that they basically dissipated and squandered energy and could have achieved much more and of more significance had they restricted themselves a little.

Rejection without Reason

The plea to concentrate on a few focal points, if possible on only one, is often met with opposition and rejection which is sometimes emotional and aggressive. As far as objective arguments go, there are hardly any that can be raised against the principle of concentration. The main objections are as follows. *Firstly*, concentration is just not possible in the modern working and organizational world. *Secondly*, it causes a person to become one-sided and leads to narrow specialization. *Thirdly*, it is detrimental to motivation, and, *fourthly*, creativity. The first objection is to be taken seriously; the others are more likely excuses or symptoms of misconceptions and mistakes with regard to management.

---

18 See Frank Welser-Möst, in *Profil*, No. 16, 1999, page 174.

It is true that it has become *difficult* to concentrate on a particular issue in today's working and organizational world. I said earlier that no other profession is so subject to the menace of wasting time and energy as management. However, it is precisely this that is the essential reason *for* the importance of this principle.

I admit that there are situations in which even the most disciplined person cannot work sensibly, and by this I mean in a concentrated way because their environment simply does not allow it. There are bosses who contact their subordinates – first and foremost their secretaries – every ten minutes for some reason or other, who call them, ask them into their office, and, at any rate, disturb them in their work. Under such managers, people *work* hard but usually little is *accomplished*. In this case, good management is confused with bustling activity. In such conditions, a person would have to suffer or endure the performance destroying behavior of a superior or leave if possible. Hence, undisciplined *bosses* are the first, most important, most frequent, and most obvious reason for the non-applicability of the principle of concentration.

This does not render the principle itself invalid; in fact, exactly the opposite is true. But it does establish a reason for the aforementioned, often aggressive rejection. If someone at a seminar brings up *this* objection, I can be very sure that I am dealing with this type of undisciplined manager; they feel, understandably, that their self-perception is under attack. Of course, they do not see themselves as undisciplined but as particularly dynamic, meeting the requirements dictated by the spirit of the times and role models in their own way. Unfortunately, the truth is something totally different, and the need for change is obvious.

The *second* reason is usually the *organization*. There are certain forms of organization that facilitate concentration and others that make it virtually impossible. The matrix organization belongs to the latter category. In a matrix structure, it is almost impossible to concentrate on anything. Therefore, it is an *obstacle in the way of productivity*. It is the opposite of what it is considered to be. It may be modern but it represents anything but progress.

Sometimes there are market structures and businesses in which the matrix organization is unavoidable because there is no alternative at present. The matrix should, however, never be the first choice in matters of organization; it should be the last. If it is proven that nothing else functions, then go ahead … in God's, or better still, the devil's name. Matrix organizations make it *difficult* for people to be effective. But good management means the opposite, making it *easy* for them.

The *second* objection mentioned above is not valid. The root of this opposition is the difference between the specialist and generalist discussed in the last chapter. It is based on the *wrong* concept of a generalist, and it is an *irrational* rejection of specialization. When we realize that specialists are required, that actually only specialists exist anymore, that specialists are only a problem when they are not integrated into the service of the whole, this objection becomes meaningless.

The *third* objection, that concentration has an adverse effect on motivation, is based on an incorrect concept of motivation and a misconception of the purpose of organizations. As I have already mentioned several times, organizations must effect performances and produce results in the area in which they are working and for the purpose for which they were established. Only a few, if any, have been established for the purpose of motivating people. One organization is intended to heal people, another to produce environmentally friendly detergents, and the purpose of a third may be to humanize conditions in women's prisons. Concentration on the main issue, on the purpose, is always required for the organization as a whole and for the people working in it. Therefore, the first task must be concentration. Whether this is incompatible with motivation is a totally different issue.

As the connection between motivation and performance has not, to date, been clarified in any way, contrary to what is generally assumed, my suggestion is that we should take care of concentration *first*. There is no doubt that people, especially the young, expect their work to be varied, but these expectations cannot, unfortunately, be met very often, and, if they are, it is possible only to a limited extent. The primary task of organizations is not to offer young people variety, unless it is in their capacity as customers.

Finally, we have the *fourth* objection, that concentration is detrimental to creativity. It may be detrimental to that which may be more accurately called *wild* creativity. This, however, is usually useless in any case, if not actually harmful. There is no dearth of *ideas* in the world, contrary to what is always being loudly proclaimed. What the world lacks is ideas that have been realized; this is something totally different, and what is required to realize these ideas is, in fact, again concentration.

The life and working methods of those people who are *rightly* considered to be highly creative – well-known musicians, painters, writers, sculptors and scientists – is replete with examples and proof that the *opposite* is true. With a few exceptions, they all concentrated *strictly* on one issue. It is precisely in this group that we most often find systematic working methods and that pathological form of concentration that can amount to self-sacrifice, leaving room for little else. The piece of art, the work, the task – that is the only thing that counts, and brings success, sometimes after many setbacks and failures.

One of the most impressive examples is Thomas Mann. During his active life, he worked without exception and with systematic stubbornness and total concentration every day, from nine to twelve in the morning, resulting in an astonishingly small output of one to one and a half pages per day which, however, eventually added up to a monumental body of work. Even Michelangelo and Franz Schubert are worth mentioning, as are all the others who have left behind their deeds and works and not just good intentions, noble resolutions and impressive plans. It is worthwhile studying their working methods, if we are interested in effectiveness and not satisfied by attributing it all to their "genius"[19].

Examples of Application

By means of a few examples of its application, I would like to explain the effect of the principle of concentration as clearly as possible.

1. Time Management

Most managers, irrespective of the type of organization they work in, have problems with time. I will say more on this subject later under the heading "Personal Working Methods". For now, I would like to focus on just one aspect. No matter how long and how hard managers work, their most frequent complaint is that of not having enough time. Working more and harder is obviously not the solution to this problem. The only solution lies in the principle of concentration.

The reason is as simple as it is frequently overlooked. The time that managers talk about only *seems* to be "their" time. The way managers

---

19 See Wolf Schneider, *Der Sieger*, Hamburg 1992, passim.

utilize time is largely *determined by others*. 70 to 80 percent of the time does not belong to *them* but to *others*, their customers, their own boss, their subordinates and colleagues, their secretaries, their financial analysts and, increasingly, the media. What remains at their disposal is a small segment of perhaps 20 to 30 percent to use as they think *fit* with regard to their tasks.

However, they cannot achieve *a lot* in 20 to 30 percent of the time, even if they put in an 18-hour day, which, in any case, is not advisable. Therefore, they need to concentrate on the crucial issues. That is easier said than done. It requires hard and risky decisions. Mistakes will be made time and again while attempting to settle the question of *what* we should be concentrating on. Nevertheless, we must make up our mind to identify areas of emphasis if we want to achieve results. The only choice is between leaving many things unaccomplished, thereby achieving significant results in a few areas and not achieving anything at all.

The psychologist George A. Miller[20] conducted studies on the extent of people's control span . He presented his findings in an informative article with the suggestive title "The Magical Number Seven Plus/Minus Two". Seven plus/minus two things per unit of time – that is approximately what a person can undertake, keep a check on, and, to some extent, control. The only way to cope with more than this is sequentially, one after the other, doing the second only after the first has been dealt with.

My suggestion is that we should adapt ourselves to the seven *minus* two rather than to the seven plus two things, and sometimes it must be even less. I know managers who attend to only *one* issue per unit of time. They are remarkably successful. Even these people fret that there are many things which they cannot do, that there is much that remains to be done for which they are basically responsible and which they would be happy to do. These people, too, sometimes make a choice which subsequently proves to be wrong. Nonetheless, they concentrate on less because they know that it is the only way to achieve anything at all and the only way to set in motion and effect anything in the prevailing state of complexity, dependence, and hectic activity.

Strangely, many managers refuse to believe this. Some managers are proud of being permanently engaged in a "war on many fronts". Their

---

20 Refer to his article with the same title in: *Psychological Review*, 1956, 63, pages 81 and 97.

work balance sheet is exceptional; their *performance balance sheet,* on the other hand, is deplorable. A "war on many fronts" can indeed be *waged,* but it cannot be *won.*

The principle of concentration applies to *everything.* If we ask someone what sport they play, and they list 15 different sports, we can be sure of one thing and that is that they are either bad or, at best, average in all of them. On the other hand, if someone replies that they do not get much time for sports after work, therefore, they only play a bit of tennis, then they will probably not be world-class players but it is quite possible that they will not be easy to beat.

2. Management by Objectives

The second important case of application of the principle of concentration is *management by objectives.* There is most probably no organization that has not already looked at this management method in one way or another. Unfortunately, there are not many, which have been successful with it. Why? More will be said on this subject in the next section. The most important reason is that people take on *too much* that is *too different.*

When I have to introduce management by objectives in an organization, I start with a short exercise where I request that the ladies and gentlemen present write down all that they wish to accomplish in the next year. Without any further comments, I give them approximately one hour for this. Without exception, the result is the same. Eight out of ten come back after an hour with two, three or even four dense pages. Two of the ten, on the other hand, come back with half a page, on which there are two or three points. We can be absolutely sure that these are the real *professionals* and that whatever they have noted are the really *important* things, and the ones they really want to accomplish.

Admittedly, there are also important points in the first group's dense pages, but these are concealed in a maze of trivial issues. Then, during the year, when they are caught in the mad rush of day-to-day business, they lose sight of the priorities. These recede from their attention. In the end, both groups have worked hard, there is nothing lacking in this respect nowadays. However, the first group has only *worked,* whereas the second group has *results* to show for their work. The success and effectiveness of management by objectives depends on the principle of concentration on a few things.

3. The New Productivity Problem

The third example of application of the principle of concentration is an increase in *productivity*. This is possibly the most important. In order to understand this, we must make a distinction between the productivity of *manual work* and that of *knowledge work*. The productivity of manual work or of industrial workers has, in the last 100 years, increased in a sensational way by 2 to 3 percent every year. No one could have even imagined this when productivity first became a topic for discussion. The key to this success is the question: *What should be the maximum time for a piece of work?* This is the core issue in all methods for increasing productivity in industry with the emphasis on "maximum".

However, due to the success achieved, the productivity of manual work is no longer the problem today. This "war" is over and it has been won. It should be noted that this was done in the face of sometimes bitter opposition from the unions which, for a long time, failed to understand that improvements in productivity were the prerequisite for a higher income for the worker. The new "theater of war" is the productivity of *knowledge workers*, those people whose asset is no longer their manual skillfulness but their knowledge. They are the most rapidly growing group, and, in developed countries, they will soon form the majority or at least the largest individual group in the total workforce. However, their productivity is, as always, *very low*. It must be improved dramatically.

For this, however, the previous question is not appropriate, a radically different one is required: *What is the minimum time I will require to complete this work?* The emphasis here is on "minimum". However, the word "uninterrupted" must be added to the question. Hence, the complete question is: *What is the minimum uninterrupted time I will require to complete this work?*

We still do not know much about the productivity of mental work. Its importance has only just begun to sink in. Nonetheless, one thing is clear. Mental work requires *large units of time* – time blocks – of *undisturbed work* in order to be effective. This does not pose a problem for industrial workers, as their whole work structure does not permit any interruption whatsoever. Industrial workers, whether at the assembly line or working in independent groups, are not disturbed by the telephone during their work, and I have never heard of a heart surgeon interrupting an operation to attend a meeting. For knowledge workers, however, constant interruption is the rule.

Let me give an example. If product managers have to make a marketing plan for a particular market, they can usually state exactly how long they need for this, if they have some professional experience. Let us assume that they estimate the time required as approximately five hours as it is a small market, and because they do not need to begin from scratch but already have sufficient material, data and experience. Five hours is equal to exactly 300 minutes. Of course, the arithmetic is always correct. However, to work on the task for five hours with full concentration and undisturbed is something radically different from working on it for ten minutes per day for a month. In both cases, 300 minutes have been devoted to the task. The first way leads to certain *success*, the second to *disaster*. The time used is the same but the result is completely different.

These three completely different cases of its application should be sufficient to satisfactorily demonstrate the practical relevance of the principle of concentration on a few things. They illustrate the wide diversity of areas in which this principle can be applied and how important it is. Concentration is one of the most important keys to results and success. It is the most important principle for coping with overwork and constantly increasing requirements. Furthermore, it is the only sustainable way to bring under control that element which heads the list of most managers' problems: stress. Concentration does not mean "working continuously" or "doing nothing else but work", as is sometimes mistakenly thought; concentration means working without distractions and disturbance on only one issue, therefore, working effectively. Quite often effective people go through long periods of inactivity, phases of lethargy and unproductive times. This was the case with Wolfgang Amadeus Mozart, Richard Wagner and Franz Schubert. However, when they worked, they worked with total concentration. Thus, Mozart and Schubert were both able to leave behind a monumental volume of work despite their phases of stagnation and their premature deaths.

The principle of concentration can be *generalized*. Wherever results are apparent, there is concentration. In hospitals, it is not simply patients being treated, but *one patient after the other*. For that period of treatment, which can be short, perhaps even too short, the entire attention of the medical staff is directed towards *one* patient. The great symphony orchestras do not have an *extensive* but a very limited repertoire. They can play a dozen different composers but not with that mastery required for peak performance, and which today's knowledgeable public, spoiled as they are by television and compact discs, have come to expect.

When I was a student, I thought I could study a textbook and listen to music simultaneously, that I had to be listening to music in order to be able to study at all. This was an illusion. Either I had read the text and understood it without having paid much attention to the music or, vice versa, I had really listened to the music and just looked through the text. My children have allowed themselves to be guided by the same illusion at the same age. The principles of effective working are not inborn; initially, most people are instinctively inclined towards the opposite.

Anyone who wants to convince us that he can effectively deal with 15 different things simultaneously is either a beginner and can be helped, or he is incompetent and can no longer be helped. The principle of concentration is applicable to people; however, it is also applicable to *organizations*. In the main, attempts to form conglomerates and diversification strategies have failed time and again. They are made with optimistic regularity, four times in recent history, and each time they were considered the height of far-sighted strategy. Each time, they failed and usually in a dramatic manner. The apparent success of the Japanese conglomerates, for example Mitsubishi, has been cited time and again against this argument. However, even this company was not able to withstand the crucial test of the Japanese economy, and had to radically reduce its vast range of business activities.

Effective organizations, good institutions are *single-purpose* systems. They are single-purpose tools, as are any tools that are useful or any single-purpose devices. Anything else leads to bad compromises, at best to mediocrity and, at worst, to failure. And this happens *despite* superhuman efforts. The cause of failure is not a lack of effort and application but the *dissipation of energies*. The tragedy lies in the lack of success in spite of great effort.

Fourth Principle

Utilizing Strengths

What Counts Is Utilizing Existing Strengths

The emphasis here is on "existing" strengths, not on those that must first be developed, and the essential element is "utilizing strengths" and not "eliminating weaknesses". This must be emphasized because most managers and particularly, it seems, personnel experts are primarily concerned with the opposite of what this principle demands: on the one hand, developing something new instead of utilizing what is already available, and, on the other hand, eliminating weaknesses instead of utilizing strengths.

In my opinion, all the principles dealt with here are equally important. However, if I were forced to talk about one individual principle, I would probably choose this one because this is the principle that is disregarded most often, and the consequences of doing so are serious. The principle of utilizing strengths has far-reaching implications for everything that has to do with people – their selection and training, job design and recruitment, performance appraisal and potential analysis. If this principle is *followed,* the consequences are extremely positive. They are *destructive,* if the principle is not taken to heart, or if people even work actively against it which is usually done with the best of intentions but has disastrous effects. A considerable part of that which is termed tragedy in the existential sense is related to the disregard or ignorance of this principle.

I maintain that the negative impact of ignoring this principle cannot be avoided, and I also maintain that it *is* universally ignored, that the majority of those working in personnel management, in spite of, or even due to their ingenuity and the discipline's apparently scientific nature, are on the wrong track.

This is all the more remarkable as practically everyone agrees with this principle as soon as it is stated. There is certainly no lack of lip service, people really do seriously agree with this principle, and it can be justified without difficulty. Therefore, there is no opposition to this principle, but still the action *taken* is in such complete contrast to it that it would be right to term it a genuine paradox.

If the principle of focusing on strengths is followed consistently, many of the instruments of policy normally used and considered essential by personnel managers can be dispensed with; their function can become simpler, leaner, and not only cost-effective but also effective. On the other hand, if the principle is not followed, the efforts of even the most well-developed human resource managers generally fall flat.

Fixation on Weaknesses

In conversations with managers, I not only ask them the questions mentioned earlier, I also ask them: *Tell me a little about your subordinates. What sort of people do you have? What are your colleagues and your boss like?* It is as if the floodgates have opened, there is a deluge of information as they tell me about their deficiencies and weaknesses, everything that the people cannot do, how their colleagues are idiots and their boss is a failure...

In a strange way, the human brain and, particularly, our perception seem to work negatively or destructively. We are most aware of what does *not* work *because* it does not work and because it therefore creates difficulties. The deficiencies seem to be etched in our consciousness because they create problems, require a solution and require effort. It is a well-known fact *that* human perception is selective. What is not always clear is *what* we select as relevant for perception. In this context, it is the weaknesses and inadequacies of other people.

However, we can be very certain that constant moaning and groaning about people's deficiencies, be it those of subordinates, colleagues or bosses, customers, suppliers or even ourselves, is firm evidence that we are dealing either with someone who does not yet know what really matters in terms of management issues, or with an incompetent person. The beginner can be helped, as I have already pointed out in another context, by giving him a new and correct focus. An incompetent person can no longer be helped. Where people are concerned, they are a *liability*.

If people are observed with our principle of focusing on strengths in mind, we would, and it is almost too trivial to mention, almost unanimously reach the verdict that everyone, even those who seem the least capable, has strengths, probably not many, and most often just one. Furthermore, we would find that even the most capable people, who are capable of giving peak performances, have a number of pronounced weaknesses. It is not a trivial issue but a tragic one that we concentrate first and foremost on weaknesses, and then do everything in our power to eliminate them.

This is a *successful* strategy but, unfortunately, this success has negative connotations. Let us imagine that a person has shortcomings, for example in communication skills or team working skills or in one of the other qualities that are, with or without justification, required today. We devise a program that is designed to improve and develop their abilities; we send them to seminars or for coaching. This will, of course, have an effect. After a few of these measures have been taken, they will have made great progress in some areas, and improvements will be noticeable in others, their shortcomings will no longer be so pronounced, and the problem will have been diluted. The person will have become *better* but in what sense? They will have become better in the sense of *"less weak"*. They will have taken a clear, noticeable step, but towards what? Towards *mediocrity*. As a subordinate, they will have become "easier to take care of"; earlier they used to create difficulties three times a day every day, now this happens just once every third day. This is considered progress, and we feel justified in adopting this kind of strategy.

Making Strengths and Tasks Compatible

However, what is far more important is that, due to the overwhelming focus on weaknesses and their elimination, we have, in all probability, failed to explore the employee's *strengths*, what they are *capable* of doing. This is the first duty of a manager. The second is to design the tasks for this person so that, as far as possible, they are compatible with what this person is capable of doing.

This is what is meant by, and achieved by, the principle of focusing on strengths and utilizing strengths: *Deploying people in areas in which they are already proficient.* This is what we can also observe in all effective, successful, good managers. They show little or no concern about people's weaknesses. These do not interest them, not only because they cannot achieve anything with them, but also because they doubt that they can do anything to change them. These managers look for the strengths that already exist, and then they organize jobs and tasks in such a way that those strengths can be deployed.

In training and in actual practice, there is a lot of talk about adaptability and flexibility. However, the burden of adaptability is usually placed on the people themselves. People are expected and required to change, not the organization. When it comes to modifying the organization in the way we are discussing here, the willingness to change decreases considerably. Suddenly operating according to dogmatic organizational theory is preferred, which means, for example, that organizing must be done independently of people.

Admittedly, it is *not* usually *easy* to implement what the principle of focusing on strengths demands, but it is *highly effective*. Most probably, any endeavor to do this will not be totally successful. However, to the extent that there is some success in making tasks compatible with strengths, two results are assured. *Firstly*, the "famous" peak performance will suddenly be achieved. I have already stated at the beginning of this book that this is of little significance to me and that I do not think very highly of the constant use of superlatives in management; nevertheless, peak performances can be achieved, and they will be achieved only where there are strengths. At any rate, they certainly cannot be expected in areas where people have their weaknesses.

Secondly, something more important may be observed. The problem of motivation would never arise, and it would not, therefore, have to be dealt with. The problems of motivation simply *disappear*. No one requires motivation to be good in areas where he is good, or where his strengths lie. On the other hand, I maintain that there is absolutely no way that a person can be motivated to be good and achieve something in areas in which he is weak.

It should be noted that, as a side effect to some extent, this would also eliminate accusations of "slave driving". There is no harm at all in demanding higher performances in areas where people are proficient. But it is inhuman to demand it of them in areas where they are weak.

This inhumanity begins with the demand that people eliminate their weaknesses. This alone usually requires an enormous and occasionally even superhuman effort. By itself, it would not be a significant problem because of the hope that the end would justify the means. However, this hope has usually proved to be false. To have no weaknesses as a result of their elimination is something entirely different from having strengths. The elimination of a weakness does *not* automatically mean that a strength will evolve, although many seem to assume this, it merely leads to a lack of weaknesses. If someone has no weaknesses in a foreign language, according to educational standards, it cannot be inferred that this is his obvious strength, that he is capable of outstanding achievements as writer or translator.

The question of whether it might be possible to find a particular strength hidden precisely where a person appears to have a weakness is asked strangely often, and it always contains an assertion or at least a hope. In principle, this cannot indeed be ruled out, but experience shows that such cases are very rare. The fact that, as we learn from the Bible, Saul became Paul is not an indication that weaknesses can frequently be converted into strengths but rather it is the story of a miracle. People are entitled to their own opinion on this issue. For argument's sake, I do not want to rule out the possibility that miracles do happen, and, when they do, we should make use of them; what I do rule out, however, is that we can rely on them, and that they can be expected in management.

Of course, it is possible that some people may be mistaken in their assumption that they have a particular weakness. Most of us, especially when we were younger, did not have any reliable information on our weaknesses and strengths, not even well-founded suppositions, rather we had hopes, desires, and illusions. The ability of most people to objectively assess themselves ranges from questionable to miserable. The more the educational system and schools followed the path of supposed educational progress and, consequently, refrained from performance appraisal, clear comparison of objectives and results, and setting clear boundaries and standards, the more could be expected that people would become increasingly unable to make a realistic self-assessment. Therefore, they are not only incapable of assessing what is perhaps the most important issue for their personal success in life, namely the issue of their weaknesses and strengths, but they also fail to understand the importance of the issue itself. Hence, it is possible that in reality there is only a supposed weakness and that it may actually conceal a strength. This case, however, differs completely from one in which there is an actual weakness and not a supposed one.

Let us now look at the other side of the issue. In contrast to the efforts and the usually miserable results associated with the eliminating of weaknesses it can often be observed that far less effort is required to really achieve something with a strength that at least shows signs of being present. Relatively speaking, it usually takes very little effort for a person to become better, and perhaps even very good, in an area in which they are already good, compared to what is required to achieve even mediocrity in an area where they are weak.

This asymmetry, which is to be found almost everywhere, must be utilized in management. Please note once again that I am talking about management and people in organizations. If someone takes a *personal* decision to concentrate his efforts on eliminating his weaknesses instead of utilizing his strengths, it is his private and personal decision, although I would advise against it even in this case.

Should Weaknesses Be Ignored?

Does focusing on strengths mean ignoring weaknesses? By no means, that would be naïve. Weaknesses must be known, but not for the reason most people want to know them, that is in order to eliminate them. They must be known for an entirely different reason, in order *to avoid making the mistake of deploying people in areas in which they are weak.* Hence, focusing on strengths does not mean being unrealistic, naïve or idealistic.

Good personnel management, that is everything that has to do with human resources, must, in principle, be designed and developed in the same way as the training of athletes. Sports teachers working with children or young people will let them try out all the sports for which they are eligible for a period of time, while they observe them. After this test phase, they will speak to the children individually. To one they may say: *You are a sprinter*, and they will then guide the child towards the sprint competitions. Their training program will include practicing the start over and over, as this is crucial for the success in the sprint disciplines. To another child they may say: *You are not a sprinter. Your discipline is more likely to be long-distance running. I am not exactly sure of the distances that would suit you best, but at any rate the shorter distances are not for you*. The training program for this child would include less training for the start of the race as this is unimportant in distance running. No one has ever won a marathon because he or she was "faster off the mark". The coach will train the athletes to build their stamina and to run the race tactically, everything, in fact, which is important for long distance running.

In doing so there may be a certain type of apparent elimination of weaknesses which always leads to misconceptions. The training will deal with and attempt to eliminate those deficiencies which stand in the way of the complete development and utilization of the strengths. Therefore, a sprinter's starting technique will, in all probability, always have to be worked at with the objective of bringing it up to the optimum level. However, this will not make the sprinter a marathon runner. A good coach would never enter a high jumper for the track events or a swimmer for the shot putt. Athletes are selected by *focusing on strengths*, and their discipline is chosen according to their strengths. This does not remove the need to perfect every detail required for actual peak performance.

No Personality Reform

All that I have said so far is a plea *against changing* people, above all changing their *personality*. Far too many managers are constantly trying to change people. It is not stated explicitly; rather it is given a refined touch by calling it personality *development*. However, in reality, it usually amounts to an attempt to change the personality.

I consider this to be *wrong* for a number of reasons. *Firstly*, there is the *moral* issue of whether this is acceptable. In my opinion, it is not. Perhaps this issue is not considered to be particularly important. I do not want to discuss it at length here. However, we must be interested in the *practical* question: Is it *in any way* possible, and is it possible within a *reasonable period of time?*

The different aspects of personality are formed and are, to a great extent, inflexible by the time people join an organization as employees around their late twenties; and this is even more true when they reach an age, in their thirties, when they begin to be considered for management responsibility. For the sake of the claims made by many psychologists, and although I have my doubts, I will accept that modifications in personality and character are possible in the early childhood years. However, this becomes progressively more difficult with increasing age, and, at the age of 30, as mentioned earlier, it is well nigh impossible.

Please note that I do not believe that people cannot change *themselves*. They can if they really *want* to. However, this happens very rarely and only under certain circumstances; most likely in the event of great misfortune and under some pressure, seldom due to insight. If a person's marriage fails, they may ask themselves whether they were partly to blame, and whether they should do certain things differently the next time around. However, as long as things are "life and business as usual", few people feel the need to change, especially as this requires considerable effort. Similarly, I also accept that there are professional groups whose objective, in spite of all the difficulties, is to change people, theologians for instance and psychotherapists. However, the results do not seem to be particularly convincing to me.

Time and again, political leaders have also attempted to do the same. We cannot overlook the fact that some of the greatest and bloodiest disasters in history have been the outcome of attempts to change people. Communism in the former Soviet Union and Mao's Cultural Revolution as well as the Catholic Church in Latin America and elsewhere wanted to create a "new community of people". Therefore, there are certain professions and institutions which consider it acceptable to change people. I do not wish to comment on this here.

What is certain, however, is that this is definitely not one of the tasks of management. Even if it were possible in principle, which I doubt, experience indicates that it would take too long for the effects to manifest themselves. *The task of management is to accept people as they are, to determine their strengths, and, by appropriately designing their tasks, give them the opportunity to work in areas where they can accomplish something and achieve results with their strengths.* Anything else cannot be justified on *moral* or *economic* grounds. We cannot change a dairy cow into a sheep. Therefore, the cow is expected to give milk, good milk and in sufficient quantity, and it is not criticized for its inability to provide wool.

Why Focus on Weaknesses?

Why do most people focus on their weaknesses instead of concentrating on their strengths? This may be primarily due to the following reasons. *Firstly*, it is *easier* to discover people's weaknesses rather than their strengths. Weaknesses attract attention because they are troublesome. No exceptional intelligence or experience is required to find out what a person *cannot* do. Above all, no intensive interaction with the person is required to determine this. On the other hand, all this and more is required, often on a large scale, to identify strengths. An interest in people is needed, in the individual, in order to discover strengths. Aside from any other factors this is time-consuming.

The *second* reason is perhaps the conditioning received in school days. As institutions, schools, and I say this without criticism, focus on eliminating weaknesses. They do this because no one can know where the children will work as adults. Therefore, every child must be equipped with a minimum of those skills which they will probably require wherever they go, or, to put it more precisely, the mastery of which will make it possible for this person to gain entry into the working world. To put it plainly, a person must be able to read, write and add up in order to become a member of the modern society. If a child has weaknesses, in mathematics for instance, every teacher will attempt to eliminate this weakness and urge the child to practice more mathematics. This is only for the good.

Therefore, school education imparts the *ability to work* but does not make a person *proficient*. No one is successful simply because his ability to read, write and add up meets the educational standards of his school. People are successful and effective because they have strengths and deploy them, not because they lack weaknesses. Therefore, the truly *great* teachers also, either willingly or unwillingly, have to reduce and smoothen out the rough edges of a weakness. However, they will primarily pay attention to what a child can really do. Their attitude could be expressed along these lines: *Unfortunately, your son is not very good at fractions, and, therefore, he has to practice if he is to achieve the required standard for the class. It is highly unlikely that he will ever become a great mathematician. However, I have noticed that your child is excellent at languages. Concentrate on this ability and ensure that he has the opportunity to deploy it properly later...*

Learning from the Great

So-called "great" people, in whatever way we understand the exceedingly misused, well worn and, ultimately, meaningless word "great", were usually very limited people. They had many conspicuous weaknesses and most of them were able to do only one thing – but they did this *excellently*.

Thomas Mann could write and nothing else; this is true of most other writers. Picasso could paint, but nothing else, which is also the "fate" of most other painters. Mozart could compose and nothing else; this was also true of most other composers. Mozart was quite naïve in the ways of the world, but this was of no importance because no one ever expected anything from him other than music. Stories about Mozart's incompetence in other areas are uninteresting to everyone, because they are insignificant in the face of his outstanding strength.

It is the same situation in practically every field. Whether it is in the field of music, painting, sculpture, literature, politics, science, or sports, the outstanding work produced by people has almost always been limited to *one very narrow* field. The famous physicists were – and remain – primarily physicists; the mathematicians were good at mathematics and the industrial chemist at chemistry.

It is true that there are a few people with multiple talents, but they are rare, and it can be said of only a few that they possessed talent of a sufficiently high level in several different fields to be able to produce achievements of some distinction in each of them. Of all the people whose lives can be reconstructed reasonably well there are perhaps three dozen people whose strengths have been proven in several fields, and these include Julius Caesar, Benjamin Franklin, E.T.A. Hoffmann, Friedrich II, and, inevitably, Goethe and Leonardo da Vinci. This in no way implies that they were also capable of achieving the same level of success in each of those fields.

It is neither possible nor is it necessary for the purpose of this chapter to discuss in detail the various attempts at analysis, which are problematic in any case. Caesar does seem to be a man who attained great heights in several, very different fields, so does the Hohenstaufen emperor, Friedrich II, if all that is "attributed to him", which is partly exaggerated, is actually true. Friedrich Nietzsche, who appears in the list as a philosopher and musician, did achieve notable success as a pianist and composer among his friends. Franklin was probably an extraordinary man in reality, and we can reliably say of Goethe and Leonardo, as mentioned in the previous chapter, that they would have benefited from having been more selective in their work. Goethe's theory of colors of which he was very proud – but what was he not proud of? – is somewhat embarrassing, as was at that time, too, especially his dispute with Isaac Newton over it. Georgio Vasari, Leonardo's biographer, passed a pithy comment about him, saying that he began a lot of things and finished only a few. In my opinion, this is a fitting judgment even centuries later.

There is another historical figure with multiple talents who was refreshingly wise and familiar with the requirements for effectiveness. That was Michelangelo who, though he was capable of many things, was so clearly aware of his real strength, sculpture, that he resisted every temptation, as much as was possible, to be distracted from it. The signature with which he signed the contract for the painting of the Sistine Chapel in 1508, after putting up tough resistance against Pope Julius II, "*Michelangelo, Scultore*" proves this better than any scholarly treatise.

Whatever is applicable to "great men" as a rule, apart from just a few exceptions, applies even more to those who are somewhat less "great". Anyone who wants to or has to achieve something must restrict themselves to what they can do and to the field in which they have their strengths. Even then, it is difficult enough to work and be successful. To concentrate on weaknesses and eliminating them amounts to a waste of time except for a few exceptions which I shall discuss later. Furthermore, even if the attempt is successful, it usually leads to a lack of *objective* results and achievements though the effort involved may be enormous in the subjective sense.

At the risk of appearing insistent, I wish to once again point out that we are talking about management and people *in* organizations. It has always been my experience that people lose sight of the context, which I view as valid and relevant, all too easily and tacitly transfer these ideas into the private sphere. If someone has as his personal objective the development of a "well-rounded personality" and, therefore, works on eliminating his weaknesses, it is his personal decision, and thus not under discussion here. I would not advise this because, all too often, the "well-rounded" personality is synonymous with "all-round average person, but very nice".

How Are Strengths Recognized?

After all that has been said so far, it is perhaps less surprising but all the more tragic that there are few support systems in management that enable or encourage people to discover their strengths. Even on those rare occasions when this is discussed, the way in which people believe strengths are discovered is systematically misleading.

The reason for this lies in the almost universally accepted opinion that someone is good at something, if he likes doing it. This is also a standard question for career advisors: *What would you like to do?* Children are asked this question on the assumption that the answer will provide an indication of the profession they should choose. Most people find this view so plausible that hardly anyone thinks of doubting it. Nevertheless, it is wrong. There is not even the slightest correlation between *liking doing something* and *doing something well*.

So where does this idea come from? There is a strong correlation between *disliking doing something* and *doing something badly*. If something is done with dislike, it seldom leads to great achievement. This is due to very banal reasons; people put off doing it, do not work at it, do not go into it in depth, therefore, they do not gain any expert knowledge and experience. As the problem does not solve itself, they take it on at the last possible moment and "stage" it hurriedly with improvisation and a minimum of effort. From the indisputable fact of this correlation, people deduce – *e contrario* – that the opposite is also true, *liking doing* and, *therefore, doing something well*.

However, attention must be paid to something totally different, and, consequently, the question must also be framed in another way. Sometimes the assumption can be turned around: *Because a person does something well, he likes doing it.* With this insight, we can get somewhere. However, this is still not the really crucial factor. The right question and, for most people, the one that decides their fate, as it is critical for their success is this: *What do you do easily?* The truly important correlation exists between *do easily* and *do well*.

The best example of this is Albert Einstein. It is said time and again that Einstein was a bad student. This gives foolish parents an apparently good reason to excuse the bad performances of their children in school with the comment that Einstein, nevertheless, won the Nobel Prize. It is hard to imagine anything more ridiculous. Einstein was a *good* student; he was particularly good at physics and mathematics. Admittedly, he had problems with a few of his teachers because he was an awkward student, but not because he was a bad student. He found mathematics and physics easy, and, in these subjects, he achieved great success almost effortlessly. However, what had he enjoyed doing, what had made his heart beat faster, what had been his burning passion? That was music, and especially the violin. He would have given an awful lot to have been a great violinist. However, despite all his practice, he was never anything more than mediocre. Einstein did not possess the coordination and skillfulness required for the violin.

Einstein is a good example of the facts, but we do not actually have to cite him to know them. All we have to do is what many personnel experts unfortunately never do; we have to *observe* people. There are countless people who play tennis, golf or some other sport, or pursue a hobby with the same passion that Einstein played the violin without achieving a certain standard. They enjoy doing it, and, compared to genuine perform, they do it poorly. On the other hand, in the case of real professionals, it can be observed that the "enjoyment" aspect – their pleasure in the activity – often decreases as the task becomes increasingly routine, and yet they are good despite this. Or, in other words, they do not require the "enjoyment" aspect to be good and successful because it is easy for them to do. It matters little whether pilots or doctors enjoy doing their work because they are professionals. Nor are they asked about this; it is not of interest to either the passenger or the patient.

The question of what is easy for a person to do becomes very important not only because of the increased chances of success in this field but also due to the risk of making the wrong correlation. The positively diabolical thing is that people are *not aware* of what they find *easy to do*, precisely *because* it is easy to do. And because they are not aware of it, they pay no attention to it and do not use it. They overlook the most important thing that will ensure effectiveness and success (in fact relatively easy and quick success), and due to this success they could also possibly achieve fulfillment, happiness and meaning, too, precisely because it is a strength.

I have already mentioned that disregarding or ignoring the principle of focusing on strengths is one of the causes of existential tragedy. The tragedy is that people in their ignorance of the correlation discussed here overlook or underestimate their strengths and, at the same time, suffer because of their weaknesses, or use their energy to eliminate them. They do not even make any attempt in spheres in which they can attain easy success, and, in areas where they work on themselves, often with a tremendous effort, success is denied to them.

At this point, we should recall the first principle. What matters in management are the results. In this regard, I made a few observations on the subject of "work should be enjoyable". It is not difficult to see that there is a direct link between this demand and the question of how a person's strengths are recognized, that is to say between "having fun" and "enjoying doing", and that both are tragic errors that are the basis of a destructive and erroneous theory discussed in many books and seminars on management.

Types of Weaknesses

In order to clearly grasp the importance of the principle of focusing on strengths, perhaps a few additional comments would be helpful. In particular, a few distinctions need to be made. Not everything that appears to be a weakness *is* a weakness in the sense discussed here. There are deficiencies that can and should be eliminated. Essentially, there are five types of deficiencies that appear to be weaknesses. Four of these can, to a great extent, be eliminated or improved upon.

The *first* are gaps in *knowledge*. A substantial proportion of these deficiencies can be eliminated with training and learning. Anyone who needs to know English for his occupation can learn it. If a person does not have a talent for languages, he will probably not be very good, he will always have a terrible accent and will never be able to read Shakespeare in the original, but this is not usually necessary. Even people who have little talent for languages can, in general, learn one of the common foreign languages well enough for practical purposes. Just as a person, even if they have not studied business administration, can acquire a minimum knowledge in the areas of organization, strategy, and accounting. These are areas of knowledge without which people face difficulties today, not only in a company but also in many other organizations.

The *second* type is *skills*. People can learn to operate a computer keyboard, set up the agenda for a meeting, write a proper report, and make a presentation. People can acquire a minimum of presentation skills, even if they may never be adequate enough to enable them to become great speakers. This applies to all the skills that are normally required in an organization today, just as we learn to drive, which is a useful skill when living in a modern society, even if we will never compete in a Formula 1 race.

Thirdly, it is possible to acquire a certain amount of *understanding* of and *insight* into other roles and fields. Biochemists can learn to accept that the pharmaceutical industry must also market its products and, therefore, requires marketing experts, even though they themselves would be totally at sea with advertising slogans. Human resource experts can understand that numbers and figures are required for certain purposes in a company. They may never be able to decipher a balance sheet, and for them accountants will always be suspect. However, a minimum of understanding, from which mutual acceptance and perhaps respect can grow, can and should be acquired.

The *fourth type of deficiency* is certain characteristics that appear to be weaknesses but are often just *bad habits*. These, too, can, to a certain extent, be eliminated. They include things such as a chronic lack of punctuality, a tendency towards careless work and negligence, or the bad habit of never completing a piece of work.

With this last category I have come close to the type of weakness, which I think is difficult or impossible to remove. For example, there are people who frequently have problems with other people and cannot get along with their fellow men. This cannot be substantially changed even with a lot of training. We cannot convert a solitary person into a really good team player. Fortunately, this is not important; it is of no consequence, if and as long as such a person is assigned tasks that must essentially be carried out alone. The assertion that everyone must be a team player these days and that there are no tasks that can be carried out alone sounds very modern and in keeping with the spirit of the times, but is simply wrong and is evidence of a blatant lack of reflection and unexamined acceptance of simple statements. Usually, this also indicates a lack of familiarity with actual practice. There are people who are excellent in a team, who in fact even need one to do themselves justice, but are quite at a loss when left on their own. On the other hand, there are people, who do not consider teamwork as the epitome of achievement and productivity, but rather as complicated, slow, unproductive, and ponderous. Though they comply with team discipline when it is demanded of them, they are nevertheless not particularly good in a team, whereas they can produce some excellent work when left alone, when they can work on a problem in a concentrated manner and without having to make allowances for others.

We will seldom be able to change a typical thinker, someone with an analytical or conceptualizing way of thinking, whose strength lies in getting to the heart of the problem mentally or developing solutions into a particularly effective doer whose strength lies in implementation. Organizations need both, but both competencies are so rarely found in one and the same person that we cannot pin our hopes on finding such a person. There are people who seldom have conflicts with others but have difficulties with numbers all their lives. On the other hand, there are people who have a special affinity for only numbers and nothing else, certainly not other people. In order to be effective, some require a definite systematic, almost algorithmic method of working which would be stifling for others.

In the Bible we learn that God created man, but that is wrong and it is not only wrong because of Darwin and the theory of evolution. That would be a subject in itself. However, whether it was God or evolution, *individuals* were created. No two people are alike, no two people work in the same manner, and no two people perform in the same way. Therefore, the type of weaknesses described here as the really important ones that are difficult to eliminate are more accurately the idiosyncrasies of personality, character and temperament, all less precise terms and less well researched fields than we would like. Fortunately, this does not play a critical role in this context.

The Two Sources of Peak Performance

Once managers accept and act in accordance with the fourth principle, numerous tenacious problems disappear which would otherwise prove difficult to solve even with a great effort were this principle disregarded.

However, this is not the only consequence. Suddenly it is possible to deliver performances that were formerly out of reach. Among other things the ways in which the aforementioned *peak performances* can be achieved become clear. If we look into the question of how topnotch performances are really achieved, there are always two things that stand out. The first is a *clearly recognized strength,* and the second is *uncompromising concen-*

tration on it. As is clear, peak performance results from a union of the third and fourth principle.

If people want results, they must *utilize strengths.* If they want to utilize strengths, they must *accept* that they have many, usually significant, weaknesses. They must try to *compensate* for them, which does not mean eliminate them. Weaknesses must be rendered insignificant, irrelevant. This is the purpose of organization. Whatever else may be achieved through organization, its primary function is to utilize strengths and render insignificant the weaknesses. This is also applicable for what is perhaps the most important sub-unit of every organization, the team.

Let me express this quite clearly. If, and for as long as the attitude, perhaps even the culture, in the organization is molded in such a way that people say: *Though Mr. Müller is an excellent gear design engineer, he is a difficult man, he is not cooperative, he cannot work in a team, he is not motivated, we want to let him go…*, a fundamental mistake is being made, one which goes against the spirit of good management. This issue should be turned around: *Mr. Müller? A thoroughly difficult man, not cooperative, cannot work in a team, is not motivated… But the man is such an excellent gear engineer that it is my task as his boss to ensure that he designs gears day and night. If he cannot get on with the world, then I shall assume this responsibility for him. This man is not on our payroll because he is a pleasant man, it is for one reason only: the fact that, with his designs, he can give us a lead of three years over our competitors…*

There is *one* important exception to the principle of utilizing strengths, which I shall cover in the chapter on the fifth principle of effective management.

Fifth Principle

Trust

What Counts Is Mutual Trust

Though the fifth principle is directly related to motivation and corporate culture, it *refutes* the prevailing views of these issues rather than supporting them. What is more, this example shows how, on the one hand, commonly held opinions are totally misleading and, on the other hand and far worse, how they almost completely overlook something much more important.

How can we explain the fact that there are managers who, if we take the textbooks as our standard, do everything wrong and nevertheless have a good, often excellent, working environment in their departments? On the other hand, how can we explain the fact that there are managers who, again according to the textbooks, do everything right, know all the motivation theories and behave accordingly, but have a bad, often miserable, working environment in their departments?

Every time I got to the root of this issue, the factor of *trust* came to light as the solution to the riddle. If and to the extent that a manager has been successful in gaining and keeping the trust of those around him, his subordinates and colleagues, there was nothing essentially wrong with the working environment or the corporate culture. If there was *no* trust, all efforts to improve the corporate culture or the level of motivation were useless, and even had an adverse effect sometimes; subordinates considered the measures taken in this respect to be dishonest, manipulative and, frequently, as a particularly refined form of cynicism.

The fifth management principle can be derived from this: *What matters in the end is mutual trust!* It is trust that counts, and certainly *not* all the other things so often described and demanded such as motivation, management style and corporate culture.

Strangely, there is no, or only a limited amount of research and literature on trust in organizations, much less than on all the other aspects of corporate culture, which are essentially far less significant. It seems as if the humanities have, for all intents and purposes, overlooked this problem. The topic has hardly been dealt with in the standard German and English literature on motivation and in writings on corporate culture.[21] There is no reference to it in most books; in the few where there are allusions to it, such as Leavitt, it has little substance, or in the case of Warren Bennis, it is confused and ends up in the realm of the metaphysical, which is totally useless in practice.

Only in recent times, around the mid nineties, has there been an intense discussion on the topic of trust, primarily in the USA, where it has now almost become a fad which, of course, does not lend substance to the issue. Apparently, many now feel inspired to quickly write something about "trust in organizations", not with any intention of solving the problem or contributing something worthwhile but simply for the purpose of writing about what is currently in vogue. In Europe, we will soon see that people will begin to talk about trust *culture* because, for some time now, it has been apparent that everything here has to be instantly elevated to the status of a "culture", thus making it more difficult to understand what it actually means. Nothing is gained by such terminology but the word sounds so good...

Much of what is written in the literature falls under the category of *"psychologizing"* mentioned in section I, in which it is rarely understood that trust, in reality, has nothing to do with psychology and certainly not with any emotional state that can actually accompany trust or mistrust, just as everything is accompanied by emotions without there being any causal link.

It is important that I do not believe that trust should or can take the place of motivation. Rather, my assertion is that there can be no motivation where there is a lack of trust.

Robustness of the Management Situation

If and inasmuch as managers are successful in gaining and keeping the trust of the people around them, they have achieved something extremely

---

21 An exception is Dale E. Zand, *Wissen, Führen, Überzeugen*, Heidelberg 1983, page 46 onwards.

important, setting up a *robust* management situation; robust as opposed to fragile, resilient as opposed to sensitive.

Robust in what way? With respect to the many management mistakes that occur time and again in spite of every effort, all discipline and all ability. Even the best managers, and we should not delude ourselves here, commit several major mistakes every day, without *wanting* to and usually without *noticing* them. In practice, managers are not as sensitive, and this may be regrettable, as experts in theory and training, who are particularly influenced by the human relations school of thought, would like them to be. This can be assumed for all types of organizations unless proved otherwise in individual cases, and, it seems to me, this is applicable to managers of both sexes. Many seem to find it exceptionally difficult to realize this and accept it as being, to a great extent, unalterable.

Therefore, the important question is not whether mistakes are made in management or not; they occur very easily in the hectic activity that characterizes day-to-day business. Rather the crucial question is how *serious* the mistake is, if it matters, if it has consequences. A management situation based on trust is strong enough to survive and cope with management mistakes. The subordinates may occasionally grumble but they know that they can rely on their boss in an emergency. Even in organizations with trust, every day is not full of joy and happiness. There is also discord, dissatisfaction and conflict, but these do not really matter as long as there is trust.

Incidentally, something similar, and I mention this only in passing, seems applicable to two other forms of human togetherness: marriage and friendship. Neither good marriages nor good friendships are free of conflict. Their quality is not determined by the fact that there are no difficulties but by the fact that conflicts can be resolved, that they can be settled – they are strong enough to weather any storms.

How Is Trust Created?

Unfortunately, as the issue of trust has, to date, been largely ignored, not much is known about it. Therefore, I can only discuss a few points. In part, this consists of information on mistakes that should be avoided, as they destroy trust permanently. Much can be gained by just following this advice, as subordinates, to a certain extent, initially trust most managers.

Never Play the "Loser Game"

There are people who never learn to admit to their mistakes. When they are made managers, they unfortunately gain the power and the means to conceal, suppress, or at any rate, cover up their mistakes with rhetorical skill and to pin the blame on their subordinates. This, of course, does not remain unnoticed.

Not *everyone* notices it *immediately*, but when a manager makes it a standard practice, even the most stupid people gradually realize the game being played on them. Generally, people are prepared to accept failures. However, when they are expected to play a "game" in which they are not just *occasionally* the losers, but in which a win is always and systematically out of reach, they refuse to accept it.

When they always, and without exception, come off worst, and all because their superiors are always changing the rules to their own advantage, the consequences are pre-programmed. The good people and those that have options will leave the organization, and the others who cannot do anything about it because they have no other alternatives due to the age factor, for example, resign inwardly. They are physically present but work only for the sake of the money, and not for the sake of the work. They remain only "spectators", not "participants", and any trust is irrevocably destroyed.

A few simple rules can be derived from this.

- *The subordinate's mistakes are the boss's mistakes* – at least to the outside world and senior management. Managers cannot "leave their people out in the cold" without losing their trust. I emphasize the phrase to the outside world and senior management, *not internally*. If a subordinate makes a mistake, it must be pointed out to him and corrected. This can be accompanied by harsh criticism and occasionally even penalties. However, when it comes to the outside world and more senior managers, the subordinates must be able to rely on the loyalty and support of their boss.
- *Mistakes made by the bosses are theirs alone* – there are no exceptions to this. Managers must have the character to admit to their mistakes or they must learn to do so. They can certainly seek the help of their subordinates to correct a mistake, but they cannot pin the blame for their own mistake on their subordinates, at least not without undermining the foundation of trust.

These rules can be expanded further.

- *The success of the subordinates is theirs alone*: The manager should not claim all the glory for himself.
- *Managers can lay claim to any successes they have achieved through their own independent efforts*: However, the good managers, and, above all, leaders also say: We achieved it.

This may sound a little idealistic but good managers act in accordance with these rules because the trust of their subordinates is more important than their own image. I am, of course, aware that there are many managers who do the exact opposite and have still attained high positions. They may appear to have reached the top of their profession in this way, but they will never enjoy the trust of their people, and, in the long run, they can wreak great damage.

Creating Trust Means Listening

Managers do not usually have a lot of time. However, if they can even spare ten minutes for their subordinates, they should listen to them attentively and with concentration for those ten minutes. Moreover, managers are usually quite impatient people, and listening does not come easy to them. Good managers force themselves to do this. They can certainly urge a subordinate to keep it short. However, managers cannot simply ignore what people have to say and particularly what they want to say to their boss without losing their trust.

An Interest in Gaining Trust Means Being Genuine

Good managers do not pull wool over their subordinates' eyes. They do not try to play a "role" that they cannot sustain in the long run. Therefore, they do not pay any particular attention to their management style; they are genuine, with all their "rough edges". They not only hold themselves accountable for their mistakes but also for their personality, which does not mean that this should not be developed.

For this reason, I do not think very highly of the literature in which the "role" of the manager is given prominence. I am indeed aware that this is a specialist term in *sociology*, and I accept that it is useful there, but I do not consider this term to be appropriate in *management*. Roles are enacted on stage and in films, by actors, and it is precisely in this way that we understand the term in everyday life, since most of us are not sociologists. Roles played by actors are the perfect example of something artificial, of something that is *only enacted* and is *not* the way things *really* are. Even small children can tell the difference. Even if they watch a film on television, spellbound and fascinated, it is perfectly clear to them later that it was *only* a film, something enacted.

Occasionally, my colleagues from the field of sociology tell me: *But you play the role of a father at home!* My answer is: *That is exactly what I do not do! I fulfill the duties of a father, as well as I possibly can. And that is something far more serious than playing a role.* Managers have tasks to carry out, not roles to play.

Management Style Is not Important

What I have just said with regard to "roles" is closely linked to management style, and what I assert in this heading is in absolute contradiction to prevailing opinion. For most managers and, above all, many speakers at seminars, there is no doubt that *firstly*, management style is *very* important, and, *secondly*, only a *certain* style, that of cooperative behavior, is acceptable.

I, too, considered management style important for almost a decade until I became convinced that it was *not important* in reality, or at any rate not as important as it is made out to be in the countless books and studies on the topic.

The reasons for my position are as follows.

Firstly, there is no link between management style and results, except in very *artificial* situations created for games or experiments. If we differentiate between an authoritarian and a cooperative management style on the one hand and between good and bad results on the other, the following can be observed.

1. There are cooperative managers who *also* achieve excellent results. This is wonderful, and we can only wish that every organization has a lot of this kind of people as managers.

2. However, there are also those who are indeed very cooperative but do *not*, unfortunately, achieve any results. Though they are nice, pleasant, and perhaps even kind, they are not effective.
3. Then there are, of course, authoritarian managers who are *unable* to show any results. They are a catastrophe for every organization, and they should be removed as quickly as possible.
4. However, I have also come across managers who were very directorial and quite authoritarian in the usual sense of the word, but achieved *outstanding* results.

Types one and three require no explanation. People in the first category should be "treasured", and those in the third category should be quickly removed. Difficulties are encountered in cases two and four. Here we are faced with a decision between giving preference to the management style, or the results. My decision goes in favor of results, even if these are achieved at the expense of unpleasant and sometimes harsh consequences.

My recommendation is that no one should let himself be deceived on this issue by certain role-plays and exercises in seminars. There are wonderful exercises for the "training" of managers which are supposed to "prove" that cooperative behavior is *always,* and authoritarian behavior is *never* rewarded with results. These exercises are very impressive and seem to be very convincing. The other exercises available which prove the opposite, never see the light of day, unfortunately, partly because many speakers at seminars are so convinced of the doctrine of the cooperative management style that they no longer question it, and partly because an ideology is being disseminated.

To avoid being misunderstood: I, too, find cooperative people more pleasant and likeable than other kinds and, as such, I would prefer to work with the first group rather than the second. However, in management and in an organization, what we find pleasant and likeable is not the issue, the issue is what is effective and right.

I freely admit that it is possible to do the wrong thing while being authoritarian. However, a person can also do the wrong thing while being cooperative. Being authoritarian but right when it comes to achieving results is better than being cooperative, and failing to achieve them.

There is a *second* reason to consider management style to be of little importance. I maintain that 90 percent of what, in practical terms, can be understood by "management style", and the term itself is not exactly a shining example of clarity and precision, is *entirely different* from what is demanded and taught in books and seminars. An acquired and polished "style" is not important; what is *really important* is something much simpler, namely, a minimum of *elementary manners*. I do not mean highbred politeness rituals but what we might call "good upbringing", a minimum of *decency*.

Unfortunately, it can no longer be taken for granted these days that everyone will automatically have this attribute. Therefore, these manners must be taught to those who lack a good upbringing. No seminars are required; they should simply be demanded. Uncouth behavior must not be tolerated. Of course, an organization is not run on, or powered by manners, but they are the "lubricants" that enable people to live and work together.

In physics, there is a law of nature according to which friction is created when solid bodies meet. Organizations are places in which "solid bodies" – people – "meet", and this causes friction, or conflict. Even the most well designed engines require some lubricating oil for true running. Our organizations are nowhere near to being as "well-designed" as engines, and as such require even more "lubricant".

People without manners must occasionally be tolerated, but they are never respected. People who go around yelling, who never think of saying "please" or "thank you", who are unable to muster the slightest decency will receive no respect in the long run, and such people are also unable to create trust. Any communication with them is tinged with skepticism, doubt, mistrust and rejection.

Incidentally, the manners being discussed here have nothing to do with etiquette and protocol. In management, these are occasionally also significant, and if someone wants to attain a top position, he would do well to learn the basics of these in plenty of time. In top management positions, it is sometimes necessary to hold receptions, be a good host, and be able to represent the organization.

However, in general it does *not* matter whether someone can eat fish or shellfish correctly, or deal with an artichoke. The manners I am talking about here are not "courtly manners" but the basics of civilized, and I certainly do not wish to say cultivated, interaction with other people. Managers do not inflict their moods on the people around them; they do not interrupt their subordinates when they are speaking, but let them finish; they do not grumble to all and sundry about the weaknesses of those around them; they do not "tear somebody to pieces", etc.

Invariably, there is an objection that this is "style", and I am asked why I am against it. There is little sense in quibbling over words. If someone would like to term it style, he is free to do so. At any rate, this aspect is not mentioned as part of what is covered under style in books and seminars, nor does it fit into the generally accepted concept of style.

Creating Trust Requires Integrity

Character or, more precisely, *integrity of character* is perhaps more important than everything we have discussed so far. Most people will agree with this even though it is not one of the main subjects in management education. What is meant by integrity of character? What is a personality with integrity? Books could be written on this subject, and indeed many have been. Much of what is written is terribly obscure, impenetrable and metaphysical, and very complicated. All the philosophical discussion of this topic boils down to something very simple: *People must mean what they say, and act accordingly.*

Consistency is just as important as *predictability*. Most people understand trust as a general, somewhat unclear emotion or feeling. Though trust may be accompanied by emotions, this does not necessarily have to be the case, and emotions are, above all, not particularly dependable. Trust is built on the foundation of *predictability* and *dependability.* We need to know where we stand with our boss and colleagues and we need to be able to rely on this. Therefore, we require rules of the game that are valid, and words must be equally valid.

Here, too, there is room for misunderstanding. *Meaning what you say* does not mean that managers should say *all* that they *mean.* That would be naïve. Every manager, on occasion, has good reason not to talk about certain things at a given time or place. However, *if* the manager does say something, he should also mean it.

Of course, this demand does not mean that people cannot ever change their opinion. Certainly they can and very often they have to do so. In this case, what needs to be done is that the people concerned should be informed about it. I see no reason why I should not tell my subordinates and colleagues: *Until recently, I was of the opinion that X is right; I have now come to the conclusion that Y is better.* This needs to be said, rather than leaving people in the dark or thinking that they will notice it sooner or later. If a person wants to be a modern manager, he will also explain and give reasons for his change of stance. This was not previously necessary. Today, it is expected.

Whenever we meet people who are almost blindly trusted by those around them, we find that their lives are characterized by consistency and honesty. In this regard, I am always told that this can only work in simple situations, not in the complex conditions prevailing at management level or, for example, powering politics. This is a widely held opinion. Nevertheless, I consider it to be *wrong*, absolutely wrong.

An example to refute this senseless opinion is the manner in which one of the best managers of the twentieth century carried out his highly complex duties. I am talking about General George C. Marshall, Chief of Staff of the American Army from 1939 to 1945, and thereafter Secretary of State and Secretary of Defence in Truman's cabinet.

As Chief of Staff of the US Army in the Second World War he had masterfully conceived and directed what was then the largest mobilization in world history and successfully carried out possibly the most difficult military operation ever. As Secretary of State he was the founder of the Marshall Plan, which was responsible for the reconstruction of Europe, and, to a considerable extent, the rise in prosperity in the post-war period.

Marshall had to carry out his functions under difficult political conditions. He faced a lot of opposition and, to some extent, spiteful hostility (in the McCarthy era). Marshall's life and the way in which he worked, his interaction with his subordinates, colleagues, superiors, politicians in the Congress and Senate, generals in the Allied Armed Forces, difficult personalities such as Roosevelt, Churchill and de Gaulle, and even more difficult leaders such as Stalin, Chiang Kai-shek, Chou En-lai, and Mao were characterized by the utmost honesty and openness, in short, by integrity.

Marshall never deceived anyone, he never manipulated anyone, and he was respected by everyone as no other person was. He had opponents and enemies, but even they held him in great respect. His biography is well worth reading.[21a]

21a Ed Cray, *General of the Army. George C. Marshall – Soldier and Statesman*, New York 2000.

Creating Trust Means Staying away from Schemers

This is my last piece of advice, and it is the exception to the utilization of strengths, which I referred to at the end of the last chapter. Managers should not tolerate any schemers around them, even if they are people with outstanding strengths; they must part with them as soon as possible, or even leave, if they have even the slightest chance of doing so.

It is impossible to work with schemers. They poison every well, pollute every environment, and undermine every attempt to create trust. On this subject, too, there is hardly any scientific study, it seems to have been overlooked.

However, there is enough illustrative material in everyday life. And anyone who wants to study the phenomenon of intrigues, if he has not already been on the receiving end a dozen times himself, has only to read a few works of world literature or see a play by Shakespeare.

To my knowledge, it is not yet known when and why a person becomes a schemer. As far as I know, this has never been studied. But we can depend upon the fact that once a person comes to know that it is much easier to make progress through intrigues than through performance, that person will resort to this method again and again.

We should not subject ourselves to the trials and tribulations of working with this kind of person. Fortunately, there are enough decent, honest and upright people with whom we can work. Life is too short to waste it with schemers.

And if it Is Difficult?

Time and again the question arises of whether it is actually possible, especially in a big organization, to manage with a focus on trust. Honest managers are certainly not desired there.

I am of the opinion that it *is possible* to manage with a focus on trust in every organization. Trust can be built up, gained and kept, and also destroyed. The example of Marshall amply demonstrates this. By quoting his example, I deliberately took a case which is one of the most difficult, a case in which we would be most likely to expect many compromises to be made and to encounter what we know as "Machiavellianism".

I certainly do not believe that building and keeping trust is easy. I agree that it can be quite difficult to act in an open, honest and upright manner under the typical conditions in a large corporation. There are numerous obstacles, and there are difficulties; above all, there is the constant temptation to do things in another way and select what appears to be the easier way. However, as difficult as the environment may be, I see no reason why I should not be able to manage with a focus on trust in my *immediate* sphere of influence.

The issue is not whether something is easy and can be done without difficulties, but whether it is *right*. Of course, there are companies and other organizations in which honesty and openness is not desired. Though no one in these companies will admit to this, we become aware of the reality soon enough. However, the existence of such organizations is no argument for continuing with things that we know to be wrong.

Firstly, things can, in fact, occasionally be changed. Alongside all the failed reforms and reformers, there are also the successful ones. We should not aim to change and improve the world immediately; it is enough to create trust as far as possible, or better, let it grow in our immediate sphere of influence. Incidentally, we can also leave an enterprise in which this kind of behavior is not desired, especially when we are young and have several options.

Secondly, some people understand trust to mean "blind faith". I certainly do not mean this; there is no place in an organization for this. Trusting blindly is simply being naïve. There are situations in life in which we *must* actually trust someone blindly because we have no choice. However, this cannot be the case everywhere; no organization can be based on this. What I mean is *justified* trust, trust with a reason. This probably requires a more detailed explanation.

The topic of trust opens up a whole minefield of misconceptions, as has always been my experience in discussions and seminars. Some people understand trust, as mentioned earlier, to be blind faith. For such people, disappointments are inevitable. The world is not that simple, and, above all, it is not that good (in the moral sense). Others interpret trust according to the motto attributed to Lenin: *Trust is good, supervision is better*. This is the cynical variant, and I certainly do not mean this either. It leads directly to destructive mistrust, a situation with catastrophic consequences for the organization. In an organization filled with mistrust, there can be neither cooperation among people nor performance. Mistrust is one of the most dangerous "cancers" in an organization, and it is incurable except in the very early stages.

What do we mean then? Is there a third possibility? In my opinion, there is. Unfortunately, it is a bit complicated and exacting. However, it is precisely this that distinguishes good managers; they do not simply fall into the traps of common misconceptions, they reflect more deeply than others. This is why good management does not consist of just "common sense". Common sense is indeed important; with it, a person can go a long way in a company, and we should be happy if it does not desert us in the course of our university studies, for example. However, this alone is not enough.

My suggested solution to these problems is as follows.

Trust everyone as much as you can, and, while doing so, extend your trust to the limit. This is the foundation and the starting point.

Next comes what has to be done in addition to this.

a) Ensure that you always realize exactly when your trust is being abused;
b) Ensure that your subordinates and colleagues know that you will realize this;
c) Furthermore, ensure that every breach of trust has serious and unavoidable consequences;
d) Finally, ensure that also your subordinates are clearly aware of this.

What do I mean by this in practical terms? To take an example, every sensible person will do their utmost to trust their children to the fullest extent. We know how important this is for a child, how sensitively even small children react to signs of mistrust and how quickly the atmosphere is ruined.

However, we also know that it is possible to fall into the trap of blind faith. Therefore, we are well-advised to speak to the child and, depending on the child's age, say something to the effect of: *I trust you as much as I can (when you go out with your friends in the evening, for example, in matters of alcohol and drugs, or with regard to school, etc.). You will make mistakes, and there will be mishaps. That is fine, we can sort it out. However, do not, under any circumstances, ever break my trust. I will find out sooner or later, and the unavoidable consequences will be this and that. Do not hide anything from me; come to me in plenty of time if something happens, and I will help you as much as I can. If you are confused about the limits, ask me in advance, and we will find a way...*

This should be the approximate attitude, and these are essentially the rules of the game. We must then always act in accordance with them; people can watch their children a little and pay attention to signs and hints. If it has been agreed that the child should be home at 11.30 in the evening, this means 11.30 pm and not 0.30 am; and when we have agreed upon "no alcohol", this means "no alcohol" and not "it was only two beers".

Whatever we agree with our children must be decided by ourselves, and opinions can and do vary in this respect, depending on the age group, the performance of the child at school, the personality, and many other factors. We have to discuss these matters time and again with our children and explain to them why something is still acceptable and something else no longer is. Similarly, these days we also have to explain and justify certain things to our subordinates, due to the current level of information and education. This is one of the results of the democratization efforts in our open and pluralistic society, and I, for my part, welcome this development.

Once something has been agreed upon, it should also apply. We would do well to occasionally check, look into, question and ensure that our trust has not been abused.

I have one last example to clarify exactly what I mean. When I ask my twelve-year-old son: *How are you doing at school?*, he may reply: *Great, Dad, everything is fine.* I believe him; I want to believe him, and I am happy about it. I will not, by any means, assume that he is lying to me. However, I cannot believe with absolute certainty that a twelve-year-old will always and under all circumstances be able to assess reality correctly. Therefore, I will occasionally call his teacher and ask him or her: *How is my son doing?* By doing so, I will not be putting things off until the bad report is lying on the table at the end of the school year and we are faced with a problem that will be difficult or impossible to solve. My son knows in advance that I will do this, that as a father it is my duty and my right.

As a result of this, we will have a very good relationship based on trust. We will gain more insight into each other's opinions and perceptions; the number of disagreements (*"I thought, you meant..."*) will diminish; he will be given more and more leeway and freedom, and he will learn to use it sensibly and maturely. I will be able to rely on him. And one day he will come to me and say: *Dad, I have a problem; I think I have made a mistake....*, and that is when he will know that he can rely on his father completely, that there will be no argument or accusations, rather I will help him to find a solution.

To avoid any misunderstandings: What is applicable in a father-child relationship cannot, as such, be applied to marriages and friendships, or to the relationship between subordinates and managers, and between colleagues in organizations. Nevertheless, the examples can help us to understand what justified trust should be, and here the same rules are indeed applicable elsewhere.

I agree that it is not always easy to avoid falling into the trap of mistrust and to create justified trust. It demands openness and honesty, discipline and integrity, all the things I have discussed in this chapter. Moreover, I also admit that not everyone is capable of doing it.

However, I am not talking about "everyone" here but about *managers*. The requirements made of them should be higher. Not impossibly high, such as the ones we read about time and again in books and magazines, and which can, in the final analysis, only be met by saints; nevertheless, they should be higher than those placed on "ordinary people".

I am only too aware that many companies and many managers do not view this in the same light, that all too often these issues are totally disregarded. These constitute the badly managed organizations and bad managers. I see no reason to depart from the rules just because this kind of organization and this kind of person exists, and in quite considerable numbers.

People who are unwilling to examine these issues more thoroughly and adopt, to the best of their ability, an honest attitude and policy towards such issues, should not be in management positions, nor should they be promoted to them. We owe this to the people in an organization and the organization itself.

Sixth Principle

Positive Thinking

What Counts Is Positive or Constructive Thinking

It is easy to misunderstand the sixth principle. It has become a hotbed of charlatanism. However, this should not be a reason for us to "throw out the baby with the bath water". Properly understood, the discipline and practice of constructive thinking is of tremendous value, or, to put it the other way around, negative thinking and the corresponding behavior are so destructive that they should not be allowed to take hold in any organization.

In one form or another, behavior based on this principle is always to be found in effective managers. There are those amongst them, who make this principle into an almost excessive philosophy, which I advise against because this soon has an overpowering effect on other people, and can, therefore, sometimes produce the opposite of the desired effect. However, most of the people who follow this principle do not talk about it. They simply *act* in accordance with it.

Opportunities instead of Problems

In much of the literature on management, managers are seen as *problem solvers*. Consequently, various types of problem solving procedures, which are intended to help managers in their supposed core function, have been and are still being developed. I, too,[22] supported

---

22 Peter Gomez/Fredmund Malik/Karl-Heinz Oeller, *Systemmethodik: Grundlagen einer Methodik zur Erforschung und Gestaltung komplexer soziotechnischer Systeme*, two volumes, Bern/Stuttgart 1975 as well as Fredmund Malik, *Strategie*

this view for a long time and was actively involved in devising a problem solving method.

I still consider the ability to solve *problems* to be very important. However, I have changed my opinion to the extent that I do not consider it to be the first and foremost task of managers. Recognizing and utilizing *opportunities* seems to me to be more important than solving problems. If all the problems in an organization have been solved, this in no way means that all the opportunities have been utilized. Particularly in practice, there is little to be gained by resorting to the cliché that utilizing opportunities is nothing more than solving problems. I consider this to be sophistry.

The principle of positive thinking turns the managers' attention to opportunities. This does not mean that problems can be ignored, that we can philosophize them away, deny or suppress them. This is precisely one of the forms in which charlatanism and "faith-healing" have flourished with regard to positive thinking. They invite us to close our eyes to problems. This is not what is meant here.

Effective people are level-headed realists, even if they have learnt to think constructively; they look problems and difficulties straight in the eye, they are not inclined to gloss over or suppress them. However, they primarily seek possibilities and opportunities, even in bigger problems. *Is there an opportunity in this problem?* is roughly their attitude. This does not mean that this is easy for them to do. If nothing else works, they force themselves to adopt this attitude. This does not necessarily mean that they will always be successful. However, *if* there were an opportunity to be found in the tricky and perhaps even seemingly hopeless situation, people who think in this way would be the ones *most likely* to find it. The probability of finding a solution, if there is one, would be higher in their case. This by itself provides a significant competitive edge.

From Motivation to Self-motivation

Closely related to the endeavor of looking for opportunities in the most difficult of situations is the discipline of *self*-motivation rather than moti-

des Managements komplexer Systeme, Bern/Stuttgart/Vienna 1984, fifth enlarged edition 1996.

vation by someone else or from the external environment. In this case too, as in many other places, I am not talking about an *ability*, certainly not an *inborn* quality. I am therefore not referring to something that will make it *easy* for people to motivate themselves. Even with the knowledge and application of this principle, self-motivation requires a certain strength of mind and effort. In the course of time, this may then become a sort of *habit*. Whether there is a natural talent for self-motivation, I am unable to say, and neither is it important. It seems to be more of a practice, a *discipline*. Often, even in this context, it is a self-imposed obligation to which we subject ourselves because insight, reason and intelligence demand it.

Once again, this does not mean that people who do this do not suffer from periods of frustration, or get disheartened, or sometimes even fall into depression. It is not as if they were *impervious* to failures and disappointments, or, as a psychoanalyst may well believe, that they require these. They get upset, suffer just like most other people, and occasionally feel the need to withdraw and "lick their wounds". But they do not *continue* to wallow in their suffering, and certainly not in *self-pity*.

The practical application of this principle is perhaps most clearly expressed in the following statement. A well-known top manager in a European country who, for a long time, headed one of its largest companies, once said to me during a dinner: "Do you know, in the course of my life, I have simply had to learn to draw sufficient inner strength from a maximum of 10 percent positive experiences during the day just so that I can endure the remaining 90 percent of rubbish."

People, who find opportunities in problems and motivate themselves where possible and, above all, where necessary, want primarily to *change* things, they want to act, and not simply recognize, analyze, understand and passively accept. Their actions may occasionally degenerate into action simply for the sake of action, perhaps even unthinking action. However, this is neither required by this principle nor is it its unavoidable consequence.

Normally, the application of the sixth principle is very simple even if, as I so often emphasize, it is not easy. People are beset by problems, they have difficulties, and they cannot afford the luxury of ignoring them. They do not simply suffer them; they do something to change the situation.

In my opinion, there are enough indications to show that this attitude gives others the impression that they are dealing with a *mature personality*. A person who does not see the problems at all, who glosses over them and exudes calculated optimism, or who sees the problems, but then despairs about solving them or freezes into inactivity cannot be considered mature or as someone with character. Mature personalities are people who recognize problems with total realism, often earlier than others and with greater astuteness. They do not leave it at that, but ask themselves: *What can I now do to change this?*

Inborn, Learnt, or Forced?

Is positive thinking an innate quality? Are we born with it? Perhaps, but we are as much in the dark about this as we are about the source of self-motivation.

From what I know of them, most people who think constructively have trained themselves to adopt this attitude, to continue with it, and in some cases, have forced themselves to do it, once they realized the important role it could play in difficult situations. The method can vary. There are people who simply carry a note in their pocket that says: *Think positively, you idiot...* When they put their hand in their pocket, they no longer need to take out the note. Just the mere touch is enough to bring their thinking back on course, if it threatens to go astray. However, this perhaps slightly primitive method may not seem very helpful to everyone. Most use one of the various methods of *mental training,* to varying degrees systematically and regularly.

I do not wish to describe these methods in detail here. *Firstly*, because there are quite a few of them, and *secondly*, I do not consider the method to be of particular importance. In my case, autogenous training was and is very helpful. In my early twenties, I came across a small book by chance, written by a certain Lindemann, the first person to sail single-handedly around the world. He wrote about how he was able to endure the enormous physical strain of his lonely voyage, which lasted several months, without any contact with people, without being able to sleep properly, often sitting in salt water for days on end, enduring hunger, thirst, exhaustion, loneliness, and, last but not least, the uncertainty of whether he would even succeed in his venture. Among other things, he referred to a method of autogenous training developed by a German doctor[23], which

23 I.H. Schultz, *Das autogene Training*, New York 1932, 18th edition 1987.

had just gained recognition at that time. By using this method, he was able to consciously influence certain bodily functions, and this helped him in his sporting achievement. According to his account, he could thus deliberately influence his body temperature, which helped him to withstand the cold and wet, and he was able to regenerate himself in a sort of half-sleep to such an extent that he was completely fit again. This method interested me and, subsequently, I more or less taught it to myself. As a relaxation, concentration, regeneration and self-influencing method, it has since been of invaluable help to me.

However, this is by no means a recommendation. Autogenous training is useful to *me* and, according to reports, to many others also. However, there are others, who think little of this method, and for whom it is not effective. There are other methods and techniques, from simple gymnastics to breathing techniques, yoga, and transcendental meditation, which, even though they are individually very different and make very different claims, do have a *common core* in that, alongside the other effects they promise, they all promote self-influence.

Everyone has his own opinion on the transcendental elements of these methods. There are people to whom this appears to be very important. Personally, I have not been able gain much from them.

Therefore, I restrict myself to that which we could perhaps call, as already mentioned, *mental training* in the clearest and most non-incriminating way. Now this is a method that I really think very highly of. The *causes* of the effect are not very clear, as far as I know; however, there is enough *evidence* of the effect. Today, no sports coach would want to dispense with mental training methods, and the same holds true for the athlete.[24]

Almost every athlete, artist, circus performer, and anyone who has to produce peak performances has in his own way worked out a method that helps him to prepare, train and develop his abilities and skills and, in crucial moments, to concentrate, bring stage fright and jittery nerves under control, and, lastly, to mobilize his energies and concentrate everything on *one thing* – the *performance*.

---

24 See the abundant sports literature, e.g. Stefan Schaffelhuber, *Inner Coaching*, Frankfurt/Berlin 1993; Fritz Stemme/Karl-Walter Reinhardt, *Supertraining*, Düsseldorf 1988, third edition 1990; Lorenz Radlinger/Walter Iser/Hubert Zittermann, *Bergsporttraining*, Munich 1983, as well as the literature there.

The methods vary in the details and reflect, to a great extent, the natural and very pronounced individuality of this kind of people. However, what is common to all is the element of *vivid imagination*. In sports, we speak of the "idea of anticipated movement"[25], and all training methods connected with the term "Inner Games" are now based on this, e.g. The Inner Game of tennis, of golf, of climbing, etc. The basic idea is that the sequence of motions perfected in the imagination translates into an easier and better performance.

In my opinion, mental training can be understood to be a reversal of the way in which, according to current knowledge, the brain appears to form intellectual – mental – units such as concepts and terms through the so-called internalization of actions. We are indebted to the great Geneva-based developmental psychologist Jean Piaget[26] for research into this process, consisting of brilliantly simple but very imaginative experiments and observations. According to him a small child at its so-called sensory-motor stage of development keeps carrying out a sequence of motions, for example, reaching out for an object until the mental equivalent, the term or mental operation, evolves in the brain, at which point coordinated movement is mastered. Through carrying out the actual action its mental concept also evolves. Why should the reverse not be true, that through the mental image which the developing child is not yet capable of producing but the adult is, a series of motions or actions can be enabled or perfected?

This method of improving physical coordination of movement through mental training is to be found primarily in sports and the arts. However, the idea, at least in terms of the approach, can be expanded to include physiological processes as such, and also views, attitudes, opinions etc. Everyone unconsciously makes use of a part of this process, and this is in the form of deliberate action. I want to stretch out my arm to pick up a glass; the thought elements of my imagination and the command are the prerequisites for and, in a certain sense, the causes of or reasons for the successful carrying out of the action. This principle can also be used,

---

25 E.g. Radlinger, Lorenz/Iser, Walter/Zittermann, Hubert, *Bergsporttraining*, page 14 onwards.

26 Jean Piaget, e.g. *Einführung in die genetische Erkenntnistheorie*, Frankfurt am Main 1973. It is to be noted that the phases of development propounded by Piaget have nothing in common with those in psychoanalysis.

within certain limits, to change the pulse rate or the body temperature, for example.

Moreover, everyone knows that we can, as is expressed so aptly in the vernacular, "convince ourselves" to feel certain things, for example, emotions such as fear or joy, good or bad moods, sympathy or antipathy. Why should we not use this ability to convince ourselves to be motivated, develop staying power, to overcome fear, or to gain the conviction that we can do something?

There are numerous reports on how people have coped with extreme situations in exactly this way. Take for example the impressive accounts of pioneering mountaineers such as Walter Bonatti, Hermann Buhl, Reinhold Messner, Hans Kammerlander, and several others or any athletes competing in sports requiring stamina – marathon runners, triathletes, iron man competitors, etc. Moreover, there are reports of other existential situations such as people in solitary confinement for years, prisoners of war, survivors of concentration camps, and those that have triumphed over severe accidents, illnesses, other crises or great misfortune. Though a bit of skepticism may be advisable with regard to an autobiographical detail here and there, the same basic pattern is apparent in them all: *mental self-influence as a prerequisite for extraordinary physical and psychological feats.*

However, it is certainly not necessary to have to compete in extreme sports to make use of this ability. Any ordinary person can try out on themselves all the things that are applicable to extreme performance. We can lose our self-control when we first reach the "lowest point" of endurance and surrender to our emotions, giving them free rein; or we can persuade ourselves that we are nowhere near the end of our resources, gain control of ourselves and continue.

Freedom from Dependence

Everyone who produces top performances, irrespective of the field, in effect "people that break barriers", knows that a person's limits are determined *first and foremost* by the mind and that these limits can be *pushed*. They are also aware that people do not have to be slaves to their emotions, whims and fancies, feelings, moods, or their level of motivation. They know that they can influence all of this and, at least to some extent, make themselves *independent* of it.

Psychology applied in certain ways in management (which I called "psychologizing" in section I) has lead to the spread of the pseudo-scientific view that people have to be motivated to achieve something, or that people have to be motivated before they can achieve anything, or that no performance is possible without motivation. This is a view I reject. It assumes the most varied forms, as we can see, but always amounts to the same thing: *subordination to moods*. Instead of emancipating people as they pretend to, these 'psychologizing' writings and the trainers and personnel managers who advocate them achieve the opposite: They produce *dependence*.

No one has to be taught that most people, possibly all, are influenced by moods in one way or another. On the other hand, what must be taught is that *something can be done about this*. This does *not* mean, and herein lies the dividing line between what is tenable and useful and charlatanism, that a little positive thinking can move mountains, as is always promised. To move mountains bulldozers are needed. Nonetheless, our thinking changes our *attitude* towards the mountains. It determines whether we see danger or opportunity in them, and this in turn determines our behavior to a great extent.

Even if the effect is a placebo-type effect, it is of no consequence. What is crucial is that it helps, even if the *how* is still not known. However, I maintain that it is not solely, or even primarily, a placebo effect, as is occasionally asserted.

The fact that mental concepts can trigger physiological reactions is essentially a truism. The mental bite into an imagined lemon and the physiological reactions triggered by this are adequate evidence. The exact biochemical and neurophysiological mechanisms of the effect are still unclear to a great extent, since they are a part of one of the most complex enigmas: the interaction between the mind and the brain.

Apart from the aforementioned works of Piaget, due consideration must also be given to other interesting studies in a range of sciences, such as philosophy, brain research and psychology in which insights from computer science and modern developments in biology, cybernetics and systems sciences also play a role to some extent. This is one of those fascinating problems which requires input from many disciplines to shed light on its intricacies. It is likely that a pioneering new science will evolve from this.[27]

Perhaps due to the fascination it evokes, this field is also a favorite playground for pseudo-scientific nonsense. Therefore, managers must shoulder a special *responsibility* here to differentiate between sense and nonsense so that they do not unwittingly promote the spread of sectarian rubbish. That is what has happened, and still does to a great extent, for example, with regard to creativity, intuition or split brain theory. Lately, it has celebrated its comeback in the form of emotional intelligence[28] and is fascinating for the in-crowd in management.

Even if intellectual honesty and Socratic modesty demand that we respect the extent of our ignorance, it must occasionally be pointed out that we know *more*, indeed *much more*, about these areas than those who spread all types of charlatanism and esoteric drivel seem to imagine. Intellectual modesty should not allow superficial knowledge and superstition free rein. We know enough to be able to recognize nonsense, and whoever does not resist its dissemination is, at least morally, partly responsible.

Doing Your Best

Notwithstanding all the magic that we unfortunately find associated with it, positive thinking fulfills an important function. It lays the foundation that enables us to see the *opportunities* and free ourselves from *self-imposed dependence* on our moods.

The result of an attitude that is basically positive and constructive is that people give their *best* wherever they are, wherever fate, coincidence or their own decisions place them. Whether this equates to topnotch performance in an absolute sense is an open question; it is, at any rate, *my best*.

---

27 See, among others, Dieter E. Zimmer, *Die Elektrifizierung der Sprache*, Munich 1997; John Searle, *Minds, Brains and Science*, Cambridge 1984; John C. Eccles, *Die Evolution des Gehirns – die Erschaffung des Selbst*, Munich 1989, third edition 1994; Karl R. Popper/John C. Eccles, *The Self and its Brain*, New York 1977, and the literature referred to there.

28 See the informative review of the latest Goleman book by Kathy Zarnegin in *Neue Zürcher Zeitung*, No. 115, 21.5.1999 (www.nzz.ch).

This is important because far too many people seem to find *justification* for doing *little* or *nothing at all* in the limitations present in any circumstances, the limitations of the specific situation in which they find themselves; or vice versa, they can perform only when those limitations are removed. However, they do not feel they have to do this themselves, they wait for others to do it.

These people can always, and this is where the last principle coincides with the first principle, recognize what is *not* possible in a situation, what they *cannot* do, what *cannot* be achieved. They point to all the difficulties they can see or maintain that the resources, the budget, for example, are not adequate to do this or that. Their motto is *not here, not now, and not with what is available.*

They can and must be shown a different attitude: *Do what you can with what you have, where you are…* The fact that we cannot do a lot of what we want to do or have to do is clear and is basically true of every situation. The mistake lies in taking that as an excuse for doing nothing. The response must be: *At least do what you can…*

It is also true that the resources available are never adequate for everything that needs to be done. This applies, to some degree, to everyone and every organization. Even the largest organizations are subject to constraints related to money or people. This attitude must be countered with: *Make the best of what is available, and stop complaining that there is never enough.*

Finally, there are also those, who express a desire to do something, but always postpone it until *later*. Not now, but when they are promoted; not in their present position, but in the next one; not in this company, but in another. These are usually *excuses for laziness*. This type of person just does not *want* to act.

Therefore, I suggest that we should not waste our time on them. We can give them one or two chances to adopt a more positive attitude. In the case of young people, we can make more of an effort, but this also has its limits. Fortunately, there are still enough people who *want* to perform, who do not take long to understand or be taught to think positively. They are the ones we must rest our hopes on, the ones we should work with, and they must be given the opportunity to perform. They must be *held up* as examples and *set up* as the standard.

Organizations, irrespective of their type, in which we always have to "motivate", in which people always need "reasons" to do something, to stir themselves to undertake some action cannot function.

Management Quality

As I explained in section I and will mention again here, every profession is characterized by four elements: principles, tasks, tools and responsibility. Professional principles regulate, as propounded in this book, the quality with which tasks are carried out in the profession and the way in which tools required to carry out the tasks are used. Consequently, the principles of effective management regulate the quality with which management tasks are carried out. They form the core of all that, within reason, can be understood as corporate culture, or at least they should. Under certain circumstances there may be additional elements in individual cases which are related to the specific features of a particular sector of the business world, the structural conditions of an organization, its history, and its purpose. However, I do not believe that additional aspects need to be considered in most cases. I believe that the six principles given here cover all aspects that are generally applicable for all types of organizations and situations.

These principles are the core of corporate culture, or to frame it in a manner less pretentious than is usual in management these days, they are the core of good, competent and effective management. This is true in two respects. *Firstly*, it is usually the case that nothing other than these six principles is required; but without adherence to these principles there cannot be good management, and achieving a useful, enduring corporate culture that is capable of holding up under difficulties is impossible. *Secondly*, and still more important, it would not be possible to manage an organization successfully in the long term without these principles, irrespective of any other elements that may be considered necessary.

In both cases the aspect of sustainability is important. Of course, it is possible that, in the short term, for a certain period of time, if circumstances are favorable, these principles can be dispensed with individually or altogether, that they can be neglected and eroded without immediately having to face serious consequences. However, in my opinion, the long-term prognosis is, without exception, negative.

The six principles should be understood in their relationship to one another and should be followed. One cannot be exchanged for another; there is no trade-off between them. They form a set of rules to regulate behavior, with the purpose of establishing effective, professional management.

Furthermore, these principles render numerous "theories" superfluous and unnecessary. They are, therefore, the basis for a certain economy of understanding, as it is neither possible nor necessary to read and learn all that has been said and written about management. Criteria are required to decide what is to be heeded and what is not. The principles of effective management are standards for the critical analysis of management theories.

As is apparent, these principles can be learnt. They are, as I have already said in the introduction to this section, easy to understand even if they may not be very easy to apply. However, we can adopt them and learn to apply them. To a certain extent, they compensate for a lack of talent; on the other hand, if there is talent, they facilitate its full utilization. Their application leads to a distinct type of behavior. Therefore, it is relatively easy to check whether they have been understood and followed.

Part III
Tasks of
Effective Management

Preliminary Remarks

Principles are the *first* element of effective management. The *second* are the tasks carried out by managers. They are the subject of the following section.

What we are discussing here is not managers' activities as such. Hence, I am pursuing a totally different objective from the Canadian management writer, Henry Mintzberg, who attracted attention several years ago with his assertion that managers' actual activities have little or nothing at all to do with what they are said to be in certain management literature, such as that by Peter Drucker. On one hand, he is right; on the other hand, this completely misses the main issue.

This section of the book will not deal with what managers *actually* do for the entire day, but what they *should* or *must* do if they wish to be *effective* as managers. The daily routine of managers includes, and in this I am in agreement with Mintzberg, much that has little to do with management or its effectiveness. Among other things, this routine includes commitments related to carrying out, or sometimes even supposedly carrying out, *job-related tasks* such as dealing with correspondence, negotiations, business meals, covering for others, reading the newspapers, etc.

A distinction must be made between job-related and management tasks. In the following five chapters, I will cover those tasks that I believe essentially determine the effectiveness of management, and they do so in such a crucial way that they must occupy center stage in our discussion of effectiveness: managing objectives, organizing, decision-making, supervising people, and developing people. Without adopting a craftsmanlike, professional approach to carrying out these key tasks it will not be possible to achieve results in any organization.

What I have said with relation to principles is also applicable to these tasks and the tools that will be discussed later. The *what* of management is the same everywhere; the *how* can and must occasionally be very different. If this is overlooked, there will be confusion about the content and also its inherent logic.

Due to their very nature, carrying out management tasks requires not only a *knowledge of management*, but also *factual* and *special* knowledge. While management tasks are the *same* everywhere, the factual knowledge required to carry them out is very *different*. What factual knowledge depends on a number of factors, for example: the purpose and activity of an organization; the industry; the geographical area in which a person is working; the size of an institution; and, last but not least, the manager's level in the organization. All this should be obvious, but it is frequently overlooked in treatises on management, and in the general understanding of management.

For the sake of clarity here are a few examples. The first of the management tasks to be discussed is "managing objectives". This task must be carried out in *every* organization. However, the *substance* of the objectives in a company dealing with aluminum differs from those in a pharmaceutical company; the administrative body of the Ministry of the Interior has different objectives from those of the Ministry of Defense or the Ministry of Foreign Affairs, and a non-profit organization that helps young people to beat drug addiction has objectives that differ from one that looks after old people in need of care.

The same applies to the different organizational levels. It is obvious that at the top level of a company, for example, which deals with strategic issues and therefore also has strategic objectives, different factors have to be taken into consideration and, consequently, the factual knowledge required at this level differs from that required at the level of a foreman in the same company who deals with very different issues.

Another question is whether the management tasks suggested and dealt with here are sufficient in principle. I would like to leave this issue open for now and discuss it at the end. For most social institutions and typical cases, the answer is yes. However, the intention here is not to create something new. Strictly speaking, the tasks that are necessary and sufficient for management are well known. The efforts of certain writers to constantly invent something new are not amusing, they are annoying. The emphasis must be on a clear and precise understanding of the elements of each management task and not the creation of an endless string of new, meaningless words.

This is particularly important for the growing number of organizations that have *information* and *knowledge* as their most important resources. Even though their employees, compared to more traditional industries, have different and new types of professional tasks to carry out that also require different knowledge relating to their methods and content, the management tasks are basically the same. A change that is almost universally underestimated or ignored has taken place: In information and knowledge organizations management must be mastered as a virtuoso. What is required is not a different management but a more *precise*, almost *perfect* management. Traditional industrial and commercial organizations were, to a great extent, impervious to management mistakes; however, the new types of organization are very sensitive and only in the rarest of cases are management mistakes forgiven.

Basic knowledge of a manager's tasks and a certain amount of experience are required to understand the following section. For each individual task there are only a few aspects that really matter. I am tempted to talk about "secrets". However, if I am to remain true to my principles, I will have to refrain from doing so. There are no secrets. Nevertheless, this knowledge is not generally known either. The contents of this section are those practices that can be learnt from effective people – who carry out the same tasks as others, but their methods of carrying them out are *different*.

First Task

Managing Objectives

The first task of effective management is managing objectives. Immediately, an almost ideological question arises, which I do not want to answer just yet, namely whether objectives are to be *stipulated* or *agreed upon*. This question is by no means as important as is generally assumed to be. The management task is to ensure that there *are* objectives. The way in which they are set must be subordinate to the task itself.

Management by objectives was one of the first management tasks to be recognized and written about. As far back as 1955, Drucker's first book on management referred to it to a limited extent[29]; the idea had appeared even earlier in papers on military leadership. The *basic principle* of "Management by Objectives" is, by and large, not disputed. In numerous companies, particularly very decentralized ones, it is the only way to manage. Nevertheless, Management by Objectives (MbO) actually functions *rather poorly* in practice. Why is this?

There are several reasons. The *first* reason is that Management by Objectives is often considered to be a method of managing a company or an institution *as a whole* (which, of course, is part of it) and less as the task of each *individual* manager. The general objectives relating to the whole are, of course, necessary but they are useless if the organization does not operate according to the same principle at the level of each individual manager.

The *second*, probably *more important* reason, though banal, is that carrying out this task involves a lot of work if it is taken seriously. Management by Objectives is not really difficult to understand in principle. Neither is it normally particularly difficult to devise sensible objectives in the

---

29 Peter F. Drucker, *The Practice of Management*, New York 1955, 17th edition
1995. Drucker is the father of Management by Objectives.

intellectual sense. It is, above all, *labor-intensive* to consider, work out, discuss, and to make those objectives so precise that they are really practical and can fulfill their function.

Perhaps an analogy to music will help to illustrate this. If a company's mission and strategy is equated with the theme of a symphony, working out objectives can be compared to writing notes on paper. The theme may require genius, but writing the score is very mundane and, above all, laborious. However, even the greatest of geniuses have to go through this drudgery, and they have to do it themselves. No one can give someone else the task of writing down what he has in his mind and what he may not be able to explain in detail. Managers, too, must do this themselves. Certain things cannot be delegated.

The *third* reason why Management by Objectives does not usually function well is the subject matter of this chapter: There are a few practices that, though not widely known, have a crucial impact on the effectiveness of Management by Objectives.

No Systems Bureaucracy

One mistake, which explains much of the ineffectiveness so often observed, is to make a complicated, bureaucratic program or system out of a sensible and very simple principle. This means a time commitment and a paper war for the manager. Far worse, it usually results in form replacing content, with the system counting for more than the substance. What is required are the right *objectives*; an MbO *program* or MbO *system* can be dispensed with.

Therefore, what should be demanded of managers, especially line supervisors, is that they follow the *principle* of Management by Objectives. Incidentally, I am using the word "demand" deliberately. There are some things that are not open to discussion and in which people are not cooperative. Furthermore, the staff and systems experts must be prevented from turning it into a bureaucracy which may be well meaning but has damaging effects.

Personal Annual Objectives

Organizations, especially companies, have several widely differing types of objectives. They differ in the period of their effect (long, medium or short-term), their content (strategic objectives, operational objectives), their area of application (general objectives, departmental objectives, personal objectives, etc.), and how specific they are (broad objectives, concrete objectives).

Therefore, when we talk about "Management by Objectives" the phrase must be clearly understood in every organization. My suggestion is that "Management by Objectives" should be understood to mean *management by personal annual objectives*. Thus, I restrict the use of this phrase "MbO" to a particular type of objective. This is a decision taken for the sake of precision. This chapter primarily refers to Management by Objectives in this sense. In a figurative sense, however, it also applies to other types of objectives.

The General Direction

We frequently neglect to adequately inform the employees who are to be managed by objectives about the *basic* intentions, the "general heading" in principle, for the next period. We can hardly expect people to set themselves good objectives or assist in their implementation if they are not informed.

Therefore, key employees must be informed briefly and succinctly about the basic direction in which the enterprise, organization, division, profit center, etc. is to proceed. Doing so *verbally* has its advantages but it can also, as in large companies, be done in *writing*. In any case, after receiving the instructions verbally the employees should also be given them in writing. The verbal method is more effective and motivational; the written is more precise, not only at that point in time but also later, because it can be reconstructed and is thus less susceptible to arbitrary interpretations.

Basic Rules for Management by Objectives

Irrespective of how objectives are set in individual cases, I suggest that particular note be taken of the following.

Few Objectives – not Many

We almost always take on *too many* things that are also very *different* in nature. Setting objectives is one of the most important applications of the principle of concentration. I have already explained this in section II with the help of examples.

Objectives, particularly the personal annual objectives referred to here, are, along with the task to be carried out, the most important means of making people in an organization, beginning with ourselves, concentrate, focus on something; or to put it very simply: of managing them.

Anyone who is interested in effectiveness and wants to see results at the end of the year must do the exact opposite of what the majority of managers do with regard to objectives. Instead of "loading the car" with more and more, ensure that people take on *few* objectives. This question should always be asked. *Is this really important? What happens if we do not do it?*

I would like to touch on priorities in this context. Contrary to what we always hear, setting priorities is not particularly difficult, unless we have no experience to speak of. Anyone, who is familiar with an organization and has some practical experience, can usually specify quite accurately what is really important. On the other hand, what is difficult and is usually ignored is preventing the *opposite* of priorities – we could call them *posteriorities* or simply non-priorities – from throwing a spanner in the works. By posteriorities I mean all those things that only appear to be important and take up a lot of space on our desks or computers. These must be brought under control and kept under control.

It is appropriate here to remember what the past master in this field, Peter Drucker, said. *"Effective executives do first things first and second things – ?"* Not "second" as most people reply when asked to complete the sentence, an exercise I have tried out many a time. Not *"second"*, but *"not at all!"*.

According to my personal experience as a manager and leader of hundreds of seminars which I have held on this topic, and where this question is discussed time and again, this is perhaps the "bite of the apple of (management) wisdom" which is most difficult to digest. Managers find it quite unpalatable. I myself had to chew on it for a long time; nevertheless, it is the most important.

We must accept this without reservations, I am tempted to say with childlike faith, otherwise we will always experience difficulty in being effective. Too much, too different, all fleetingly touched upon, nothing really completed, nothing but compromises and half measures – this will be our situation at the end of a year. Why is it so difficult? Perhaps because it goes against the prevailing work ethic in some countries. People still believe that a lot is good. This is wrong. *What is good is doing the right thing and doing it right* should be the maxim. However, the more important reason, of course, lies in the everyday situation in organizations with their frenetic pace, which is mistaken for dynamism, with their bustling activity, which is confused with effectiveness, and with their rituals, which are taken for substance.

There is yet another, a *third* reason. Of course, we have to deal with many things that have little or nothing to do with the really important objectives and which, in reality, stand in their way. All of this, the posteriorities, the daily odds and ends, must somehow be disposed of. Effective people are, of course, not exempt from these tasks. However, they get rid of these things as quickly as possible and with a minimum of effort and time; they spend the first two or last two hours in the office doing this or do it over lunchtime so that they can then devote themselves to the really important priorities. They do not assess themselves – remember the first principle – according to the work they have done but rather according to what they have achieved, and these achievements are not related to day-to-day activities but to one, two or three important objectives.

Few but Big Objectives

Taking on less does not necessarily mean, as is occasionally assumed, working less, being lazy and "hanging around". The maxim is: *Few but big objectives – ones that are significant and count for something when they are achieved.*

As I shall explain in a subsequent chapter of this section, people develop by carrying out the *big* tasks. These are the ones that motivate them and stretch them to their limits. This principle should not remain abstract but rather should be reflected in the objectives every year. Where, if not here, will this ever be effective?

Most people have too many *small* tasks. This is detrimental for them; they become stunted, they dissipate their energies, and while they may indeed have a lot of work they have no results to show for it. Therefore, they do not experience any success, which is why they need to be "motivated". This vicious circle must be broken, not through sophistic "development programs" but through *big objectives*. The task, the job, the objective should guide the people, not the boss. The objective should be the source of authority, direction and supervision, not a superior.

What Is no Longer Relevant?

Even this third point, like the previous two, is inconsistent with prevailing opinion. Usually, we determine our objectives with the question: *What should I, must I do, or do I want to do?* However, effective people turn the question around and ask: *What should I stop doing, and what do I no longer want to do?*

First, we must get rid of the rubbish and systematically abandon previous habits, activities and tasks. Setting annual objectives not only provides the focus but also the best opportunity to systematically purify the organization, make it lean, "detoxify" it from the inside out, clear away the accumulated rubbish and make room for the new. There will be some specific details on the practical implementation of this idea in the section on tools.

I would suggest that employees be encouraged to write down the most important of these things. To *stop* doing something is as much an objective as doing something *extra*. Abandoning what has previously been done often has far-reaching consequences for the organization, and, therefore, some support measures may be required for this to succeed, such as providing appropriate information to others, as a minimum. More important, however, is the fact that, unless they are written down, these will remain nothing more than vague resolutions and good intentions; nothing concrete will actually be done.

Quantification – but not Dogmatism

Wherever possible, it should be obligatory for employees to quantify their objectives. This must always be followed up and insisted upon. There is *much more* that can be quantified than most people believe. This is because they have never learnt to do so systematically, excluding people with strong scientific or technical training. Most give up too quickly, they barely make an effort to consider the possibilities and use a little imagination; many believe that creativity and quantification are diametrically opposed to each other. The opposite is the case. Successful quantification of something that has never been quantified is the perfect example of a highly creative achievement. The absolute minimum is a quantification of time, i.e. there should be no objectives without a deadline.

I am deliberately talking about *quantification* and not simply *measurement*. The English cyberneticist Stafford Beer put it aptly: *"There is more to quantification than numeration."* We should go as far as is possible with quantification, at any rate, beyond the point where we usually stop but, and this is an important qualification, we should not be dogmatic about it.

The dogma to which we can fall prey is this: *Anything that cannot be quantified is not important – and, therefore, requires no attention.* This would be extremely hazardous for a company or any other kind of organization. It is an error that results from *misunderstanding* quantification, and is the consequence of an *apparently* scientific approach, which is completely misunderstood and is known in philosophy as "Scientism".

Experience shows that *the more important the objective for the organization, the less it can be quantified in the narrow sense of the word.* Sales, market share, productivity, cash flow, and many other things can now be quantified (this was not previously considered possible). But what is the situation like in the case of quality, customer benefit, customer satisfaction, innovation, etc.? The fact that non-quantifiable things are much more important than those that are quantifiable is true to a much greater extent in the case of non-commercial organizations.

It is like walking a tightrope. There should be as much quantification as possible, but not to such an immoderate extent that it distracts our attention from other things that are equally important but cannot be quantified. There is no general formula that can help us to find the right balance. However, in an individual case, when the circumstances, situation, product, market, technology, and, above all, the people are known, we can often quite accurately state how far we can and should go with quantification.

In any case, we must demand the maximum possible *precision*. This is also possible where quantification in its narrow sense is no longer feasible. *What do we base our assessment and evaluation on at the end of the next period in order to determine whether we have come closer to our objective?* This must be the key question. Therefore, we must train people to describe the desired final outcome as precisely as possible. A small trick is to demand the future perfect tense in the linguistic formulation of objectives. The question should not be: *What do we want to achieve?* but *What will have been achieved?* The masters of linguistic precision are good lawyers, even if they sometimes use their skill to create confusion.

Contradictory Objectives

In textbooks we can read: *Set non-contradictory objectives!* This sounds plausible, but it is too good to be true. The more important the objectives, the more contradictory they are (unfortunately). We must learn to live with this.

Setting good objectives always requires the skill of balancing and weighing the pros and cons. In this regard, Peter Drucker wrote[30]: "There are few things that distinguish competent from incompetent management quite as sharply as performance in balancing objectives. There is no formula for doing the job. Each business requires its own balance – and it may require a different balance at different times. Balancing is not a mechanical job. It is risk-taking decision."

Unfortunately, there are no formulae for this, and consequently we cannot delegate this task to our staff or a computer. It remains one of the elementary management tasks, and one that requires experience and not just knowledge.

Objectives or Measures?

In textbooks we can also read: *Set objectives and not measures!* This rule is correct as such but unfortunately it cannot always be followed. We should not be *dogmatic* about it either. There are cases in which we cannot determine a sufficiently precise objective but we can determine a *measure* that we assume from experience will take us in the right direction. There-

---

30 Peter F. Drucker, *Management*, New York 1974, fifth edition 1994, page 112.

fore, in such cases, we should adopt measures instead of objectives. What is important is not theoretical purity but practical effect. Whatever helps me to get closer to my objective is useful and acceptable.

That is *one* aspect. However, there is a *second* aspect that makes it important to concern ourselves with measures. Measures can be illegitimate, even if the objectives are not, they can be disputed on ethical or social grounds or be incompatible with the image of the organization. Therefore, we cannot simply exclude measures from the determination of objectives.

Resources

Textbook purity frequently also prevails in how we deal with resources. It is always correct to differentiate between objectives, resources, and measures as concepts. This does not mean that they cannot be dealt with together. On the contrary, I believe that they *must be* dealt with *together* on principle. This does not mean that certain secondary problems cannot be solved as part of a separate planning process.

I would propose that we should not only ask employees for the objectives but they should also state the most important resources they are likely to require to achieve them. *Firstly*, this will improve their understanding of the business or activity of the organization and its internal workings. *Secondly*, this corresponds with holistic and entrepreneurial thinking. There are no entrepreneurs, at least none that successfully survive, that do not simultaneously think about all three elements: objectives, resources and measures. And *thirdly*, it is the only way to not only set objectives but also to set *realistic* objectives, which is what is really required.

Defining objectives is not an art, provided we do not have to think about how and with what they are to be achieved. The most dangerous aspect of the discussion on vision, which has been carried out at great expense in the last few years, and one of the essential reasons for my rejecting it is that it is often far removed from reality.

Napoleon was a master of resource planning: Every time his generals submitted grand offensive strategies he leant back in his chair and inquired about such issues as how many horses were required for these strategies. Usually the generals had not given enough thought to this question. However, the question of resources cannot be left to subordinates, the "fortunes of war" depend on it.

People not Groups

Every objective must have a *person's* name on it. Effective objectives are *personal* objectives. Whether the person responsible for the objective then requires a group, a team, etc. for its implementation is another issue. This can often be decided by the people in charge, if they are sufficiently competent to make the decision. However, one person should be in charge and *not a group*. One of the most important functions of objectives in an organization is to individualize responsibility. It is precisely because organizations are collectives that responsibility must be personalized as much as possible.

If, for some reason, this is not possible (and I do not wish to rule out the possibility that this can happen in principle), and if even after serious effort, we cannot appoint an individual instead of a group, we should be very skeptical about the chances of successful implementation and entertain only modest expectations. As a result, we must keep a close *eye* on such cases, "stay on the ball", and take action at the slightest indication that the issue is "straying off course".

All Employees or only Selected Ones?

In management issues people are unfortunately far too inclined to have a concept of equal treatment that is *not properly understood*. The fact that everyone is equal in the eyes of the law is indeed an important constitutional principle and it signifies progress. But this does not mean that everyone should or can be equal in the eyes of their boss. It has been my experience time and again that the common belief is that if it is useful for certain employees to have objectives, the same must be true of *all* employees. Thus, there is a compulsive search for objectives to be set for doormen and part-time staff. This usually leads to absurd situations, which render the whole principle of Management by Objectives ridiculous and without any credibility.

I do not, of course, rule out situations in which a doorman can have sensible objectives, such as when new security systems are installed which he must learn to operate. However, he will not usually require any objectives to carry out his duties well.

Therefore, careful consideration must be given to the issue of which employees should have objectives and which should not. This is a genuine management decision, which will keep changing from year to year.

Individual Application

A second type of individualization is more important, namely the individual *application* of Management by Objectives. This idea applies to almost everything in management.

Experienced staff cannot and should not be managed in the same way as the inexperienced. In the case of the *inexperienced*, whether they are too young to have gained experience or are new to the company, the manager must thoroughly check the objectives they intend to achieve, what they perceive to be their priorities, and what they consider of secondary importance. Great stress must be laid on precision and quantification. The manager must discuss their objectives with them thoroughly and examine in great detail their analysis of the relevant resources. Objectives are a useful means, perhaps the best vehicle to find out mutual expectations and ideas.

On the other hand, *experienced* people who the manager has known for the last eight or ten years, and of who he knows how they react and particularly how they work, require much less management. In such cases the manager can be content with less precision and also with less discussion. Therefore, there should be *no unnecessary egalitarianism*! For an experienced employee it is very demotivating, even insulting, to be subjected to the same procedures as young and inexperienced employees. After all, they have already proved their capabilities, and also that they can be relied on.

The more Difficult, the Shorter the Duration

As already mentioned in this chapter we are primarily talking about management by annual objectives. These are only secondary in determining the *direction*, the course of an organization. That must be determined by long-term objectives. However, annual objectives determine the *effectiveness of the implementation* of long-term objectives. In difficult situations such as business turnarounds, rescue operations, managing acquisitions and mergers or management crises, we must sometimes work with objectives that have a considerably shorter term. In general, the more difficult the situation in which the organization finds itself, the shorter should be the timeframe for objectives. In extreme cases weekly or daily objectives can and should be set and even shorter timeframes can sometimes be required.

The situation is similar to handling extreme physical performance. When it is a question of survival, whether this is within the context of accidents, disasters, or generally in life or death situations, our thoughts are not focused on the distant future but on solving the immediate problem, surviving the next hour or the next day. Less dramatic but equally illustrative is what people experience when they stretch themselves to the limits of their personal performance capabilities, for example in sports. When we come close to the limits of exhaustion in a sport that requires stamina – running, cross-country skiing, or cycling – we do not, as an experienced athlete, think: *just another 20 kilometers* but: *just to the next bend...* When we reach it, the thought is: *...just until the next tree...* In this way, in small units taken one at a time, great objectives can be achieved if we believe we have already reached the end.

Objectives Must Be Specified in Writing

A remarkable number of managers dislike the requirement that certain things should be in writing. They associate it with bureaucracy. This may be justified in some cases, but it is not true in the case of objectives. Each person's objectives must be documented in writing and as precisely as possible. This certainly does not mean more work, as is the frequent objection. On the contrary, it saves additional work, namely the effort expended later to eliminate misunderstandings, mistakes, and communication problems. Moreover, the documentation of objectives is absolutely essential for a subsequent performance appraisal.

No great effort is involved. One page usually suffices if we adhere to the practices suggested here. If we need to write more, it is indicative of the fact that the objectives have not been considered and determined professionally, and this again makes their successful implementation doubtful.

Stipulate Objectives or Agree upon Them?

Countless books have been written on the question that was not answered at the beginning of this chapter, whether objectives should be agreed upon or stipulated. However, this question is certainly not as important as the scores of books on the subject would have us believe. The job is to *ensure that there are objectives*! This is the management task.

For obvious reasons there is much to be said for *agreeing upon* objectives, wherever this may be possible. We are aware of the positive effect this has on motivation; people are more inclined to do their utmost for something if they have participated in its inception.

However, to set sensible objectives by agreement, *two conditions* must be met *together: good employees and a lot of time*. If even one of the conditions is not fulfilled, it will be difficult to reach an agreement that is more than a pseudo-consensus. At any rate, it is important that we do not adopt a dogmatic approach to agreeing upon objectives. There will always be situations, in which we must at some time, say: *We have now discussed these objectives for six weeks, and regrettably we have not reached any consensus, even though I have done everything in my power to facilitate this*. What now? This is the situation in which the objectives themselves are even more important than agreeing upon them. They must then be *stipulated*, even if this does not seem to be in keeping with the modern view. At any rate, under no circumstances should there be a situation where there are no objectives simply because it was not possible to reach an agreement.

Cooperative management is almost always better than autocratic management, but there is also, as I explained in section II, cooperation that does not yield any results. The emphasis must be on management. Participation is frequently and mistakenly understood to be an end in itself. It serves a purpose which does not consist of imparting the "feeling of having a say". Its purpose is to *make responsibility a part of the task*.

Thus, there are good reasons for participation. But once again it is not an end in itself. There can be not enough participation or there can be too much participation. Not enough participation usually leads to a lack of responsibility. Too much participation, on the other hand, frequently leads to a lack of performance. We can discuss any topic to the point of distraction. Unfortunately, there is once again no general formula by which we can determine what is "too much" or "too little". In individual cases, we can usually state quite accurately where the dividing line lies between these two extremes.

A company is not a democracy, and this is true of most other organizations in society, even of those that believe that they should act in a particularly democratic way, because they champion the cause of democracy, such as political parties or unions. The fact that we organize society itself and the state based on democratic principles is no indication that this is the optimum form for other types of organization. These issues are always confused or mixed up, with consequences that are equally as damaging for the state and society as they are for its organizations. I will return to the issue of participation in relation to decision-making, where it is almost more important than is the case here.

Objectives are essential for every organization. The management task of managing objectives and Managing by Objectives determines the effectiveness of an organization in a crucial way, and nothing else can compensate, if it is not carried out. It also determines the effectiveness of each individual, and this is by no means restricted only to the business world. It is objectives that define when work becomes performance. Basically, we cannot speak of performance without having objectives. Objectives give human effort direction and meaning.

Which Objectives?

Setting objectives is a management issue. However, the objectives a person has are not directly related to management itself, but are related to the specific organization in question, its purpose, and its situation. I have already discussed this in section II with regard to the principle of focusing on results, and I would like to revert to it again here.

Of course, it is not a case of just *any* objectives; the *right* objectives are required for the specific organization. Companies have objectives that differ from those of non-profit organizations; institutions operating at an international level have objectives that are different from those of organizations operating at a national or local level. Whether, as a manager or as an agent of the institution for which he or she is working, a person selects big or small objectives, abstract or concrete ones, visionary or down-to-earth ones, the setting of these objectives has less to do with management logic and more to do with the situation in which the organization finds itself, its purpose, the organization's previous objectives and results, its history, its competition and partners, its customers and the recipients of its services as well as the self-perception of the people involved and their own situation.

For these reasons only qualified general statements can be expressed about organizations' objectives. As I mentioned in section II, each type of organization requires at least two types of objectives: those related to people, thus related to the staffing of the organization, and those that have to do with money, because every organization requires people and money.

The following are typical areas for objectives, and are applicable to companies, but also to many other organizations in a figurative and appropriately modified sense: market position, innovative work, productivity, attractiveness for suitable people, liquidity, and cash flow as well as profit or revenue requirements. These constitute the minimum areas or dimensions for which an enterprise requires objectives; others can be added such as those related to environmental, social or political fields.

Second Task

Organizing

The second task of effective management is organizing. Effective people do not wait to be organized; they organize themselves for their own benefit in their personal tasks and their area of responsibility.

Once again I will limit myself to the most important things here that, in my experience, determine the effectiveness with which this task is carried out, and this is largely independent of any specific circumstances. The structure of companies and most other institutions in society will, if the signs are not deceptive, be one of the most widely discussed topics in the coming years, an ongoing problem for which there are not really any solutions at present. Many organizations are experimenting and in most there is great uncertainty. With the exception of those companies that run a simple business, and those institutions that have a very simple task, all are, in some way, involved in organization. The changes that are taking place in the economy and society are forcing us to reconsider these structures increasingly frequently. However, it seems to me that no one has a ready solution at present.

Therefore, this chapter is not about the future macrostructure of an institution, but about that which should *always* be given attention in organization, regardless of the stage of development or restructuring a company or any other institution may be at.

Warning against "Organizitis"

An ever increasing number of managers follows a strategy of constant reorganization and restructuring, so that "things are always on the move". I fail to understand this; I consider it to be wrong. It has nothing to do with sensible organization, it is a disease – let us call it "organizitis". It primarily occurs in people who believe they should be "dynamic" at all costs, or in those people who wish to be featured in the media. In any case, it is a mistake made by corporate and also personnel managers.

People can certainly cope with change, but they *also* require periods of calm and stability to *perform productively*. Anyone who changes and re-organizes for the sake of change risks a clear erosion of the company's results and will produce "wait-and-see attitude", lethargy, and anxiety.

Organizational changes can be compared to surgical operations on an organism, a *living* organism and *without anesthetics*. Surgeons are in a considerably better position than managers; they can at least put their patients under anesthetic. *Managers cannot do this.* The manager's "patients" are fully aware of whatever is coming their way and they react accordingly.

Good surgeons have learnt that they should not operate unless strictly necessary. Only when all other means are futile will they take up the scalpel. Good managers behave in the same way. *They do not reorganize unless it is necessary,* and *if* they do have to, it is only after proper preparations have been made, and after the procedure has been thoroughly thought out and all the necessary support measures have been taken.

There Is no such Thing as "Good" Organization

Most people, especially inexperienced ones, have the idea in their mind that there are forms of organizations that function *without friction*. Whether management or business administration will ever find such forms is uncertain. At any rate, we do not yet know of any.

All organizations are *imperfect*: They *all* produce conflicts, coordination problems, problems with regard to information, areas of interpersonal friction, a lack of clarity, interactions, and all the other possible difficulties. In my opinion we would be well advised to assume that there is no choice between good and bad organization, but there is a choice between *bad* or *less bad. Compromises* are necessary in every organization.

Furthermore, we can rarely select a "pure" form of organization. These exist only in textbooks. Real organizations are practically always a combination of several "pure" forms; they are *hybrid structures*. There is nothing negative in this, unless you happen to be a purist. There is no need to be alarmed, if we arrive at a hybrid form as the best solution to an organizational problem. However, many people do get alarmed due to the misguided notion that they must follow a theory. In reality, they move further and further away from a practical and useful method of organization.

All too often managers overlook the fact that there may be other solutions for problems which are thought to have only organizational solutions. What is overlooked most frequently is that most problems, while it may not be possible to solve them immediately, can be alleviated more quickly and easily with better management, i.e. the suggestions put forward in this book, than through structural changes.

In this regard, I recommend the following rules. The *optimum* position can be achieved in areas where "good" organization (I use this word now despite the reservations just expressed, but in quotes) is combined with good management. However, this is a *rare* case. If *both* factors are negative and there is bad organization with bad management, we are faced with an almost hopeless case. These represent the two clear cases.

What is the situation like when one of the two factors is good and the other is bad? In my experience, if it is the management, the craftsmanlike professionalism that is bad, it can *never* be rectified or compensated for by "good organization". In the reverse case remarkable results can often be achieved. Time and time again, I have observed that managers can give outstanding performances, even in bad structures.

There are managers who do not let miserable organization stand in the way of giving their best, and thus achieve results in the face of all adversity. Of course, they get agitated about the ponderousness, the bureaucracy, the slowness or whatever the problem may be (usually it is several problems simultaneously), but they fight or muddle their way through.

The Three Basic Issues of Organizing

In all fields there is a risk of not seeing the woods for the trees. In organizing it is easy to get lost in a maze of objectives and criteria that are to be met by the organization. The worst thing that we can do is to *overload* an organization with requirements. The *more* the requirements, the *less* the organization can *achieve*.

Effective organizations are, as I have already mentioned in section I, *single-purpose* structures. Whether they can be *simple* is another issue. If they are, it is all for the good, but even single-purpose devices or machines can be very complex. "Simple" or "single-purpose" are often confused with one other. For example, a fighter aircraft is a single, purpose system, but it is certainly not simple. Its application is very restricted, but it performs its function better than any other device.

Essentially, there are *just three questions* to be answered; these are the basic questions for all forms of organizing. They protect an organization from being overburdened and overtaxed. These questions have been formulated with a company in mind. However, they are applicable in general when modified appropriately.

1. *How do we organize ourselves so that attention remains focused on that which the customer pays us for?*
2. *How do we organize ourselves so that the employees really do what they are paid to do?*
3. *How do we organize ourselves so that the top management really does what it is paid to do?*

To some extent the organization forms a bridge between these three questions. Here is some further information on the questions. Every company these days professes to have a profound belief in customer orientation. However, it has not, by any means, been realized. *Firstly*, because it is not easy to determine what a customer is really paying a company for. *Secondly*, even if we do know, there are numerous ways of organizing that completely disregard the customer instead of making him the focus of attention. An example that clarifies both the first and second questions is that of an insurance company, whose sales staff has to carry out administrative work in addition to selling policies. All analyses show that the sales staff of numerous insurance companies can, at the most, devote 40 percent of their time to customers; the rest of the time, a larger percentage, has to be spent on a widely differing range of administrative work. Therefore in reality, the customer is not the center of attention nor are the employees doing what they are really paid to do.

With regard to the second question, it is worthwhile to regularly question employees about their contribution. You may remember the question formulated in section II: Why are you on the payroll of this company? In an astonishing number of cases we either receive *no* answers at all or the answers are very *vague*. However, we also find time and again that organizations *hinder* employees in their work rather than really supporting them. Quite frequently the obstacle is the boss.

The *third* question for organizing refers to the things on which the top management actually spends its valuable time. Are the *actual* top management tasks really being carried out? Or does the top management get engrossed in day-to-day business? Does the organization really enable the top management level to tackle those problems that can only be solved with a view and awareness of the whole? Or is so much time and energy spent in just keeping the organization going that everything else gets neglected?[31]

Symptoms of Bad Organization

As I said at the beginning, firstly, we should not reorganize for the sake of doing so, and secondly, the only choice is between bad or less bad forms of organization. Keeping this in mind, when should we *still* consider a change in the organization? Which symptoms indicate a *real* organizational problem?

There are people who, without any thought, attribute *every* difficulty to an organizational or structural problem and immediately call for organizational changes. As managers we should never *succumb* to this line of reasoning. Of course, there are difficulties, problems and conflicts every day in every company. But only a *few* are *caused* by organization. On closer examination we will usually (or quite often anyway) come to the conclusion that *management* is more to blame than organization.

Organizations should not primarily be assessed according to the problems that they produce but according to those that they do *not*. The organization that we have today may create difficulties, but what difficulties would occur in any other organization? Through reorganization we can almost always solve the existing problem. *However, how many new and different problems are created by this course of action?* This question should also be taken into consideration along with the many other aspects.

---

31 See my book *Wirksame Unternehmensaufsicht, Corporate Governance in Umbruchszeiten*, section 2, second edition, Frankfurt am Main 1999.

The fact that organization is the actual cause of problems is strongly indicated by the presence of a few symptoms. If these symptoms are present, we should seriously think about organizational changes.

Increase in Management Levels

This is the *clearest* and most *serious* symptom of bad organization that requires change. This insight began to gain recognition in the nineties and is accepted and relatively widespread today. However, it took a long time to reach this situation. How else is it possible to explain the fact that people are vociferously calling for the reduction of hierarchies and eliminating three, four or five levels at a stroke? These levels must, at one time, have come about and been accepted, otherwise there would have been no need to remove them now. Nevertheless, they should never have been allowed to come about in the first place.

The rule is: The *lowest possible number of levels and the shortest possible channels*! We must *strongly resist* any temptation to create additional management levels. It is possible that, after thoroughly examining the circumstances, we come to the conclusion that another level is really necessary. However, this should only be done as a *last* resort.

Each additional level renders mutual understanding more difficult, creates disturbance in the channels, distorts information, falsifies the objectives, and steers the attention of the employees in the wrong direction. Each level means additional stress and is another source of inertia, friction and costs.

Constant Talk about "Cross-Departmental Work"

This is also a danger signal and an indication of the probable existence of organizational problems. "Cross-departmental work" *sounds* very modern; and it is often supplemented by the demand that people should think "interrelated".

In reality, "interrelated" thinking will be increasingly necessary, because our world is becoming more complex. But this is in no way desirable. It is extraordinarily difficult, and only a few people can master it. Even intensive training does not lead to any overwhelming success. For most people cross-departmental work and interrelated thinking place requirements on them that they simply cannot meet or can meet only with great difficulty.

Therefore, the *basic rule* must be *totally different*: *The organization is right if very little cross-departmental work is necessary*. We are properly organized if cross-departmental work is not necessary at all.

I am aware that this is not always easy and sometimes cannot be done at all. A lot of thought must be devoted to organizational solutions in order to follow this rule. However, this should be the guiding principle against which the unavoidable and necessary compromises are measured. Process-oriented organizational forms are leading the way in this direction, and re-sourceful use of information technology will facilitate useful solutions.

Lots of Meetings with lots of People

The "circus of meetings", which can be observed in so many organizations, is also a strong indication that something is wrong with the organization, and this evidence should be taken seriously.

It seems to be almost inevitable that more and more meetings are now required. This is by no means a desirable or even necessary development. Only seldom is real work accomplished in a meeting. The actual work is done before or after the meeting. And every meeting (especially a productive one) necessitates another three meetings.[32]

There is a *clear rule* for this, too; it is frequently misunderstood, but that is precisely why it is important. The rule is: *Minimize the necessity for personal contact in order to achieve something*.

I am talking expressly about minimizing the *necessity* and not the *opportunity*. The employees should, of course, have *adequate*, even *numerous* opportunities to interact with each other, their colleagues, superiors etc. Therefore, it is appropriate, usually even necessary, to create opportunities for contacts by way of a suitable layout of the building, the arrangement of workstations, the cafeteria or canteen, company events, and also by occasionally "turning a blind eye". However, if eight or ten people always have to get together to deal with any issue, because we are organized in this way, to coordinate and agree upon a course of action before anything can actually be done, then we are *not* properly organized.

---

32 Refer to section IV.

Overstaffing

The most productive resource, as always, is an able, competent employee who is *allowed to work* and is *not hindered in any way*. I know that this does not sound very modern in the age of task forces and teamwork. Nevertheless, I think that this issue should be given some thought. What is important is not whether something is *modern* but whether it is *right*.

If *several* people are always occupied with the same task, the organization is *bad*. Fortunately, the worst excesses have been corrected to a large extent by the years of recession in the recent past. The staff reductions that became necessary as a result of the economic situation have opened the eyes of many people. However, there is still much to be done. To date only completely obvious overstaffing has been corrected. Further pruning of the staff, which could be possible through clever reorganization, has yet to be carried out.

Necessity of Coordinators and Assistants

It is likely that some coordinators are required in every company today, especially in the larger ones, and there are managers who really do require an assistant, not just as a status symbol. However, the number of these jobs must *always* be *minimized*. They must be the *exception*. Anything extraneous is a sign of *incorrect* organization. People are quick to focus on status and position, academic titles and diplomas instead of on results. They concern themselves with what is interesting, not with what is important. And the costs rise, not primarily because the assistants and coordinators cost money, but because they *waste the time of all the other employees* and *keep them from their work*. We see analysis rather than action.

Lots of Jobs with "a Bit of Everything"

"A bit of everything" is not a good maxim, even for putting together a meal. It is *disastrous for people's work* and a serious organizational problem.

Ideally, jobs should make the employees concentrate and focus on one task, which should, however, be a big task. A well-designed and organized job directs the person's *complete* attention and energy towards the achievement of *one* objective. Anything else leads to a waste of time and dissipation of energy.

I know that this is unpopular, but it has proved to be correct, and it is the *only* way to help people achieve real, convincing, visible *successes* that can be held up for all to see.

Usually, we do not have to worry about variety. Even the best jobs, requiring the greatest concentration, provide enough leeway and spring enough surprises every day to keep the employee from getting bored.

Jobs that have "a bit of everything" provide an *escape route from performance* and *responsibility*. They make it impossible for employees to attain the one thing that is *important*, that they need in order to be motivated, respected, and possibly even satisfied and happy, and that one thing is *clear results* of which they can be proud, and as a result of which they can count on the lasting *respect* and *appreciation* of their colleagues, superiors and subordinates.

If one or more of these symptoms exist, we should seriously begin to rethink the organization. There are *other reasons* that prompt us to reconsider structures, such as the growth and size of an institution, the acquisition of new companies, the necessity of alliances and joint ventures, the control of succession issues at the top, etc. These problems, which are due to external factors, are usually given more attention than those discussed in this chapter.

Finally, to recapitulate: If, on the basis of the symptoms presented here, we reach the conclusion that reorganization is necessary, the required changes must be carefully thought out in advance, and then carried out *quickly* and *without compromise*. Hesitation and indecisiveness discourage the supporters and empower the opponents of the necessary measures.

Speed is important so that after structural change everyone can *resume work without being disturbed, the productivity that always suffers during restructuring is restored, and thus the humane conditions required by people to work properly can also return.* A company does not survive because it is constantly being reorganized; its survival is based solely on its performance, which will hopefully be considerably higher *after* reorganization than it was before. However, we must be prepared for the fact that, even afterwards, there may be situations that cause friction. Competent management that is focused on effectiveness is still required, even after reorganization.

Third Task

Decision-Making

One of the essential tasks for managers is decision-making. It is not their only task, as is implied in the science of decision-oriented business administration in the German-speaking countries or as Herbert Simon has suggested in the USA. Managers have several other tasks that have little or nothing to do with decision-making. But decision-making is the most *typical* management task.

Only managers make decisions. Anyone who makes decisions *is* a manager, irrespective of his status, designation or position. And the reverse is also true; irrespective of his position, status, the associated privileges and authorizations, if a person does *not* make decisions, that person is *not* a manager.

A decision brings everything together; everything is focused on the core issue. Decision-making is not the sole task of a manager, but it is the most *critical – the task that makes or breaks the manager.* Therefore, I will be devoting more space to this task and especially those aspects that are seldom, if ever, found in the relevant literature and popular case studies. This discussion covers the correct use of participation and consensus as well as issues related to the implementation of decisions.

Misconceptions and Mistakes

We might think that, given its importance, all managers *analyze* all aspects of decision-making extremely intensively, that they *train* their decision-making skills, apply a decision-making *method,* and approach this task with the utmost caution. Unfortunately, this is rarely the case. Coupled with this are a few widespread *errors, misconceptions,* and *mistakes* that adversely affect the quality of decisions. They are *easy to avoid,* if we are aware of them and disregard a few clichés.

The Illusion that the Problem Is Clear

Most managers come to a decision, in the narrow sense, *far too quickly.* They believe that the *issue* on which a decision has to be made and the *problem* involved in the decision are clear. I suggest that we should let ourselves to be guided by the premise that *the problem is never clear, it must first be found.*

This is the first and most important task in the decision-making process. I am, of course, not talking about small, unimportant decisions here, ones that do not have any consequences. What I am discussing here are the big, really important decisions that have consequences in which the problem is *never* really clear at the outset. It has to be deduced or distilled usually from a maze of data, suppositions, claims and vague ideas.

Sales are declining; is there a marketing problem, or is it related to the quality of the products? Is the pricing wrong, or is the advertising at fault? Is it due to the competitors' products, the economic situation, or does our sales force lack punch? Is it one single factor, or do several factors constitute the cause, and if so in what proportions?

Textbooks give the well-meaning advice: *Start with the facts!* But what are facts when it comes to making a critical decision? We cannot begin with facts but at best, with *opinions* about facts, and this is something totally different from the facts themselves.

If the problem has not been correctly understood, the correct decision can never be made. Even very refined processing, analysis, and evaluation of the individual elements of the decision cannot lead to the right decision, if the problem itself has not been understood.

Most people are reluctant to remember solving mathematical problems at school. Many faced difficulties with them and indeed had less of a problem with the calculations themselves than they had with understanding the problem. This is why all good teachers work with two categories for marking such problems; one is for "correctly understanding the problem", and the second is for "solving the equation correctly", and more marks are allocated to the first category than to the second.

If the equation has been incorrectly solved, the error can easily be found and corrected. However, if the equation itself is incorrect, all our efforts to manipulate the equation will not yield any results.

What is it all about? This must be the first and most important question, and we must, if possible, take our time and consider the issue thoroughly.

The Illusion that Someone Who Makes a Lot of Decisions, and quickly, Is a Good Manager

Most managers are inclined to hold this opinion. Even at the top level there are people, who have the Hollywood image of managers in mind, with seven telephones on their desk, one receiver clamped between their ear and shoulder, another in their hand, a third ready in front of them, people who travel around the world buying and selling, giving instructions and orders. This could be true in the case of a foreign exchange dealer; otherwise it is pure Hollywood and has *nothing* to do with good management and good decisions. It is a caricature of a manager.

Really good, effective managers make *few* decisions, but they are made after *proper consideration* and are *well thought out*. They know that risks are involved in decisions and that they have consequences which always include the desirable and *not so desirable ones*. They also know that *correcting* the *mistakes* from a poor decision takes up much more time, work and energy than is required for the labor-intensive decision itself.

Of course, there are times when good managers are forced to make a swift or improvised decision. If so, they make it. However, they *avoid* this situation as much as they can. They do not let themselves be pressurized into making decisions.

Quick and, therefore, usually spontaneous decisions are often justified by *intuition*, and it is very tempting for even the best managers to be proud of their intuition.

Nevertheless, really good managers have a very ambiguous relationship with intuition.[33] No doubt there is something like intuition that is accompanied by a very strong *feeling of subjective certainty*. However, the prob-

---

33 Confer the informative exposition in Edgar F. Puryear Jr., *Nineteen Stars. A Study in Military Character and Leadership*, Washington, DC 1971, page 361 onwards.

lem is not whether intuition exists or not, but it is of knowing *in advance* when our intuition is *right* and when it is *wrong*. Though subjective certainty is often a very *strong* feeling, it is a very *dangerous* adviser. It can be right or wrong in equal measure.

Therefore, good managers use their intuition like everyone else, but they are aware that they *should not rely* on it. It is this that differentiates them from ordinary people, not a greater degree of intuition.

The American general George S. Patton was very famous and notorious for his quick decisions which, on the surface, seemed to be spontaneous, intuitive, and split-second decisions. He has been attributed a "sixth sense", and in retrospect it can even be said that it seldom failed him. His "snap decisions" were almost always right. They played a decisive role in the success of the Third US Army commanded by him in Europe during the Second World War.

How was Patton able to do this? Was it a natural talent, an innate ability? No, it was something *totally different*. Patton had spent a lifetime training in his profession and *preparing* for his task (a task that he could not know, if and when it was to be carried out, and what it would be like in detail), and this learning and preparation was so thorough that it was almost unparalleled.

Patton had already served as a lieutenant colonel in the American Expeditionary Force during the First World War. He knew the conditions in France inside out. During the course of his training he spent some time in France in 1913 at the École de Cavalerie. He had personally visited the sites of battles from previous wars on French soil, patrolled the open country with maps, knew the geographical situation like the back of his hand, and had a three-dimensional image of the land fixed in his mind. In their training at West Point the cadets were given the following type of task. *It is 2nd July, 1863, 16.30 hours in Gettysburg. What is the situation like at this point in the battle, and what is going to happen in the next two hours?*

Patton had solved these tasks with pedantic thoroughness. His apparently intuitive "snap decisions" were not the result of a natural talent, but of very hard work, extremely thorough expert knowledge, and a lifelong preoccupation with the question of how to command an armored force.

When Patton was once harshly criticized for his quick decisions during the Second World War, he said, "*I have learnt the craft of war for more than 40 years. If a doctor decides during an operation to change his objectives, to close this artery, cut deeper or remove an additional organ that is also diseased, he is not making any snap decisions, but ones that are based on knowledge, experience and long years of training. I do exactly the same."*[34]

As can be seen, there are people who can decide quickly *and* also correctly. Of course, they also exist in the business world. Yet how many can say with a clear conscience that they *really* possess the *level of preparation* that is necessary, and that *detailed knowledge* of the business that eventually enables them to develop a *reliable* "sixth sense"?

Certainly not the young manager, fresh out of training, and certainly not those managers who believe that they are "managing" 26 totally different divisions in highly diversified corporations; most certainly not people who are members of 17 different boards of directors or supervisory boards in completely different sectors and who know each enterprise only on the basis of three or four meetings they have attended there.

I am aware of the fact that it is possible to be *too slow* in reaching a decision and thus paralyze the company. However, it is also possible to make a decision *too quickly* and cause a disaster. Assessing the right amount of time and thoroughness is one management problem that does *not* have a problem-solving formula. What is required for this is *judgment* (that can be sharpened), *experience* (for which time is needed), and a lot of *expert knowledge* (that cannot be substituted with slick maxims).

I recommend that *two* types of decisions in particular should *only* be made in one way, *slowly* and *very thoroughly*, and they are *decisions related to personnel* and decisions on *remuneration systems*. Quick decisions in these two areas are *almost always wrong* decisions. And the consequences are catastrophic.

Too Few Alternatives

The third mistake that is often made is that we are far too easily satisfied with the existing alternatives.

Effective managers start with the premise: *There are always more alternatives than we know of at the moment.*

---

34 See Edgar F. Puryear Jr. *Nineteen Stars. A Study in Military Character and Leadership*, Washington, DC 1971, page 382.

Of course, they also know that we must, at some point in time, stop looking for alternatives, and that the search for alternatives can be taken to an extreme. However, they are never satisfied with the first good alternatives that occur to them or are submitted to them. They have no inhibitions in rejecting even what seem to be their subordinates' best analyses with the question: *Are there any other alternatives?* They know that by doing so they are not exactly making themselves popular; but they also know that this procedure is an essential element of conscientious management.

I wish to emphasize again that I am not talking about the unimportant but the really important decisions. A complete or as complete as possible examination of *all* the alternatives is naturally time-consuming and costly. This is also one of the reasons why good managers make only a *few* decisions. They concentrate on the principal decisions, precisely because they know that good decisions involve an enormous amount of work and time.

The Opinion that the Decision Itself Is Important

Of course, decisions are important, otherwise this chapter would be superfluous. And good decisions are also difficult.

However, the decision itself is, relatively speaking, far *less* important and also *less* difficult than a completely different issue to which most people pay very little attention, and that is the *implementation* of the decision.

If we were to get even one dollar for every decision *made* at management level but *not implemented* on any given day in any country, we would be rich. Decisions are made, recorded and announced, and then they vanish into the bowels of the organizations and never lead to any results.

Effective managers make the implementation of a decision a *part of the decision-making process*. Their idea of a good decision does *not* end with making the decision itself, it *also* includes the implementation phase.

As difficult as making a decision may be, its implementation is even more difficult. Even the best decisions can go awry in the implementation phase. They may also go wrong due to the type of implementation. The decision can be misunderstood, distorted, perverted, or sabotaged.

Therefore, good managers always bear in mind the subsequent implementation at each step of the decision-making process. They review *in advance* the people who will be involved in the implementation of the decision and what these people will need to know so that they can understand and then correctly implement the decision.

Therefore, they also include these people in the decision-making process. They do not do this primarily for some motivational reason or as some vague endeavor to adopt democratic procedures, but to facilitate the implementation and to ensure that the implementation is *as effective as possible*. Thus, participative decision-making is important for managers but for reasons that are completely *different* from those that are usually mentioned in the literature.

Furthermore, good managers place great value on the follow-up and follow-through. They make sure that the important things are really *done*; they do not rely on verbal or written reports, they see to it personally.

This is why they approach with exceptional conscientiousness those decisions that are known to involve a great deal of *change* and whose implementation will necessitate a change in the behavior of the employees. They do not make such decisions until and unless they know about the training the employees will have to undergo, as well as the information and the new tools that will be required to implement the decision.

The Opinion that Consensus Is Important

Another mistake or misunderstanding is the widespread opinion that *consensus* is essential for the management of an organization. Above all, there are major mistakes regarding *how* consensus is to be reached.

Of course, in the *final analysis consensus* is important at the *conclusion* of a decision-making process. Decisions reached through consensus always have a far greater chance of being implemented than others. However, many managers have a pronounced tendency to strive for harmony, and certain psychological theories lend support to this behavior. Even the best managers, as I always emphasize, are only ordinary people, and many of them would rather avoid dispute or conflict. Therefore, they try to reach a consensus far *too quickly* and *too early*. This coincides with the fad of consensus *culture*.

What is really important is not consensus but *dissension*. A *sustainable* consensus that does not fall apart when difficulties occur in the implementation (as they always will) is not achieved through seeking harmony, but only through *expressed* dissension. There are only *three* ways to express dissension, and these are *openly, openly* and *openly.* As difficult and troublesome as this can occasionally be, there are no other options.

Alfred Sloan[35], the long-standing head of General Motors referred to earlier, had a crystal clear understanding of this. He made *dissension* a *systematic method* of decision-making at General Motors. The meetings of the decision-making bodies of which Sloan was the chairman were usually quite heated. At one of these meetings Sloan ascertained that there was universal agreement on an important decision. He once again made certain that everyone apparently shared the same opinion on the issue. Everyone nodded his or her head. Then Sloan said something to the effect of: *If that is the case, then I suggest that the meeting be discontinued right now – and we take some time to arrive at different conclusions...*

Sloan knew very well that decisions made by acclamation could rarely be the right decisions, that consensus existed, only because no one had done their homework thoroughly. He wanted dissension, and he had actively sought it. His procedure had *method*; and Sloan was clear that managers were paid to offer *differing* views on important issues. After scores of discussions with "consensus culture apostles" I have come to the conclusion that they simply cannot understand this concept. Typically, none of them has ever had the opportunity to manage an enterprise; in fact, they have never participated in any important decision-making. I have since given up on these discussions, as they are meaningless.

For good managers quick consensus is positively *unnatural.* They do not trust the "peace". They know only too well that differing views do exist in the background and will come to light if an issue is examined thoroughly. They also know that this dissension will appear in the implementation phase, if not sooner. They want to know in advance who is for and against, how people actually view the issue, where the "pockets of resistance" are and why. They provoke *systematic dissension* in order to reach, as mentioned earlier, a consensus that will be sustainable even in the implementation phase of the decision.

This costs time and money, and occasionally emotions are involved. Furthermore, a manager does not exactly win popularity this way. Never-

---

35 See Peter F. Drucker, *Adventures of a Bystander*, New York 1978, second edition 1994, page 256 onwards, especially page 287.

theless, it leads to *better* decisions, and *better* results in implementation. This is what counts.

The Mistake that only *Complicated Methods* Lead to Good Decisions

Young, newly trained graduates in particular who have learnt complicated methods such as utility analysis, operations research methods etc., are prone to make this mistake.

Some people are *fascinated* by the complicated methods, while others let themselves be *misled*. Many people are *impressed* by them. The issue is not whether something is fascinating or impressive, but whether it is *effective*. There are problems that require complicated methods for their solution, but these are the *exception*, not the rule.

Most decisions can be made with the help of a *simple* procedure, a simple sequence of steps. What is important is that none of these steps is systematically omitted and that each step is carried out carefully, thoroughly and conscientiously. Certain methods and techniques can be very helpful for each individual step, but they cannot replace the actual decision or the path to the decision. Their biggest advantage is not that they can replace decisions but that, with their help, information can be organized, or more precisely, data can be processed and organized in such a way that information can be derived from it.

The Decision-Making Process

In nine out of ten cases a good decision can be reached by adhering to a simple procedure, a sequence of steps.

The steps are:

1. Accurate definition of the problem,
2. Specification of the requirements that must be met by the decision,
3. Identification of all the alternatives,
4. Analysis of risks and consequences of each alternative and specification of boundary conditions,
5. The resolution itself,

6. Inclusion of implementation in the decision,
7. Setting up feedback: follow-up and follow-through.

1. Definition of the Problem

The first step in every decision-making process must be the *thorough* and *complete* definition of the *actual* problem. We should not be satisfied with either symptoms or opinions. We must look into the underlying facts and causes of those symptoms and views.

There are people who think it smart to assert with furrowed brow or raised forefinger the apparently scientific argument that we cannot find facts and causes, because everything is so complex or so interwoven, or because there are philosophical issues involved. I can only advise strongly against being impressed by this kind of fashionable statement.

We *can*, if we really want to, find the facts and causes in many cases at any rate, and to a sufficiently accurate degree for practical purposes. Some people talk about complexity and philosophy simply in an attempt to hide their lack of education and expert knowledge, and occasionally their laziness, which prevents them carrying out the work necessary to ascertain facts and causes.

I believe I have worked long enough in the field of complex systems to be able to say this. In most cases it is not necessary to elevate a difficulty that admittedly exists to the status of an insurmountable obstacle.

The biggest difficulty is *not* the complexity; neither is it the *incorrect* definition of the problem. Most managers are able to ascertain quite quickly when a problem has been misunderstood. The greatest trap is the *plausible*, but *incomplete* or only *partly* correct definition of the problem as well as the frequently observed behavior of being satisfied with the definition far too quickly, often due to a lack of time. Here, there must be room for the attitude that distinguishes good managers from others; this consists of a sense of responsibility, sense of duty, thoroughness, and conscientiousness.

The minimum that should be considered in defining a problem is the *classification* of the problem; is it an *isolated* case, or is it a *fundamental problem*? The importance of this distinction is that, depending on whether it is one or the other, the type of solution and the decision to be made will be *radically different*. The solution for an isolated case or an exceptional problem can be *pragmatic* and ad hoc, related to just this case. We can also improvise here. This problem will never occur again, *if* it is really an isolated case.

On the other hand, a fundamental problem requires a *fundamental decision*. We must find or specify a policy, a principle or a rule to solve it. These types of decisions involve more far-reaching consequences than an isolated case, and, therefore, they must be made with more care. Pragmatic "snap" decisions and improvisation will usually cause long-term damage in this case.

What is this actually all about? This must be, as already mentioned, the key question, and we must *take the time* to answer it. One of the typical mistakes made by many managers is answering *too quickly* and *without enough thought*. The time taken for this step is a good investment. It is well-known that the Japanese, who I do not consider as an example to be emulated as was once the trend, take an enormous amount of time in this first phase of the decision-making process and thoroughly clarify the issue. Contrary to what is often asserted, there are not too many *real* differences between Japanese and western management. This is, however, one of the differences.

There is *only one* way not to fall into the trap of defining the problem incorrectly: *The definition of the problem must be repeatedly examined in the light of all available facts*. If the definition of the problem does not include all the facts observed, it is not yet good enough.

A typical and informative case of misunderstanding a problem is the example given by Drucker[36] of the US automobile industry in the seventies, when the issue of safety in cars was being widely discussed, and about which there were even Congressional hearings. Managers did not realize, or did so only much later, that the issue was not about "safety when used correctly" but something totally different, namely "safety even when used incorrectly". Other examples worth studying are almost all military conflicts, from the Trojan War to Vietnam, to quote Barbara Tuchman[37], and today a few others can be added, from Grenada to Chechnya. In most of them at least one side misunderstood the real problem. In recent times the

---

36 See Peter F. Drucker, "The Effective Decision" in *Harvard Business Review*, January/February 1967, page 94.

37 Barbara Tuchman, *Die Torheit der Regierenden*, Frankfurt am Main, third edition 1984.

handling of claims for compensation by Holocaust victims can be included in this series of cases, in which people had great difficulty in recognizing the real problem, and some could not understand it at all.

3. Defining Specifications

The second step is to identify as precisely as possible the *requirements* this decision must meet. The key question for this second step must be: *What would be right?*

Two points are particularly important here. *Firstly*, the definition of the specifications must *not* be focused on the *maximum* requirements to be met, but the *minimum*. The minimum requirements that are to be met by the decision must be clearly and accurately defined. Any effects of the decision above and beyond this are welcome and will be accepted gladly. However, the thinking must be as follows. *If the decision to be made does not even meet the minimum requirements, it is better not to make it.* The reason for this is very simple: Every decision involves work, risks, and difficulties. It throws the organization out of gear. The risks involved are clearly disproportionate to the minimum effect, if it is determined in advance that the latter is questionable.

The *second* point that we must keep in mind concerns the handling of *compromises*. I have already addressed this issue to some extent in section II. The pitfall here is *premature* integration of compromises into the decision. The question must be: *What is right?* and not: *What suits me best? What is acceptable? What is the most pleasant or easiest? What can be implemented the best?*

Settling for compromises will always happen soon enough. First, we must think about what is correct and what would really solve the problem. In politics especially, this principle is only rarely understood. The fact that we must (almost) always make compromises *in the end* is clear and does not need to be specifically emphasized. However, this does not mean that we should *begin* by making compromises.

The specifications must combine both these points and define what we could call the *minimum ideal state* that the decision should bring about. It is precisely *because* we will be *forced* to make compromises at a later stage in the decision, and particularly in the implementation, that this procedure is necessary.

I recall that there are *two types* of compromises: *right* and *wrong* ones. We can differentiate between the two only if this question has already been considered: *What would be right for this company in this situation?*

The *occasional* wrong compromise is not usually of great significance. However, a *series of wrong compromises* is dangerous, because this leads to a maze of constraints. Organizations in which no one asks what is right and in which people begin by making compromises fall into bad habits. One day we must say X, Y and Z, because we had already carelessly said A, B and C earlier. The famous "constraints" will be constantly quoted as an alibi and excuse for other lazy compromises. In reality, most people caught in these constraints simply do not know how to reach decisions.

It should be noted that the same action could be a wrong compromise at one time and a right compromise at another. When two people are hungry, sharing bread is the right compromise. However, sharing a baby would be a wrong compromise. King Solomon knew this when he suggested this compromise to two women, each of whom maintained that the baby found was hers. Through this suggestion he was able to find the right mother. Real mothers would not settle for such compromises.

There is little that distinguishes good from bad and competent from incompetent managers so clearly as the ability to distinguish between right and wrong compromises. The key to this is the accurate and scrupulous definition of the minimum ideal state.

3. The Search for Alternatives

The third step in the decision-making process is the search for alternatives. Two mistakes are made here. *Firstly*, we are satisfied with the first alternatives that we find. However, effective managers know that there are always more alternatives, and therefore they force themselves and their subordinates not to be satisfied right away.

The *second* mistake is discounting the *zero option*, the status quo as an alternative. The status quo, the present situation, is naturally *also* an alternative. Often it is not the best; that is why there is a problem, and a decision must be made. But this is not always the case.

Some managers allow themselves to be *pressured* into making a decision and making a change by those around them. They believe that they have only fulfilled their task, if they always take steps to bring about a change or something new. However, this can be absolutely wrong.

The status quo may show signs of imperfection and may have difficulties. But its *greatest advantage* is that we at least *know* the difficulties. A new alternative may give the impression that it will remove all the difficulties. Perhaps it will even deliver on its promise, but we should always assume that it will bring its own difficulties and problems; we do not know *yet* what these will be, which is why everything seems to be perfect. These difficulties then become clearer in the implementation phase.

When I arrived in Switzerland as a young Austrian, my attention was drawn to the relatively frequent use of a word which I had never heard in Austria. The word is "Verschlimmbesserung". It indicates an *apparent* improvement, which in reality leads to a *deterioration* of the conditions. It is worthwhile to verify whether the alternatives will actually make things worse instead of better.

4. Considering the Consequences and Risks of each Alternative

The fourth step is usually the most labor-intensive part of decision-making, the systematic, thorough, and careful consideration of all the consequences and risks involved with *each* alternative.

The following points are important.

1. We must first consider the length of *time* to which the company would be committed with each alternative, and how *reversible* the process is.

   Decisions that bind a company for just a *short* time or those that can be *easily* reversed can perhaps be made more casually. On the other hand, those decisions that will decide the course of the company for the long term and will be difficult or impossible to correct need to be made with that much more conscientiousness. One obvious example is investment decisions in a company.

2. Every significant decision, and only significant ones are being discussed here, involves risks. This is unavoidable. Therefore, it is very important to know the type of risks involved.

   This certainly does not mean using primarily, and as a basis, the complicated and sophistic theoretical analyses of probability which are used less frequently than specialists would like to believe. What is important is differentiating between four types of risks. *Firstly*, the risk involved in all businesses; *secondly*, the additional risk that we *can afford* to take, which will not kill off the company if it takes effect, and which, therefore, can be taken; *thirdly*, the risk that we *cannot* afford to take because the changes brought about by that decision could lead to a catastrophe; and *fourthly*, the risk we *cannot* afford *not* to take because we do not have a choice, there are no other options – in short, the risk that has to be taken with all its consequences.

Furthermore, the so-called *boundary conditions* must be defined for each alternative. They could also be called assumptions or premises.

At some point in time the search for and analysis of the alternatives will have to stop. Nevertheless, it is highly improbable in practice that we will know everything that we actually should in order to reach a decision in a so-called "rational" way – that is justified beyond all doubt.

Even after thorough analysis there will always be things that we do *not* know, and we must make do with *assumptions* about these issues. These assumptions constitute the *boundary conditions* for each alternative. They must be properly identified and documented because they are indispensable in providing insight into when a decision that was right in the beginning became wrong and untenable due to circumstances.

If one of the boundary conditions comes into play, there are serious consequences. In this case, we should not, even with slight corrections, stick to the original decision. We are faced with a *completely different* situation that usually requires a *new* and *different* decision.

Let me give an example. Even the best experts cannot say what the dollar will be worth in twelve months. (If someone did know, he would not be on the payroll of an organization, a bank or another institution for long.) The only thing that can be achieved after a great deal of analysis is an educated *guess* on the future trends or a fluctuation range, etc.

There comes a time, when we must put an end to the analysis and make an assumption. It could be: According to what we know, the dollar should not fall below xy euros. This is the boundary condition. Now, if the dollar actually falls below the specified mark, there is a new situation that demands a new decision. In most cases it makes little sense to try to "manipulate" the decision and its consequences. A *new* decision must be made under the *changed* circumstances. It is for this purpose that the boundary conditions must be specified in writing.

The question that leads to the definition of the boundary conditions is this. *What are the circumstances that will make us accept that we have made a mistake?* It is a sign of incompetence to defend and justify the decision in the light of the changed circumstances.[38] Good managers react quickly and sensitively to the emergence of boundary conditions. Though it is a problem, by following the sixth principle they see it as an *opportunity* to make a new decision.

There are countless examples that demonstrate how a lack of analysis, specification, documentation or non-adherence to boundary conditions has led to catastrophes which could have been avoided – the Vietnam disaster for the Americans, the Schlieffen Plan in the First World War, the behavior of the German Field Marshal von Rundstedt and his general staff with regard to the Allied invasion of Normandy. Even in the Brent Spar affair, no one on the outside could have established that the Shell managers had specified boundary conditions. They only reacted when they were faced with a full-blown disaster. The decision, which was perfectly correct in the beginning, turned into a wrong decision due to the circumstances.

5. The Resolution

If all these steps have been carried out carefully, we *must* and *can decide* because we have done everything humanly possible to reach a decision.

We make this resolution not on the basis of methodical games, or scores we have been presented with, but because the problem, its specifications, the alternatives, and consequences have been analyzed thoroughly and conscientiously. Therefore, we have reason to believe that further analysis and study will not yield any further significant information.

Naturally, there are always people who do not decide even *then*. They are *irresolute*. Irresolution is a weakness that is frequently found in managers. They always want *more* analysis and studies; they want *more* consultants and always want to discuss the matter with *even more* experts. In reality, this is just an attempt to *conceal their own irresolution*.

---

38 This is my suggestion of how the falsification criterion in science can be used in management practice. Those familiar with the writings of Karl Popper or Hans Albert can easily make the connection.

Such people are not suitable for management. They may possibly be carrying out their other tasks very well, but in this critical task, which is specific to managers, they are failing – they do not make any decisions. This case is clear and simple because the solution is known and because there is no other solution.

I would like to make a recommendation that is useful for this fifth step. I advise my clients to give themselves the opportunity to listen to a special and very cheap consultant after all the analysis has been completed – *the inner voice*.

How they do this depends on the individual. Some people need to "sleep on it", to put it informally. Others take a long walk alone in order to think it over one more time. Still others may go into an empty church (without their mobile phone), in order to reflect on and review everything, perhaps even to commune with something they believe in (contrary to many so-called intellectuals, I have nothing against this, because it helps many people).

Therefore, the way this is done may differ from person to person. If my inner voice clearly tells me: *There is something wrong here*, I will not hesitate to start from the beginning. Of course, I am aware this is *not always* possible. Things have perhaps progressed too far, and a decision *must* be made now.

I also know that it is exactly this recommendation that some people will welcome as an excuse for their irresolution; nonetheless, I am making it. There is only a thin line between "listening to an inner voice" and "justifying irresolution". I have no formula to help deal with this situation. Once again, it is one of those situations in which experience, proper judgment, an ability for self-assessment, and a certain amount of modesty are crucial.

This inner voice could also be called *intuition*. As I have already mentioned, I do set some store by intuition. However, I use it in my management concepts with the utmost *caution*.

- *Firstly*, because all research findings in this field show that intuition can be *wrong* as often as it can be right. I have already mentioned this.
- *Secondly*, because I do *not* consider intuition to be a scarce commodity, as do its proponents. Everyone has something that they call intuition, presentiment, feeling, mood, or inspiration. This is not the problem. The problem lies in knowing *in advance* whose intuition will prove to be *right*. I have already shed some light on this issue, too.

- *Thirdly*, I do not use intuition as a substitute for thinking and hard work. Intuition has its rightful place, *not at the beginning* of a decision-making process, but at the *end*. It is only when all the homework has been done, and more work will not produce anything useful, that intuition is appropriate.

6. Implementing the Decision

Most people believe that a decision has been made, when a resolution is made. In this regard, even the textbooks do not have much to offer. However, the really essential part of the decision comes only after steps six and seven. Unfortunately, a large percentage of even those managers who have very conscientiously carried out steps one to five fail here.

My suggestion is that we should not call something a decision while it is still a resolution, but only when the resolution has been translated into clear and correct results. The results must, according to my suggestion, be included in the *definition* of the term decision, even if this is unusual.

Therefore, the sixth step consists of the following. *Firstly*, specifying and recording in writing the critical measures required for the implementation of the decision. *Secondly*, making a *person responsible* for each measure, and *thirdly*, fixing *deadlines*.

Resolutions are implemented by people carrying out measures at a set time. There is no other way. Without this step we do not have a decision. Strictly speaking, we do not even have a resolution. We merely have good intentions and illusions that sound good.

There do not have to be many measures, nor do they have to be worked out in detail. I said that the *critical* measures have to be defined. Usually there are only a few of these. If we are interested in implementation and results, we do not leave this to the lower levels of the organization or our subordinates. We leave the detailing and the final touches to them, but not this fundamental element.

The measures to be specified should, above all, include the answers to the following questions.

1. *Who is to be included in the implementation?*
2. *Therefore, who needs to be informed of the decision, when and in what way?*

3. *Who needs what type of information, tools, and training so that they understand the decision, its implementation and its consequences, and can thus make an active contribution?*
4. *How do we intend to monitor, check, and control the implementation of the decision? How should reports on the decision be prepared?*

Clear, unambiguous responsibilities must be specified. This means that each measure is to be assigned to a *person*, and not a *team*. Whether this person then requires a team to implement this measure is another issue. A team will be required with greater frequency in the future. However, the responsibility must lie with one person, and this brings us very specifically to the question of what this person needs to know and be able to do, and what competencies this person needs to have to actually assume this responsibility. This is the *practical, effective* way to run and manage organizations, not the abstract definition of tasks, areas of authority and responsibility otherwise known as job design. That is also important, but jobs do not run and control organizations.

The critical *deadlines* are a further part of the decision. The right timing is an important element of each decision. My recommendation is to set *tight* deadlines. The reason for this is simple. *Every* deadline can be stretched, but none can be *advanced*.

If a very tight deadline is extended, the decision to do so will be welcomed by everyone in the organization; advancing the deadline leads to stress and chaos, irrespective of the reason that dictates this necessity. If this is only necessary, because the manager failed to consider this in advance or ignored the above recommendations, that manager also risks losing credibility.

Therefore, step six is the *action plan*: *What, who, by when?* The action plan is to be kept as *evidence* or filed under "pending" in the office where the decision was made.

7. Setting up of Feedback: Follow-Up and Follow-Through

We should not lose sight of a decision and its implementation. Effective managers treat the decisions they have made like a dog does a bone.

They keep a close track of the issue, ask for reports about the progress of implementation, any difficulties encountered, and the results. Above all, they personally check the progress and satisfy themselves that the implementation is making headway. They *follow through* consistently until the job is done, until it is *completed*.

From time to time they notify all those concerned and involved of the status; they make results and successes *visible*, even if they are small in the beginning, because they know that visible success is one of the greatest motivators.

They do not talk in abstract terms about feedback, as is considered so modern today, but they embody feedback. Effective managers have a deep distrust of abstract "communication". They go personally and talk to the people; they want to see things personally and, if possible, adopt a hands-on approach. Thus they acquire, over a period of time, a degree of expert knowledge and familiarity with the situation that cannot be achieved in any other way.

Participation in the Decision-Making Process

An inextricable part of everything to do with decisions is the question of the *participation* of the people concerned in this process, the question of *participative* or even democratic decision-making processes.

This question has at least *two* aspects.

1. In the *first* case, it is not a single person but a committee, an *executive committee*, for example, consisting of several people that is responsible for making the decision as per the procedural rules or legal stipulations.

   Normally, in this case, there are appropriate provisions that stipulate how any existing disagreements in such a committee are to be handled, should the need arise. In other words, what is the proportion of votes required for a resolution to be adopted. However, in the case of really important decisions, everything possible should be done, irrespective of the formal rules, to reach a *unanimous* decision. Time is required to reach the required consensus.

   If a decision is not unanimous, but has been made with a majority of votes, the question of how the *defeated minority* should behave arises. The way I understand it, the defeated minority must behave *loyally* in this case and do everything they can to ensure that the decision is implemented according to plan. Active or passive opposition or just mere hints of the fact that they are not really in favor of this decision, can cause great damage, even if those hints are very subtle. If they are totally against the decision, perhaps the only solution to the problem lies in *leaving* the organization.

2. The *second* case concerns the issue of *participation by the employees* of an organization, in as far as they have to participate in the implementation or are affected by the consequences of the decision. Participative decision-making and general participative management has been one of the most widely discussed topics in the last decade. A considerable if not major part of this discussion is *ideological* and is on the wrong track. Another part is related to *motivation issues*. Even though there is no convincing evidence that participation has a positive effect on motivation, it at least seems plausible.

However, there exists *an* extremely valid reason for participation. It is the only way in which much of the *knowledge* available in the organization can be incorporated into the decision. A decision can hardly be any better than the knowledge that goes into making it. Therefore, it is in the best interests of those managers who want to make good and correct decisions to use as much of the knowledge and powers of judgment available from the employees as possible.

Though the *rules* for this are simple, the *procedure* may not always be.

1. Those people who will be playing a key role in the *implementation* of the decision must, as far as possible, be able to participate in the individual steps of the decision-making process, such as the definition of the problem, the preparation of the specifications, the search for alternatives, the analysis of consequences, and risks as well as the definition of the implementation measures.

2. However, the essential questions are never: *What would you decide?* or *What would you do in my place?* The employees *are not* in the position of the managers and, therefore, *cannot* respond to this question with a clear conscience. Even answers given with the best of intentions are irrelevant. Such questions are, in fact, a clear indication of management weakness.

The *essential* question must be quite different: *How do you view the situation from your perspective, from the point of view of your func-*

tion, your training and experience? This is the only, quickest and most effective way to consider the *multi-dimensional* aspects, which almost always exist, of a problem for which a decision is to be made, and to gradually attain something that corresponds to a *holistic* and *integrated* understanding of the problem and its possible solutions.

The American president Harry Truman a master of decision-making, practiced this with great consistency. For important issues he would carefully consider all the ministries, authorities and institutions that could or should contribute to the solution of a problem. Then he would call together the people concerned and ask each person, beginning with the most recent recruit: *How do you see this situation?* and he always emphasized: *Don't give me a recommendation, give me a description of how the problem looks from your perspective.* The application of this method is not particularly difficult, but it requires time, and this means that the decision-making process should start as soon as possible.

3. The decision itself, however, must be made by the manager(s) who is(are) *responsible*. Truman never left anyone in doubt that it was his exclusive, personal task to make the decision. *"I will have to make the decision,"* he would say, *"and I will take as many of your opinions as possible into consideration. But it is my job to make the decision and I will let you know what it is."*

This was his method of reaching effective decisions, and he was possibly the most effective American president in the twentieth century. His method also included the early identification of the quarter from which resistance could be expected in the governmental organizations, the unions, industrial associations, in the Congress and Senate, and in the media. As a result of this he could take these things into consideration and, if necessary, create more understanding with the right information and suitable arguments, achieve a reasonable compromise, and devote special attention to those areas of implementation that held the greatest pockets of resistance. With this procedure, he won the trust, respect and credibility of even his opponents and those against whose interests he had to decide.

Few men in history have been so ill prepared for a task of this proportion and difficulty as was Truman, who, as vice-president, had to step into the shoes of Roosevelt on 12th April, 1945. Roosevelt had never discussed anything with his vice-president. Truman, who had to assume the mantle of Roosevelt, had had absolutely no training for the task ahead of him, and he had no experience with the problems he was immediately confronted with, nor was he well-versed in the ways of the British, the Russians or even foreign policy. He did not know Churchill or Stalin personally, nor had he ever met any of the other important foreign politicians.

Truman had no qualifications or talent. Furthermore, all the influential newspapers in America were against him from practically the first day, and no one before or after him has been so ridiculed and run down. But no one has been as *effective* or so *quickly* familiarized himself with his task and its numerous facets as did Truman. He lacked experience in these matters and also talent, but he knew *how* to reach *decisions*; his *methods* and his *principles* of decision-making were crucial factors in his effectiveness.

Truman's method is the method used by *all effective decision-makers.* They devote themselves to their task and the responsibility that comes with it, even if they sometimes feel isolated. They do not dilute the responsibilities in the organization with questionable motivational considerations or a social and romantic misconception of democracy.

Fourth Task

Supervising

The fourth task is the most unpopular and, in a certain sense, the most controversial. Contrary to common opinion, most managers are reluctant to supervise. Therefore, people who advise against supervision are usually very welcome, regardless of the quality of their reasoning.

An example is given here that is representative of a widespread school of thought. A German writer who reached cult status in the eighties and the early nineties (we hear little or nothing about him now) devoted a lot of space in one of his books to advising against supervision and the advantages of an "organization freed from supervision". Perhaps sensing the question in the mind of the reader, he asked the rhetorical question of whether it was too good to be true. And rhetorically he gave a negative answer, at the same time supporting his answer with a practical example of success: the BCCI bank. This bank, too, is hardly mentioned these days. However, at that time it was the talk of the town, as the largest ever criminal case of the systematically planned bankruptcy of a bank in which thousands of people were cheated of their savings...

There Must Be Supervision

If we are interested in the quality of management, we *cannot*, with a clear conscience, advise against supervision. *Whether* we should or should not supervise should not be a matter for discussion. However, *how* it can best be done can, of course, be discussed.

Arguments that are frequently put forward against supervision are that people do not like to be supervised, that it has an adverse effect on motivation, and that supervision encroaches upon the personal freedom that is so important these days.

I can agree with the first argument. It is true that many people do not *like* to be supervised. This, however, does not mean that we can or should dispense with supervision. People do not like to do many of those things which, nevertheless or precisely because of this, are important and have to be done. Many of the scandals in the business world would never have been possible with more careful supervision; this is also true in the case of air or rail accidents, or of disasters in nuclear reactors or tunnels, for example. With alarming regularity inadequate supervision is identified as one of the causes.

Supervision *can* have an adverse effect on motivation, this, too, is correct. However, this *need not* necessarily be the case. It is possible to supervise in a demotivating way, and I must admit that this is far too often the case. The reasons for this are as easy to recognize as they are to remove. It almost always comes down to sheer thoughtlessness, sometimes coupled with an inadequate understanding of the management task involved. Of course, there are also cases, though they are rather rare, of intentional abuse and harassment, and occasionally these even amount to sadism. This, however, has no causal link to the task of controlling as such. Mistakes are made, but almost all are avoidable.

Finally, we have the argument relating to personal freedom which clearly does not take everything into account. Being supervised does not mean having "no personal freedom". Whether personal freedom is necessary, where it is to be created, to whom it should be applicable, and where it should not be granted, are all issues that have little to do with supervision. They are related to organization and, far too often, unfortunately, to ideology.

Even if maximum personal freedom is granted, for whatever reasons, supervision is still a must, *firstly*, to check whether this freedom is being used *at all*, and *secondly*, whether it is being used *correctly* or abused. If there is too much talk about freedom in an organization, skepticism is called for. It is often the case that people do not even use the freedom that they have. In almost every case I have come to the conclusion that the freedom given was, in fact, much more than was actually being used.

Therefore, supervision is a must. The best form of supervision would probably be *self-supervision*, which means enabling as many people as possible in an organization to supervise their own work as far as possible.[39] Even the question of how we can achieve that is of great value. Reflecting on it often leads to a radically altered and better understanding of an organization. However, even this would not dispense with the necessity of supervision, because we would have to occasionally check whether people are, in actual fact, supervising their own work and whether they are doing so effectively. The best example is speed checks on traffic. As every vehicle is equipped with a speedometer, all drivers should be able to regulate their own speed. As is well known, not everyone does this.

Trust as the Foundation

The importance of trust has already been discussed in section II. In this context it plays a particularly important role.

Supervision must be based on trust, first and foremost in two areas: in people's *capabilities* and in their *willingness to perform*. If we cannot trust that these requirements will be met, the problem is not one of supervision but a totally different one, for example a staffing- or recruitment-related problem.

I feel that this situation shows another reason for not making a constant effort to motivate. If there is a lack of capability and willingness to perform, little can be achieved with motivation. Trust in the existence of these two conditions for performance is necessary for motivation as well as for supervision.

Of course, this trust should not be blind trust. It must be justified. In section II I have already explained the difference between justified and blind or naïve trust, and therefore, I will just briefly touch upon the important aspects here. As far as possible, we should trust, if possible even beyond those limits that we feel comfortable with. However, we must ensure that we find out whether and when our trust has been abused, and we must also ensure that our subordinates know that we will find out and that this will have serious, non-negotiable consequences.

---

39 This is by no means a new insight. Peter F. Drucker, the "inventor" of Management by Objectives, clearly realized this from the outset, in 1955, in his book *The Practice of Management,* New York 1955, 17th edition 1995. The title of chapter eleven of his book is not "Management by Objectives" but "Management by Objectives and Self-Control".

How Do We Supervise?

As I have already mentioned, there are various ways and methods of supervising. Once the necessity of supervision is accepted, the "how" becomes significant in several respects – its effect on motivation and corporate culture as well as financial viability. Far too many checks, especially in the business world, are useless but involve a lot of expense and are sometimes even damaging.

The Smallest Number of Checks

Formerly, there was no need to particularly emphasize this point because it was difficult enough to even make checks. The information required for proper supervision was almost impossible to obtain or entailed high costs. Therefore, there was little danger of excessive supervision. Rather, the opposite was the case; there were not enough checks. Today, the reverse is true. Information, or at least data, is available in abundance. The expense involved in obtaining it is negligible compared to what it used to be. Today, we must take an active stand against excessive checks.

We should restrict ourselves to checking the *least possible* number of variables. Anything else *firstly*, creates confusion and, *secondly*, prevents people from doing their work. An organization does not exist for the sake of supervision; this is not what a company is paid to do. Therefore, the question should not be: *What can we supervise?* Instead it should be: *What should we – definitely and necessarily – supervise in order to give us enough justified trust that nothing important can go "off course"?* Therefore, the guiding principle should not be the capability of computers, which is as good as unlimited with respect to checks, but an adequate level of certainty for practical purposes.

The way managers deal with voluminous controller's reports is a good illustration of what I mean here. They begin to glance through the report, stop at a certain point, then they continue and stop at another point. And so it goes on. In this way, they filter out five, six or maybe ten variables. It is these that they then use to manage their department. Why are they presented with hundreds of figures when they really only use around a dozen – and these are usually sufficient? The greater part of a typical controller's report contains, at best, *data* for the managers. From this they filter out what they regard as *information*. Not only do they *not* require the rest but it also *confuses* them and wastes their time. It is for good reason that cars are equipped only with those instruments that are really necessary. Therefore, ergonomic principles must be taken into account when developing checks.[40]

An objection that is raised at this point is that it is not always possible to leave it to people to decide on the number of control variables they will use for supervision. This is, of course, true. Therefore, there will always be cases in which a works manager, for example, will have to be told that, although the half dozen variables he or she has used so far were adequate, he or she must, in the future, take another three, four or five variables into consideration for certain reasons. If it is really necessary, the subordinate is also informed and must also be trained to deal with these additional variables if required. Nevertheless, what is applicable is *the minimum required and not the maximum possible*. This is all the more important as we are always inclined to veer towards the excessive as a result of the ease with which data can now be obtained.

Samples instead of Complete Investigation

Wherever possible, managers should work with samples. Few other fields have made so much progress in the last few decades as that of statistics. In my university days carrying out the arithmetical operations required for the use of statistical methods was still a laborious process. With the help of computers this is no longer a problem now, and, above all, it is a field in which the computer can really be utilized to its full capacity, which is not usually the case elsewhere.

Let me give an example. Unfortunately, it is an inescapable fact of life that we must enter each and every expense record for bookkeeping or tax

---

40 The article by George A. Miller on the span of control mentioned in section II comes to mind. Anything over and above the "magical number seven plus or minus two" defined by him leads to "overload", in this case to "information overload", which causes stress and is one of the main reasons for what is called "human error" in accidents. General cognitive psychology and ergonomics converge here. For engineers and designers in engineering, it is natural to note these things and take them into account in the construction and design of technical devices. In management, these are just as important, if not more so. However, here they are seldom, if ever, taken into consideration.

purposes. However, such a procedure is not necessary to check our expenses. Any small number of samples can be sufficient to provide almost the maximum level of supervision. A properly carried out sample check in which perhaps 5 percent of the expense records are examined very thoroughly and completely confers, in practical terms, a sufficiently high degree of probability that there has been no abuse of expenses. Even if a minimal amount of wasted expenses still slips through the net of statistical control, this is more than compensated for by the low cost of the supervision itself.

The only area of management in which the advances made in statistical control have been utilized adequately is in quality assurance. However, the same methods can be used in many other areas, in warehouse management and logistics, in fieldwork, in all forms of expenditure control, in time management, etc.

According to a report that appeared in the gazette some time in the nineties, the American Ministry of Defense spent more money on processing and checking official trips than on the trips themselves. The report stated that a drastic reduction in number of officials required was now being sought, and computers were to be used instead. In this way, they were hoping to reduce the costs of checking the travel expenses by half. This was considered to be a positive endorsement of the introduction of management methods in the administration. The first part of the report describes a catastrophe. That such a thing can come to pass reflects a complete failure of the administration. The second part, however, is not to be hailed as a management success; it is an absurdity. A 50 percent reduction in costs in *such* a case is still gross wastage. Such cases should get by with supervision expenses of 5 to a maximum of 10 percent.

Action-Oriented instead of Information-Oriented

Meaningful supervision must be directed towards controlling people's *behavior*. There is an old principle: *People behave as they are controlled.* On the other hand, most supervision is, politely expressed, information-oriented. The guiding question is not: *What should the people do?*; it is: *What do we want to know about them?*

This question is wrong, as is amply demonstrated by the aforementioned example on the statistical control of expenses. From a *technical point of view of supervision*, it is wrong to collect and evaluate more information than is really required to control the expenses. It is *economically* wrong because the costs far outweigh the benefits. It is also wrong from a *management* point of view because this is precisely the kind of thing that causes psychological damage and ruins motivation. Information-oriented controls are considered, with some justification, *snooping*. Most people, even without training in complex statistics, can differentiate between the amount of supervision required to maintain a certain order – for adherence to regulations or to control a process –, and the other very different form of supervision that tends to be more like an Orwellian state of total monitoring.

To take an example, it has never been my experience that the employees of an organization, such as a bank, have anything against the work of auditors. It is clear to everyone in a bank that an internal audit is necessary. No one thinks of it as spying or as demotivating. On the contrary, we would be surprised if a bank had no audits, and then, perhaps, not quite so surprised if there were cases of fraud. Anyone with any common sense and knowledge of life would expect and predict it. It is not without good reason that the Lord's Prayer contains the line *"...and lead us not into temptation..."*.

No Surprises

For supervision to function properly, it is necessary to enforce the principle that no employee in an organization should conceal any problems which will come as an unpleasant surprise to the boss when they can no longer be hidden. The maxim should be: *Report at the first sign of anything that threatens to develop into a problem.*

In the early stages we cannot only cure most diseases, but also solve most management problems or at least reduce their impact. In the advanced stages this is very often no longer possible or requires excessive expenditure.

An organization in which this principle is not applied or is not understood cannot function for long. In this regard, I am tempted to talk about corporate culture, such as the culture of openness. However, I will not do this because it is far too vague for me, and it is certainly not required here. General openness, and this does not contradict what has been said earlier, is neither necessary nor possible. Openness is related only to very special, specific issues.

Comprehensive Supervision of Ongoing Issues

What must be rigorously supervised, without exception, are *ongoing issues*, which we call *"Pendenzen"* in Switzerland. Managers must train those around them not to forget or overlook anything that has been decided upon.

How this is done can vary considerably in individual cases. Some do it themselves by writing everything down and checking it daily or at least weekly. Others let their secretaries check on ongoing issues. One person may use a computer to do it, while another uses stickers. The "how" is not important here. What is important is that it is done, and that each person with whom the manager works knows that the issue has not been forgotten.

Of course, this does not mean that everything will always be *done*. That is hardly ever possible. However, an issue does not remain unattended to because it has been forgotten. It remains unfinished because it has been decided to leave it that way, because the circumstances have changed, because priorities have had to be changed, etc., and not simply because it has been "overlooked and forgotten".

Reports Are not Enough

These days, reports on almost anything can be obtained quickly and easily. This is the result of information technology. Ten years ago the preparation of a report involved a considerable and not always justified expense. This is why we seldom made reports. Today, we no longer have this restriction and thus tend to go to the other extreme. There is a profusion of reports in every organization, even on the most nonsensical things. This alone would not constitute a problem because the expense involved, though considerable, would still be tolerable. The problem is something totally different: The easy availability of reports *encourages us to rely on them.*

However, experienced managers have learnt that there can *never* be effective supervision through reports. Of course, they do not discontinue their use of the reports, but neither do they rely on them; they *go to the place concerned and find out for themselves.* I have already referred to this in the chapter on decision-making.

Even the best report, whether verbal or written, contains only that which the writer of the report can see or has made enquiries about. This is the *first* thing that adversely affects the *reliability* of reports and the *accurate representation of reality* contained in them. The *second* and more important is that not everything that needs to be known for an assessment of the facts can be available in the form of a report. Only that which can be *described* can be included in a report. And not everything that can be perceived can be described. These two functions do not always coincide; in reality only a small proportion of what can be perceived can also be described. Experienced, competent managers know this, and, for this reason, they never miss an opportunity to take a closer look at the issue themselves. The more delicate the issue is, the more *critical it is to success,* and the more *novel* it is, the less they rely on reports.

The fact that managers can lend *weight* to the issue and also achieve many other positive side effects with their personal presence is of secondary importance. The essential reason for looking into a matter personally is the discrepancy between *perception* and *description*; motivational reasons or reasons attributed to corporate culture, as is argued time and again, are by no means the motive for doing this. At the most, as mentioned earlier, they are welcome additional effects.

There are countless examples. Perhaps the most impressive can be found in military history; military action generally more than meets the criteria which demand an inspection in person rather than a report: Military matters are delicate, critical to success and novel. We know that all good commanders, regardless of their nationality, have never missed an opportunity to inspect the front. Their decisions had to be based on reality, and none of them relied blindly on the fact that the reports, which they received from their staff in abundance, quickly and professionally carried out, could present the reality sufficiently accurately. The higher the command, the more difficult it was to find the time and opportunity to visit the front. Therefore, the visits were not perhaps very frequent, and the good commanders were distressed by this and found it very oppressive. Nevertheless, they did what they could.

The same can be observed in politics, and the business world, too, has examples of this. One of the most classic examples is the habit of Alfred P. Sloan of personally selling cars a couple of times a year, as an ordinary car salesman, because he knew that not even a very refined reporting system could substitute for personal observation.

Benevolent Overlooking

Another method should also be mentioned. Even though this chapter *advocates* supervision, this does not necessarily mean that we should *always* react *immediately*, if we notice that something is contrary to our expectations. There are cases in which it is more prudent to stand by and monitor a situation, to observe how it develops, and wait. In everyday language, it is occasionally possible to "turn a blind eye". We know that something is not exactly the way it should be, but this does not mean that action is necessary, and certainly not frenzied action.

Perhaps the issue will sort itself out; perhaps we can help it along a bit from a distance, without making a big song and dance about it. Perhaps it is important that the people involved are able to save face. There are situations where, for legal reasons, immediate action must be taken, but there are others that we can benevolently overlook, at least for a time.

There is no general criterion that can help determine the type of behavior appropriate in any given situation. However, in an *individual case*, a decision is almost always possible. How we react depends on experience, shrewdness, proportion, and perhaps also our humanity. It is one of those situations that crop up from time to time, and are so typical in management, which could be likened to walking a tightrope.

Supervision Must Be Individual

Finally, we come to another important aspect. Supervision must be related to the *individual person*. Here, the bad practice of excessive egalitarianism, or perhaps we should say the ideological rubbish, is particularly damaging. There is a great difference between supervising people who we have known for years, who have never blotted their copybooks, are paragons of correctness and reliability, and, therefore, do not really need to be supervised, and supervising people who we do not know because they are new to the company or have not proven themselves, of whom we know nothing and who, therefore, must be supervised. This is not because we basically mistrust these people but because we do not know them, and neither do they, and this is a point to be noted, know the company or us. Supervising in the first case is *insulting*; in the second, it is a mutual education, i.e., it trains a person, shows him or her the ropes, and therefore also sets a trend.

Measurement and Judgment

Essentially, these few things are enough to properly carry out the task of supervision in most situations that occur. They are the principles according to which supervision must be carried out. As is apparent, they are very simple. However, their application in individual cases may not be so simple.

Last but not least is a point that is usually unclear and leads to serious misconceptions. Supervision is easy as long as *measurement* is possible. The quantification on which measurements are based can be very exacting and necessitate substantial scientific and technical efforts. On the other hand, the checks as such are easy. They are only difficult when measurement in the usual sense is not possible. And because they are difficult, checks are not done beyond what is quantifiable, or they are usually considered impossible, according to the motto *what cannot be measured cannot be checked either.*

I consider this to be a grave error and a fundamental misconception in management. If and as long as measurement is possible, management and managers are not really required for the task of supervision. In this case computers can be used. It is precisely when measurement is no longer possible that managers must assume the task of supervising with the help of another procedure, not through measurement but through *assessment* and, ultimately, *judgment.*

This inevitably leads us into the whole philosophical maze of objectivity, subjectivity, reliability, relevance, repeatability, justification, etc. To my knowledge, these issues have not yet been resolved[41], and perhaps in the strictest sense of the word, they cannot be. However, it is precisely because of this, and this is seldom understood, that managers are required. Though managers cannot solve the philosophical side of these problems, they can eliminate them through their decisions, with the help of their powers of

---

41 There are, of course, suggestions for solving this problem in philosophical and epistemological literature. I prefer the position of critical rationalism, particularly the writings of Hans Albert, which have great practical relevance. However, these solutions are by no means universally accepted. In recent times it is rather the variants of subjectivist and relativist constructivism which I consider to be irrational and of neither theoretical nor practical use that are gaining ground, usually enriched with hermeneutic "spawn". They are obviously attractive to people who believe that unclear and fuzzy thoughts and speech are a mental achievement.

judgment, and on the basis of their experience. This is admittedly not a very satisfactory procedure, and if there were a better one available, it would probably be used. However, in the organizations in society we cannot wait until science, or even philosophy, can solve these problems.

We must act one way or another. Even inaction is, *in fact,* an action; not making a decision is also a decision. Here we encounter one of the most important practical differences between science and management, which I have already drawn attention to in section I. Once more it is appropriate to emphasize that management is a profession in which experience is important, and that this is not really the case in every profession.

Upon closer examination the difference between measurement and evaluation is not actually as great as it is sometimes made out to be, and I have explained it here for the sake of emphasis. Measurement is based on many, non-justifiable conventions, on practices that have been settled on because they were suitable in some way. Only a layman believes that measurements can be exact. Measuring tapes, scales, and clocks are very inaccurate, scientifically speaking, which has led to the constant refinement of measurement procedures. *Accurate enough for the current purpose* is the maxim that is followed.

We can talk about *measurement* if, after establishing a procedure, even inexperienced people achieve almost the same results if they just keep to the *procedure.* On the other hand, we talk about *judgments* when experienced people achieve almost the same results if they keep to the *rules.*

The clearest example of this can probably be found in the legal system. Judges are required, because legal cases cannot be decided in any way other than through the judicial process. It is clear that inexperienced people would be completely lost with the procedural rules. It is also clear that, even in the case of very professional application and great experience, judges do not always reach the same decision. By and large, however, judges with the appropriate training and experience in judicial processes will arrive at the same or at least similar results.

Hardly anyone would claim that judicial proceedings in constitutional states are an unsuitable means of ascertaining a result, because they are based on judgments and assessments. Even if the proceedings do not have the same type of objectivity as measurement, and even if we prefer to call the judgment in a judicial process subjective, delivered by people and dependent on people, the process is not *arbitrary.* Subjectivity is not the problem, but being arbitrary would be.

If a young judge were to deliver judgments time and again that were set aside or considerably revised not just occasionally but regularly in the appeal courts, no one would think of changing procedural law on account of this. The young judge would be given more training, cautioned to be more careful and, if there was still no improvement, withdrawn on account of incompetence and given a role, where he or she would not be able to wreak any damage. Anything else would be absurd for the practice and science of law.

The situation is totally different and indicative of the overall state of affairs in management. The lack of ability shown by inexperienced or incompetent people does not necessarily prompt the adoption of practical measures for better training, better fulfillment of duties and ultimately transfer or dismissal, as would be a matter of course in the case of other disciplines. Rather, there is a tendency to introduce some complicated methods, to resort to metaphysics, charlatanism, and transcendental rubbish, to replace experience and ability with intuition and emotion, and, in doing so, move even further away from a practical solution to the problem. The whole issue is regularly supported by the involvement of pseudo-science.

A small but typical episode may clarify this. As part of a training program for higher-level managers in a company that employed several thousand employees, I had to hold a seminar on the principles and tasks of effective management. Among other things, I occasionally displayed my skepticism about the importance and reliability of intuition and feelings. Apart from the managers, all with degrees primarily in the fields of science and technology, there were also three employees from the training department. One of them spoke to me in one of the breaks. With a certain amount of regret he stated that what I was propounding here was all very interesting but, unfortunately, much of it could not be quantified, could not be measured. I confirmed this and asked him why this was important and what conclusions he had arrived at. He felt that this was precisely why we had to do many things intuitively and with the help of feelings. To make sure that I had understood him correctly, I followed this up with another question on where in particular intuition and feelings could be used. His answer was in the selection of employees in personnel management, for example...

The man who was still quite young and, as I discovered later, very inexperienced had not the slightest inkling of the existence of such things as well-founded judgment, sharpening our powers of judgment, and judgment resulting from experience. Even if it is a sensible idea that there is a continuum which has, at one end, quantification based on measurement and (just) feeling at the other, there are quite a few intermediate stages in between these extremes consisting of judgments justifiable on various counts. This episode would not be worth mentioning and could have been assigned to the category of "uneducated people" had this view not been characteristic of a prevailing way of thinking and had not the people in such positions, in management training, been the cause of great, almost irreparable damage. After the coffee break I took the opportunity to conduct an experiment in which I asked the person to share his thoughts and concern with the others and put the issue up for discussion. It was shattering to note that not one of the participants who, as I mentioned earlier, were people trained in science and technology, held an opposing opinion. Without any contradictions they all accepted the postulated opposites of measurement and feeling as reality.

In summary, wherever we can measure, we should. The fact that some things cannot be measured should not be reason enough to do away with supervision altogether. Where we cannot measure, we must judge, and this requires, for want of better options, managers with experience and those who carry out their tasks, in this case supervising, conscientiously and carefully.

Developing People

Hardly any manager would dispute that people are an organization's most important resource. At least no one would openly dispute this. What a manager really thinks about this is another matter. Sometimes we cannot help thinking that an organization without people, if that were possible, would have its advantages. It is the people who are almost always the cause of difficulties, mistakes, failures, lapses, conflicts, etc. Machines or computers, once they are functioning, do so without many problems. They never get tired, they do not require motivation, they do not have any difficulties with communication, they are psychologically robust, they never get sick, they do not need holidays, they do not develop any group dynamics, and so on and so forth.

Factories that are devoid of people are almost a reality. However, for everything else we still require people, at least for the time being. Therefore, one of the foremost management tasks is developing people. This is the task of *every* manager, not just personnel experts.

Properly functioning personnel management is valuable in many ways, but it cannot develop people, at least not where the individual manager, the direct superior, is failing. Even the best human resources management cannot replace the training and development work of the manager in an organization, whereas in the reverse case, if the individual managers do their part, personnel management is perhaps not completely but almost superfluous or can devote itself to other tasks. In such a case, personnel management will then concentrate on the basic conceptual issues and certain service functions.

In the final analysis people can really only develop *themselves*, just as only they can change themselves. This is not only the quickest but also the most effective way. It is particularly true for the development and skills required to achieve *exceptional* performances. Practically all the real performers in history *developed themselves*. Occasionally they had teachers, but they were far fewer in number than people are inclined to believe. They found themselves models that they tried to emulate. To a much greater extent, they had mentors who urged them to be active in areas where they had their strengths. Above all, they had benefactors or customers who provided them with the opportunity to demonstrate their ability. One of the most well known examples is that of Pope Julius II, who played such a role in the lives of Bramante and Michelangelo. Not only in art, but also in politics and the business world, in sports and in science, we find more examples of people who developed themselves with the support of mentors, patrons or sponsors than are mentioned in textbooks.

People instead of Employees

In this chapter I deliberately do not talk about the development of employees, because this would give a very limited perspective. Organizations have more than just employees, whether they like it or not. This is being increasingly understood. Perhaps organizations will always *search* for employees, but they will end up with *people*, as Max Frisch once more or less said. Therefore, there is no choice in this matter, just as there is none on the question of whether we should develop them or not. They will develop in one way or another; the only question is in which direction. An organization is *in fact* a place we pretentiously call a "learning environment". Therefore, we can only influence *what* people learn but not *whether* they do.

Individuals instead of Abstractions

Almost everything that has to do with the development of people must be done at an *individual* level. I have emphasized this repeatedly in this book, and it is particularly important here. It is *individuals* that are developed, not abstractions, aggregates, or averages. There is no commonality. I have observed that it is remarkably difficult for most managers to accept this, even though it is blatantly obvious.

People always make generalizations on issues that cannot be generalized, and they always group things that do not belong together. This is one of the main reasons why, to date, many of our hopes for the development of people, particularly in the new didactic methods, psychological theories and procedures, have remained unrealized. It all begins with the wrong ideas about how people learn, even though a lot is already known about this in principle. The ideas about learning, which most people carry with them throughout their lives, are influenced by their early experiences in school where everyone learns in the same way. This kind of learning may be suitable for primary school children, although there is room for doubt even here.

However, as adults, people learn and develop in very *different* ways. One learns by listening, another by reading, and another by writing. Some learn best when they are teaching, others learn by doing. Some learn from their mistakes, others from their successes. Hence, we must find out the best way in which an individual learns, if we want to help in that person's development.

This calls into question the numerous extensive human development programs. *Because* they are so extensive, these programs are inevitably *standardized* to a considerable extent. In these programs many things have to be designed in the same way for many people. However, this is clearly moving away from individualization. This is the *first* reason for the questionable nature of these programs. The *second* reason is that those things that are actually most suitable for generalization remain almost completely overlooked.

Whatever the methods and organization, there are *four* essential elements that must be taken into consideration for the development of people in organizations. If these are ignored or neglected, all our efforts will either have disappointing results or none at all. These four elements are: the task, the existing strengths, the manager, and the placement.

The Task

Even though it may sound banal, and even though this insight is not new, it obviously needs to be emphasized over and over: *People develop with and at their tasks.* This is the first and most important element. Training programs lose meaning, if there is no task at the end of the program *for* which a person has been trained. This is one of the most important differences between learning at school and learning in an organization as an adult. The fact that we learn "for life" at school may sound plausible, though even this is difficult to ascertain because it is so terribly abstract. This type of learning is not appropriate later. Adult learning is oriented towards a specific goal, and that is why it is much better and more efficient, even if each person learns in a different way.

It seems to be easier to design extensive and demanding training and development programs than it is to find a suitable task for each person. I regularly question how each individual will be assigned after the completion of the program. Only very seldom do I receive a concrete answer. It is always something to the effect of: *These are the people with great potential*, or: *for higher management roles*. However, this is already clear *before* the start of the development program, otherwise the people concerned would not have been selected for the program. The specifics are usually unclear because the matter has often not been given any thought.

If a task is to effect the development of people, it must meet a few requirements. It must be bigger and more difficult than the previous task. While it is possible to ask too much of people, it is certainly not easy. Most people can do a *lot more* than they give themselves credit for. That is why they should be given the opportunity to do so. Therefore, the task does not have to be linked to a higher position or better pay, which is neither necessary nor is it always possible. It is not even wise. In fact, I consider it to be *harmful* when people's development is organized in such a way that it is always or usually linked to *promotion* and *payment*. Even though it may not always be meant in this way, it is frequently understood as such.

Firstly, the task itself must be bigger, more comprehensive, more difficult, and more demanding. *Secondly*, it is necessary, as far as possible, to aim to create a situation in which getting a bigger, more demanding task is considered an honor, a privilege, and a sign of recognition; this should be an essential aspect of corporate culture in every organization. The development of people must be separated from moving up the corporate ladder if it is to be effective. I know that this is not easy and that it contradicts almost universally accepted expectations and customs. I have not, to date, come across a single paper on this aspect of corporate culture, which I consider a dangerous and thoroughly misleading tendency.

What must be emphasized is the *opportunity* to *do something* and to be responsible for doing it. The task must be a *challenge*[42] for the person; therefore, to put it metaphorically, it must be a size larger than the previous task. And there should be a more direct, more personal *responsibility* attached to it. "Participating" somewhere, "being involved" in a project, "being part" of a team, etc. usually do not meet these requirements, or not well enough at any rate. Therefore, particular care must be taken to ensure that the person's individual contribution is clear and identifiable. The question should be something along these lines: *What should we hold you responsible for in the coming period?*

If we want to develop people, we must demand something from them; this is the exact opposite of customary practice, namely offering them something. In this case, too, I am certainly not assuming that this is easy to achieve. On the contrary, it is difficult, it is unusual, and it goes against practices that I consider to be wrong. I am all too aware that in times of a tight labor market, as is periodically the case, or in certain sectors and fields, compromises must be made in this respect.

Nevertheless, we should not miss any opportunity to correct the mistakes of former times in which even young and inexperienced people were offered "the earth". To see this we only need to look at job advertisements in the past and, to a considerable extent, the present. They always follow the same format. Very little is written on what "We expect", and what there is, is quite general, but under "We offer" there is a long list of very specific and very extravagant perks. This spoils people, particularly the young ones, and it hinders their development. They develop materialistic and demanding attitudes, often without wanting to or noticing it, and which managers complain about shortly thereafter and want to replace with "entrepreneurial behavior". However, it is too late for that; the seeds of trouble have already been sown by the organization itself.

I do not wish to generalize from my own experience. However, I have observed that there are still enough young people who *want* a challenge. And if the signs do not deceive, people look back and remember those teach-

---

42 This does not contradict what I said in section I about the people constantly "look for challenges". It is an undisputed fact that people require challenges to develop themselves. In the former case, challenge is a means of self-actualization and, quite frequently, an excuse to escape from any responsibility for results.
I admit that differentiating between the two is not always easy nor is the difference obvious.

ers and former bosses in particular who demanded *a lot from them*. What we remember is being challenged to the limit, and we do so in a positive light. Whenever possible, I ask participants in my seminars to state, usually in writing, the people they have learnt the most from and why. With almost unfailing regularity the answers correspond to my assertion. Incidentally, there is only *one* common element in the curricula vitae of effective performers. They all went through similar types of formative experiences early in life – they successfully coped with a task without at first believing themselves capable of doing it, thus, without having been *challenged before*.

Whether or not there is a link between developing people and *job rotation*, as is often suspected, I will leave an open question. There are phases in people's lives, and there must be in those of future *managers* in particular in which it is important to get to know other fields and functional areas – not in order to master them or be active in them but to gain an understanding of them. What seems important to me is not the *variety* of jobs, which is what job rotation normally means, but that the jobs are *bigger*.

Musicians provide the most illustrative examples of this. We would hardly expect violinists to play the clarinet, for example, for two long years and then change over to the trombone for the sake of their development and because they want to become good musicians. Their development, and the challenges they face as a violinist, is essentially furthered when they are given more difficult pieces to play, when they participate in demanding performances and have to tackle works by different composers and from different musical trends – but they do all this as violinists, of course. Instead of being fourth violinist, they eventually graduate to being the first. This is not a "higher" position though it is often linked to greater recognition; a first violin is a long way from being able to become conductor of an orchestra, and most never achieve this. There is no such thing as "rotation".

An element of development that must be incorporated into a task from the start is *learning* to *budget*. In section IV the budget will be discussed as a tool for the effectiveness of managers; therefore, I will only make a few comments on it here. In essence, there is practically no better means of *being trained* for a new task, a new department, or even a new organization than having to produce a budget for a sizeable section of the organization. It always surprises me that this element hardly ever features in training programs. Planning the budget for a new area of activity is not the most pleasant or the easiest of tasks, but it is the best, the quickest, and the most infallible.

Develop Strengths

What is meant by a person's *development*? What *should* we understand by this, especially when we want to make a person successful, competent, self-assured, and perhaps even happy? The link to the principle of focusing on strengths is obvious; it is here that it must be applied.

We should concentrate on the further development of *strengths that already exist*, those that are already very evident and those whose existence may be suspected on the basis of certain signs and indications. Development must be *strength-oriented*. Any weaknesses that the person may have, which are probably accurately and reliably known for the reasons mentioned in section II, are *limitations*. They exclude a person from certain jobs, or they rule out certain avenues for that person. They must be taken into account from this point of view. A sportsman, who cannot handle a ball, will not only be encouraged not to select a ball game as his sport, but he will be discouraged from doing so. He will be directed to another sport in which handling a ball is not important.

No one will ever be successful, in any sense, in his or her areas of weakness, and this also applies to areas where the weaknesses have been *eliminated*. Usually this only allows them, as mentioned earlier, to reach a level of mediocrity. People can only be successful in areas where their strengths lie. Success in these areas will be easier, faster, and more visible, and this is exactly what we mean by effectiveness.

How do we know a person's strengths? There is only one source to make any kind of reliable assessment. Though I say this at the risk of once again inviting a lot of criticism, it is *not* the tests, it is *not* the assessment centers, and neither is it the graphology experts, etc. *It is the tasks already carried out, past performance and the results achieved.* A person can be assessed by observing that person working on three to five tasks, that is to say *genuine* tasks, not simulated ones.

Therefore, we *cannot* assess very *young* people. We do not know them; we know nothing about them. The only thing that is known is their studies. Unfortunately, there is no correlation between academic results and later professional performance. Therefore, we must *try out* young people by giving them two, three or four different tasks one after the other in quick succession. They do not have to be major tasks at first; that is not usually possible in any case. In this process, if we show even a little interest and make the effort to watch their work, the first signs of their strengths and weaknesses will soon be apparent. And development must be based on this.

The reader may find a contradiction between what is being stated here and in section II, where I expressly talked about "existing strengths" and not those that have "still to be developed". This is only an apparent contradiction. Only existing strengths can be used *immediately*; anything else requires time. The immediate *deployment* of people must be focused on this. What is meant here, in complete accordance with the principle of focusing on strengths, is the fact that people's development should also be based primarily on their strengths, in this case existing and still to be developed strengths, and not on eliminating weaknesses.

Which Boss?

The third element of a person's development is the manager. The question should be: *What type of manager does this person require for his or her next phase of development?*

My suggestion would be not to classify the managers into the usual categories such as according to management style or role models. We should certainly not be on the lookout for all-around geniuses, for reasons that are now clear. The situation may be something like this: *Dr. Müller is indeed a difficult man, aloof, unapproachable, dry and a bit boring, and young Ms. Schultze will face a difficult time, if we post her to his department. The work there will be difficult and hard. He is also not particularly inspiring, and his disposition is not what young people expect. But with Müller she will be able to learn to tackle projects methodically and properly. This is Müller's great strength. There has not been a single customer who has been dissatisfied in all the ten years that Mr. Müller has been with us. No one can do this better, and no one can teach this better than he can...* This should generally be the way to look at the situation.

Please note that I am avoiding the usual jargon. It is immaterial whether Müller is "a leader" or an "integrator" or a "communicator", or any of the other labels that are, unfortunately, totally meaningless.

However, two things must be borne in mind. Potential managers, and especially those that are being considered for the task of developing people, must fulfill two conditions. *Firstly*, they must set an example: *Would I wish my son or daughter to have these people as role models?* This should be the question. If the answer is no, this person is not suitable as a manager for anyone else either.

What we are discussing here is not a universally ideal person. Such a person does not exist. The suitability of potential managers as an example must be based on two things. *Firstly*, they must be an example from a professional point of view. Professionally incompetent people cannot develop others because they have no credibility. This, of course, does not mean that the piano teacher must be able to play the piano as well as the budding, highly talented but still developing young soloist. But the piano teacher must understand something about music and also about the piano. *Secondly*, apart from professional competence, potential managers must be models or examples with regard to a certain aspect of behavior. They must be people who *carry out* their *tasks* and take *responsibility* for them. I do not know of any apt term, label or name for this. In certain contexts I would risk calling them leaders, but this term is perhaps a bit too exalted for what is meant here.

The *second* condition to be fulfilled is *integrity of character*; I have already discussed this in section II. Morally bankrupt and mentally corrupt people cannot develop other people, unless it is in the direction of moral corruptness, which develops very rapidly but is hardly desirable: *Meier is not only an excellent tax expert, he also has the right attitude toward the company, toward work, and toward our customers. Therefore, he is the right boss for Mr. Baumann who will be able to learn the maximum possible in these two years…* This expresses the integrity of character element in practical terms.

Placement

The fourth element of people's development is expressed in the questions: *Where does this person belong? What type of post should be provided for this person?* This is closely linked to the task and also a person's specific strengths, but it is not the same as them. This has more to do with a person's character and temperament.

The type of question that should be considered is: *Does this person belong in a line or a staff position?* There are people who cannot work properly under the pressure and mad rush of a line position, irrespective of what they are capable of and whatever strengths they may have. They suffer, their performance is at best mediocre, and, under certain circumstances, they can even fall ill. On the other hand, there are people who require exactly this type of environment to be productive, as they are incapable of enduring the loneliness and abstraction of a staff post.

The following is another example of framing the right question. *Is the person concerned more suited for a post with a high proportion of routine or for one with a high level of innovation?* Quite a few people require a substantial amount of routine to be proficient at their work. They need the repetition and a certain amount of security and predictability. Then they can perform excellently. Others get inured, become careless and sloppy, in a certain sense they go to seed. They require something new every day, the need for improvisation, the surprise and the "kick".

Other questions that I do not want to comment on in detail are: *Is the individual more of a loner or a team player? Is the person very precise, perhaps even pedantic, and fond of details, which is indispensable for certain tasks, or does the person's strength lie in giving broad outlines, in sketching out the concepts and the basics but not in furnishing the details?*

The task, the strengths, the type of manager, and the placement – these are the four important elements in developing people. If these are borne in mind, training programs, corporate universities and business academies will not only be effective but will occasionally even work wonders. However, if these four elements are absent completely or to a great extent, the large programs are of little use. They fizzle out despite the often enormous expense involved. And not only that. They wreak damage by adversely affecting the *credibility* of serious training and development, sometimes to the point that they are ridiculed and, even worse, engender pronounced cynicism. Unfortunately, there are numerous companies in which training is ridiculed, and if someone participates in a training program or is sent to one, it is regarded a sign of incompetence more than anything else.

Additional Aspects

There are a few other things that are important but do not require detailed discussion, as they are simple to understand.

Sparing with Praise

If we want to develop people, we must, contrary to common belief, be *sparing with praise*. Praise is, of course, one of the most potent means of motivation, and that is why the opposite of what I am saying here is usually recommended. However, it is unfortunate that the fact that praise in itself is not effective is overlooked. It has the right effect only under very specific circumstances, if it is *not heard too often* and if it comes from the *right person* and refers to the *right action*.

Being sparing with praise does *not*, and it is strange how frequently this is misunderstood, mean *never* giving praise; nor does it mean going to the other extreme and constantly criticizing. Being sparing with praise means being *sparing* with praise, that is to say only giving praise when the person concerned has really earned that praise, achieved extraordinary performance, and this happens rather rarely.

Furthermore, praise has an effect only when it comes from a person who we respect on account of his achievements or as a person. If this is not the case, the praise is considered rather ridiculous, possibly even insulting.

Praise should be used sparingly. It is equally important not to praise for things that are *taken for granted*, but only for the extraordinary, immense performance – immense and extraordinary in relation to the level of development of the person concerned.

I think little of the frequently expressed recommendation that people should be praised daily and for every type of work, even very ordinary, average and basic work. To praise an adult for being able to add, read and write fairly well is totally inappropriate. We should set standards when praising, putting the focus not only on the person directly concerned but everyone else, too. The effect on *others* is almost more important than the effect on the person directly praised. If people receive praise for bad or average performance, the consequence is that performance will, almost certainly, be undermined.

This is as true for the business world as it is for sports or school. If everything is praised, as is recommended in numerous books, advocated by management trainers, and also practiced by managers, and perhaps already begun by parents in their naïveté, then the demarcation between performance and non-performance is indistinct, everything is right and, therefore, of no value, and an organization loses its reference points.

Every reader can surely think back to his or her own school days, and, irrespective of how he or she did as students, recall the teachers who were quick to praise but enjoyed hardly any respect because of this, because the students knew that they had not produced a praiseworthy performance every day. Most people can also remember that other teacher who never said anything. The students never knew where they were with him. Then, weeks or months later, he would suddenly say: *That essay, yesterday, that wasn't bad at all...* Please note, he did not say that the essay was good, but that it was not too bad. But that meant a lot, that carried weight, that brought such a high that the student walked two feet off the ground for the next three weeks because he knew that if he had said it, it must have been good.

With regard to being sparing with praise, there are two exceptions. Younger people who have no experience, and those that have a new task and do not, therefore, know exactly whether they are on the right track should be praised more often. Similarly, people require more frequent praise in times of severe crisis. In a long-lasting and deepening crisis we should take every opportunity to prevent employees from sinking into total resignation by praising them even when it may not be totally justified.

No Crown Princes

Establishing crown princes, through a formal act or actual behavior, intentionally or unintentionally, is a serious mistake, if we want to develop people. Some people then believe that they can kiss their own chances goodbye and *give up*. They lack, at least temporarily, the motivation to continue working. Others become *opportunistic*. They not only give up but they also begin to ingratiate themselves. A third group of people focuses its criticism on the crown prince, and sometimes even its aggression; these people begin to take "pot shots" at the crown prince, often with some success. The candidate can then be unable to function or is at least battered, or will have to be imposed by resorting to autocratic action. This, however, is not a proper foundation for good personnel decisions and policy.

When it comes to promotions, the chances must be the same for everyone who is under consideration for the post and at least should be kept open until the last possible moment. All candidates must be able to show, and because the opportunity is there, also want to show what they can do and what they are capable of in principle. Each one of them is aware that only one person can get the post. This fact is clear and does not need to be emphasized.

There is yet another reason to be careful about setting up a crown prince. It has been observed time and again that so-called "potential" remains just what the word suggests, that is hopes and frequently false hopes. There is little correlation between what we believe has been detected as potential and subsequent performance. Some people go as far as to reject potential analysis as a procedure and do not base personnel decisions on its results. Drucker belongs to this school of thought with good reason in my opinion. The actual performance is the only thing that is real and concrete. Therefore, people who have achieved good results with their personnel decisions are not impressed by potential, they pay attention to performance. It is specifically "performance" and not "potential" that interests them.

No Social Classes

Just as there should be no crown princes, a marked preference should not be shown for certain classes or groups. As soon as there is preferential treatment and thus discrimination, the measures adopted for human resource development are rendered ineffective, and this often results in the opposite of what we are trying to achieve. The only things that should count are performance and results. Whenever certain posts are reserved for members of a certain group, such as academics or graduates from a particular course or from a particular university, or those with certain degrees, e.g. holders of an MBA, people's development suffers a setback. The consequences of this behavior are measures becoming ineffective, aggression, inner and outer resignation. Other examples are posts that are only open to people of a certain nationality or sex, giving preference to members of certain students societies, political parties, ethnic groups, etc. and, in family-owned companies, certain posts that are only open to family members.

These issues are now discussed primarily under the heading of establishing multiculturalism. However, I do not consider this to be essential. Whether an organization is multicultural or monocultural has less to do with its capabilities and performance than the issue of whether it is attractive to the best people. Multiculturalism can hardly be the purpose of an organization. Not even in the UN is this important, as its history shows, even though the UN would be the most likely organization to have this as a purpose in itself.

Some of the biggest *disasters* in history were due to the fact that social class determined who should occupy the posts in a society's organizations. However, what is more important, and noticed less often, is that some of the biggest successes can be attributed almost exclusively to the fact that there was no discrimination, or, at any rate, that a certain type of discrimination did not exist. In a certain way the Catholic Church is an example of this, especially certain orders such as the Jesuits. With the exception of convents the management posts were not open to women but to everyone else. (The issue of women may well decide the future importance and performance of the Catholic Church). The fact that the top posts were generally open to all is also responsible for the early successes of the German national socialists and fascist groups in other countries. The disastrous results of these groups is another issue, which has been better researched than the issue of how they could come into existence or why they exerted such a pull on many people in the early stages.

What is significant here is not the issue of the conception of man the organization had or represented, such as the issue of equality or inequality of people, but whether and in what way a person can succeed in the organization. I think it is worth noting that, with regard to issues of corporate culture, these aspects are almost never discussed even though they have far greater consequences than all those things that are given prominence.

And what about all the other Tasks ...

At the beginning of this section I left unanswered the question of whether the list of management tasks suggested here was sufficient in principle. It could perhaps be considered *incomplete*. People are welcome to supplement the list when appropriate and, above all, if they can justify adding to it.

However, I would recommend the utmost restraint in adding to the list of tasks. Usually, this just confuses and complicates matters without accomplishing very much, or it leads to a dilution, falsification and distortion of the inner logic of management. It has become a detestable trend to constantly create something *different*, something *new*, for its own sake, without thinking about whether and in what respect it will lead to *improvements* and contribute to *progress*.

My position with regard to this is as follows. Without the five tasks discussed here being professionally carried out, management cannot function or achieve any results, except on a temporary basis as a result of fortuitous events and circumstances, which cannot, however, be counted on in the long run. These tasks cannot be replaced by any other tasks. Along with the other elements covered in this book they form the core of the profession of management. Other additional tasks may be added if they can be adequately justified, and if they are linked to or involve progress. Progress must mean either a better theoretical and conceptual understanding of management or that managers are able to perform better in their profession. As mentioned, restraint is advised here.

People most frequently ask questions about the following activities, which are considered to be management tasks, or at least candidates for them: planning, motivating, informing, communicating, inspiring, implementing, enabling and empowering people, innovating, and managing change. Characteristics such as being dynamic, communicative and socially competent are inevitably mentioned in the same breath. Then, there is the school of thought that asserts that it is not management that is important but leadership. Another topic of discussion is the issue of where tasks such as marketing, research and development, accounting and personnel management should be placed. Strategy, vision, re-engineering, etc. are sometimes missed.

A concise listing makes it clear that vastly different categories have been brought together under the term "tasks", which is intended to apply to all of them. In reality, they are a very heterogeneous assortment.

The following thoughts explain my position.

1. The aforementioned activities are, to some extent, *integrated into* and *considered in* the tasks I have suggested and discussed, *or they are specific applications of these tasks*. This applies to planning, for example, which is included in a sensible interpretation of the task "managing objectives". There may be reason to consider planning as a separate task in individual cases. However, I would avoid this as far as possible; for reasons that I have explained, the tasks should be big and comprehensive in order to promote what is known as holistic thinking, among other things, and prevent excessive division of labor and thus also specialization.

    This is equally applicable to the opinion that has gained ground in recent years that it is a management task to *enable* or *empower* people. Significantly, there is no mention of why or for what purpose people are to be enabled and empowered. I do not think this task can bring about any genuine improvement. Both, if properly interpreted, are elements of people's development and training; both are related to the right way of managing objectives and to sensible organization.

    Strategic planning, corporate strategy, and, if at all necessary, visionary ideas fall under the category of special cases in the determination of objectives. These are special *types* of objectives, those that define the basic direction of the company or other organization as a whole and position it in the relevant environment. The fact that expert knowledge is required for this is obvious and has already been discussed in the preliminary remarks. The thoughts that I expressed in the first chapter of this section are applicable to these objectives, too.

2. Others of the listed tasks do not consist of *management tasks* but are unmistakably *job-related tasks*. These include marketing, personnel, logistics, research and development, and all the other functional areas

that are common, primarily in all companies. Please note that these are terms that have a limited application, which are not applicable to organizations outside the business world, or only in a modified form. Certain functions, such as personnel and finance, exist in many, if not all, organizations but have a totally different definition. On the other hand, whether and in what sense it may be relevant for hospitals or public administration organizations or the Red Cross to talk about marketing is a very controversial topic. Even within the business world not all functional designations can be used for all types of companies. There are already new types of companies, and others will emerge, for which the present range of functions and designations will have little meaning, and entirely different ones will be required. This is the case in the information technology and biotechnology sectors, and has been for quite some time in the finance sector and the numerous new service sectors. Whatever the case may be, the aforementioned tasks, though important, are not management tasks.

3. However, these demands or suggestions also fall in part into the widely supported category of *modernism*, some of which is absolute rubbish. An example of a "new" task is the demand that subordinates should be filled with enthusiasm and/or inspiration.[43] For some the skills of "creating enthusiasm and inspiring" are among the most important criteria for distinguishing between management and leadership, a difference that seems to be of great significance to them. There are indeed reasons to distinguish between management and leadership. However, creating enthusiasm in and inspiring people are not among them. They have nothing to do with either management or leadership for the following reasons among others.

Firstly, most of the work carried out in organizations day in and day out is quite trivial. This is true not only of the business world but other fields as well. A person has to possess a particular disposition to be enthusiastic about writing invoices, for example, or writing a control report, filling in or checking tax returns, or updating changes in personnel day after day. Even creating a commercial or designing a new packaging label, carrying out an endless series of tests in the laboratory in the

---

43 James M. Kouzes and Barry Z. Posner, "The Credibility Factor: What Followers Expect From Their Leaders", *Management Review*, January 1990, page 29 and following pages.

pharmaceutical industry, debugging defective software, or preparing patients for their operations can make only those people who have never done it before *enthusiastic*. Even innovations generate enthusiasm only in the beginning; once the difficulties in their implementation become apparent, there is more hard and, quite frequently, deathly-dull work than enthusiasm.

Secondly, enthusiasm is seldom if ever *necessary* in an organization. It is typical of writers who call for enthusiasm to never state why enthusiasm must be generated, why it is required or what it would change in an organization. Less surprising is the fact that they also never specify *how* enthusiasm is to be generated, what is required for this, and the preparations managers must make, for instance, if they want to create enthusiasm in their subordinates the coming week, apart from giving the same presentations, talks, etc. that are seldom convincing, let alone capable of generating enthusiasm. Enthusiasm is simply demanded as an attribute or ability; the "gullible" manager can work out the specific details. Furthermore, they overlook the fact that management or leadership is not required in situations in which people can be enthusiastic about something. Everything functions by itself. What is of undisputed importance is effectiveness and productivity, stamina and perseverance, conscientiousness and thoroughness. Enthusiasm...? Hardly.

Thirdly, as I have already explained in section II, there is no convincing evidence to support the fact that if something is done with enthusiasm, it *will* lead to better results. A business plan that is made with enthusiasm should be regarded with skepticism. It could very easily lack a sense of reality.

The demand for enthusiasm and the ability to generate enthusiasm is based on a totally unproven, untested assertion. In fact, it is usually beginners that do something with great enthusiasm until they realize how difficult it is to reach a professional level. Isn't it amazing that, while reading articles on enthusiasm, we wonder whether their authors have in mind only the mood prevalent in the organizations as holidays approach? Do they only want to describe this and not the realities of the day-to-day routine, or are they perhaps not even familiar with the latter?

The same is true of *inspiration* whose connection to either normal or creative performance is not proven, because no one really knows what it means. What inspiration required in everyday life is, and what it is for, is completely unknown. Even if we seek to identify it where it is thought to be most likely to occur – in the arts –, the concept does not get much clearer. There are artists and commentators who always attribute their performances to a higher source of inspiration, whatever the value of such statements may be. What is interesting though is that there are also artists, and not just bad ones, who emphatically dispute the importance of inspiration. Both Rembrandt and van Gogh, for example, were convinced that painting was a matter of practice. Academic studies on this subject are highly contradictory.

There is, at present, hardly any clarity on the nature and importance of inspiration. What is clear from all the relevant studies is that inspiration plays, at best, a very small role in the creation of artistic works and that most of it is hard, systematic work. Our present level of knowledge sheds little light on those things that might be used to establish a distinction between management and leadership and between managers and leaders. In my book on corporate governance I explained this in more detail.[44]

When there is so little objective knowledge about a phenomenon, we should in all honesty and fairness refrain from basing our requirements for management and managers on it, unless we do not mind being suspected of pompousness or losing our credibility.

Please note that I am against the assertion that creating enthusiasm and inspiration *are general* management tasks, or at any rate that they *have to* be. I do not dispute that there are managers who seem to find it relatively easy and are therefore able to repeatedly create a mood amongst their subordinates that may be termed enthusiasm, in the prevailing sense of the word, for even trivial matters. But this quickly wanes in my experience. Just how common such managers are, I cannot say. However, what I do know for sure is that there are many managers, who simply cannot do this and do not even try to, not least because they would appear quite ridiculous to themselves, and they know that their subordinates would also find them so. Nevertheless, and this is what is essential, they achieve excellent results.

If certain people discover that they can generate enthusiasm in people, can inspire them to come up with better ideas, improved perfor-

---

44 Fredmund Malik, *Wirksame Unternehmensaufsicht. Corporate Governance in Umbruchszeiten*, Frankfurt am Main, second edition 1999, chapter 9.

mance or whatever, that they, therefore, have a special strength, they should, of course, utilize it wherever appropriate. The fact that there are people with certain abilities does not necessarily mean that they are, *firstly*, necessary in order to be effective in an organization, and *secondly*, that these can be made general requirements. Incidentally, as the superior of a manager capable of generating enthusiasm, I would always be on the lookout for any inclination on the part of my subordinate to misuse this special ability.

4. You will notice, above all, that three "candidates" have not been mentioned here that are practically always considered management tasks: *motivating, informing* and *communicating*. I have purposely excluded them, not because they are *unimportant* but because they logically belong to a category that is *different* from that of the tasks discussed here.

   In my opinion information and communication can be better understood, if we do not consider them to be tasks, but as a means by which tasks can be carried out. Though it may be a clumsy comparison, just as money is a means or a vehicle the business world uses to operate, information and communication (and there are important differences between these that are sometimes ignored) can be seen as means or vehicles for being effective. However, in management, and this is important, it is hardly ever a question of information and communication; these are not *ends in themselves*. The purpose must be to carry out management tasks, and if information is required for this, it must be communicated. Apart from socializing information and communication in an organization are not "just for the sake of it", but are always *about something* such as objectives and their interrelationships, or about the related priorities, inner contradictions, and their best possible formulation.

   This is in no way intended to reduce the importance attached to information and communication but to assign them to their rightful place and function. Managers must clearly understand this, otherwise they will not be able to use information and communication in the right way. In management, it is always the message that is important, it is the contents and not the medium itself that matters. It may have been an interesting statement that Marshall McLuhan made when he said: *The medium is the message...*, but firstly, he was not talking about management, and secondly, if that had been the case, it would have been totally wrong, dysfunctional and damaging.

There may be cases in which McLuhan's statement would be appropriate, but these are not to be found in management and the world of organizations. What is applicable here is: *The message is the message...* irrespective of which medium is used to convey it, how it is formulated, and what coding system is used. It is the duty of every manager to ensure that the content, and indeed the right content, is conveyed and that information and communication cannot be perverted or misused.

Finally, we come to the topic of motivation. The whole world uses the term motivation; it is probably the most frequently used word in management. However, the more we delve into the issue of motivation, the more we encounter difficulties and ambiguities. The whole subject of motivation can be likened to a swamp, a glacier, or quicksand. On the surface everything seems to be all right; however, as soon as we "venture further", all the points of reference disappear.

I suggest that until we know more about motivation, we should not consider it to be a management task in the narrow sense, but the *result* of the competent performance of the tasks mentioned here. When the management tasks I have suggested here are professionally carried out, the tools are properly utilized and the principles are followed, motivation results; motivation beyond this level is not required.

However, what is far *more important* is the fact that, if the aforementioned conditions are not met or are only improperly met, there *can* be no motivation, because it has become impossible. People then consider what is normally seen as motivation and motivating to be just manipulation and cynicism.

Perhaps we should refrain from using the word "motivating" altogether. I know that most people will find this completely absurd. My doubts about whether people can really be motivated have increased with the passage of time, not decreased. It is evident that they can be *demotivated*; this does not mean that the opposite is also possible. Fortunately, there are people who can motivate *themselves* exceptionally well. This may even be true for most people, provided they are not prevented from doing so. Quite a few replace motivation with a sense of duty and performance of a contract. This also means a great deal and takes most people quite a long way.

If the management tasks mentioned and discussed in this section are carried out conscientiously, thoroughly and competently, we do not have to worry about people's motivation, at least not that of a sufficiently large number of people. I would suggest that not too much time be wasted on people who are still not motivated. Perhaps these people should seek another job in another organization.

5. Finally, I will give another explanation of the additional tasks of *innovating* and *managing change* that are also quite often demanded and have essentially the same object. This example very clearly and, I believe, unmistakably illustrates the mistake made in this thinking. I consider the following ideas to be important because many authors demand "different management" for everyone and everything. Firstly, it is doubtful whether this is really necessary, and secondly, we must also question whether managers can always succeed in learning different types of management.

Naturally, and there should be no doubt about this, every company and every organization should innovate alongside its existing businesses or activities; this should be one of the first priorities of every manager. For this reason I have often drawn attention to innovation, as a standard area for objectives, for example.

However, innovation is not an additional management task, though it necessitates the performance of the tasks discussed in a *particularly* professional way. Innovation is a *job-related task*. A new model of a car has to be developed; analogue technology is replaced by digital technology; genetically modified seeds should bring about higher yields in agriculture and greater immunity against pests; internal activities have to be combined in the course of re-engineering to new processes which are organized in different ways; customer benefits and value creation have to be redefined and documented and should play a role in determining the remuneration of employees, including those in management. All of these are innovations, some of them relate to products, markets and technologies, and others change the way the company actually operates.

In order to implement them, however, the same management tasks have to be carried out as in every other activity. Objectives are required, particularly for innovation; organization is necessary, because with innovation some things will be different from what already exists. Decisions that are particularly difficult and risky in the case of new and unknown areas need to be made. Particularly thorough supervision is necessary for innovations; the right people are required for this; they are hopefully developed, trained and prepared for their innovation-related tasks in plenty of time.

What remains to be done? I am of the opinion that there is nothing that has not already been discussed here. However, one thing must be clear: Carrying out management tasks is particularly *difficult* with regard to innovation and requires tremendous professionalism and experience. The *best* people are required for innovation, and even they cannot always handle it. The same is true for the tools of effective management covered in the next section. They are the same for innovation as for the entire spectrum of activities.

Managing innovation could be likened to the first ascent in mountaineering. The first ascent does not require *different* tasks or tools from those used for the ascent of a known route. There are the same requirements but for a totally different *level of performance*. The climber must be able to climb rocks and move on ice; a different safety system is not used nor are different ropes or ice axes. However, along with total physical fitness everything must be mastered like a virtuoso – and even then there can be problems.

In the same way that much is known and familiar in an existing, operative business, so the route in mountaineering is learnt by repeatedly going over it – there are descriptions and perhaps photographs, and the specific difficulties, the time required, etc. are known. None of this is known on the first ascent; we must depend on assumptions. In the case of innovations, too, not a lot is known about what is really important for success. This makes innovations difficult and risky; and it is for this reason that so many fail despite the best management.

As is apparent, management only needs to be learnt once, but properly and professionally. Once it has been learnt, it can be applied step by step to difficult problems, in demanding situations, and to cope with bigger tasks. By saying this, I am not asserting that the learning process can ever be completed. But this is nothing extraordinary; even in the case of a foreign language or a musical instrument, learning never comes to an end.

Part IV

Tools of
Effective Management

Preliminary Remarks

This section deals with the tools of effective management. Or, to be more precise, this section deals with the things that must be *made* into tools in order for a manager to be effective. The tools I am suggesting here are not tools by themselves. No one is born with them, nor do we learn to use them at school.

In a certain way the mastery of tools *defines* a profession. A person who knows how to work with a chisel *is* a stonemason – perhaps only an amateur or one who is just pursuing a hobby – but whether that person is a sculptor is doubtful. However, he is a stonemason, irrespective of whether he has a certificate of apprenticeship or a master craftsman's certificate, whether he is a member of a guild, and irrespective of the way he has learnt to use the tool. The purpose for which the tool is utilized is another issue. It can be used for good or for bad. That does not depend on the tool.

In order to master a tool *practice* is necessary. Indefatigable, continuous, never ending practice and training is the only way to gain mastery of tools. There is no other way. Whether what is known as virtuosity can be achieved using this method alone is another issue. In most cases a certain basic talent must also exist. However, what is essential is not the talent but what is *achieved with it*. That is what we mean by effectiveness. And effectiveness requires continuous practice, as has been shown by experience and all kinds of analyses. It can be observed in those people who have taken something to a form of virtuosity, to mastery, such as successful sportsmen and sportswomen, musicians and also surgeons, for example.

The tools that I suggest for managers and their effectiveness are very unspectacular, mundane things. This creates a problem. Not much attention is paid to them; they are not even recognized to be what they actually are. People think of complicated, more striking things. I often carry out a small exercise with participants in seminars before I start on the subject of tools. I ask them to tell me what they consider to be tools. In the last few years the spontaneous and immediate answer has been the computer. The computer is no doubt a tool, but it is a tool for practically everyone and not specifically or primarily for managers.

Then there is a pause; the participants reflect. I have never come across a joiner, locksmith or bricklayer who had to think when I asked them to name their most important tools. Managers always have to think. They are unfamiliar with the whole abstract category. Then come the answers, uncertain, hesitant, and questioning rather than answering, usually very complicated things: capital budgeting, cash flow analysis, efficiency analysis, cost benefit analysis, critical path technique, and such like.

These are indeed tools but I would suggest that they be considered tools for *specialists*. A *few* managers need to master these types of tools and methods; or to put it another way, every organization needs a few people who can use these tools. However, these things are certainly not required by *every* manager. As in other parts of this book, the principal question here is: What does *every* manager in *every* organization need, and what should the manager be equipped with in principle?

Many managers are not familiar with their tools nor do they practice their application. This is true of an astonishingly large number of managers. Some, more of a minority, think they are too good for tools; this is either arrogance or stupidity. On the other hand, most are not even aware of the existence and importance of tools. They cannot imagine that tools should also be important in their profession.

Tools are, of course, not the aim and object of a profession, even though they define it in a certain way, as I mentioned. The tools of a mountaineer – rope, ice hammer, crampons and safety equipment – do not constitute the aim of mountaineering, whatever we may see that aim as being. They are, however, necessary if we want to climb mountains.

There are seven elements that I think are suitable tools: meetings, reports, job design and assignment control, personal working methods, budgets, performance appraisal, and systematic waste disposal. These tools now assume far greater significance as a result of the working conditions in the service, information, and knowledge society. The precision and professionalism with which they are used are essential for the success of a manager.

This is not a very exciting topic. It becomes interesting, informative and sometimes very exciting when the volume of work, the working methods, and the results of managers who have learnt to use their tools effectively are compared to those who have not. It is the difference between a professional and a dilettante. What is striking is, above all, the volume of work and the high degree of complexity that managers can handle when they have mastered these tools.

As was the case with the management tasks, here too, I will concentrate on the small percentage of the material available on these topics that *directly* determines the effectiveness of the utilization of tools. If the issue is not exciting, I will at least try to make it as relevant as possible.

Perhaps one more comment on the word "tool". I have already mentioned that most managers have no idea of this category as such. Some do not seem to particularly like the word. Of course, I would have nothing against people using the word "instrument". Ultimately, it is not the words that matter.

First Tool

Meetings

Managers spend a considerable proportion of their time in meetings. Usually this proportion is far too high. 80 percent of all higher-level managers stated in interviews that they spent 60 percent of their time in meetings. And 80 percent of the managers stated that 60 percent of all meetings were inefficient and unproductive. Whichever way we look at it, this is an unacceptable situation. Meetings *can* and *must* be made productive. They *can* be a very *effective* tool provided we follow a few simple rules.

Reduce the Number of Meetings

Improvements in the effectiveness of meetings begin with the cancellation of some meetings. In most organizations there are simply *far too many* meetings. This is essentially due to the following reasons, which will gain more rather than less validity in the future due to technological change: Organizational structures are getting more and more complicated. There is an increasing trend towards working groups and teamwork. Many managers call meetings simply as a knee jerk reaction without thinking about whether they are really necessary. The numbers of specialists are increasing, but due to their narrow field of expertise, they are unable to carry out a task from beginning to end on their own; they need another five or six people to help out.

Therefore, the number of meetings automatically increases if no action is taken against this trend. Furthermore, each meeting necessitates a series of subsequent meetings. Every management meeting usually means work for each member of the management team, which in turn necessitates more meetings in the divisions and departments under them.

Hence, the first important step is to put a stop to this *proliferation* of meetings. The automatic mechanisms that lead to more meetings must be eliminated or brought under control.

Therefore, my first recommendation is: *Do not hold a meeting!* When we get the impulse to call a meeting, we should stop briefly and ask: *Is this meeting really important? Is there another way to do the work or solve the problem?* Only after careful consideration, and if there really is no other or better way, should we actually call the meeting.

Particular attention must be paid to one cause of the proliferation of meetings: *teamwork*. Since teamwork has become so *routine*, it has also become a source of *inefficiency*. Many "teams" are not teams in reality, they are groups. They are put together without thought; not enough thought is devoted to who should be a part of the team and who should not; the tasks and working methods are set sloppily; frequently, the objectives are not defined well enough. The more this is true, the more meetings will be necessary, not for the purpose of doing actual work, but to seek clarification and to deal with the sloppiness.

Though teamwork is distinguished by smooth *cooperation*, this does not mean that all team members need to attend all the meetings. *Good teamwork means that the need to hold meetings is reduced to a minimum.*

Managers who spend more than 30 percent of their time in meetings should give careful thought to how they can reduce the time taken up by meetings. And if this is really not possible, they should at least devote a great deal of attention to the effectiveness of their meetings.

Crucial for Success: Preparation and Follow-Up Work

The real work is not usually done *in* the meeting itself but *before* and *after* it. The effectiveness of a meeting is determined by *preparation*, in practical terms this means preparing the *agenda* and *implementation* of the resolutions after the meeting.

The preparation of a meeting requires time. Therefore, we should make a space for this time in our schedule to ensure we have it. Managers do enter meetings in their diaries. But surprisingly, very few also reserve time in their schedules for the preparation and follow-up work.

Inadequate preparation can, to a certain extent, be compensated for by improvisation, and experienced managers resort to this. It should be noted in passing that this is not an innate ability but the result of long years of experience. Good managers can improvise, but they do not *depend* on the skill of improvisation. They prepare, they conscientiously think about the meeting and its course, and they also know that even the best-prepared meetings do not always go according to plan. There is enough demand for the skill of improvisation even with the best of preparation.

The instrument for preparing a meeting is the agenda. There should be *no* meeting without an agenda – with one exception that I shall explain at the end.

Usually it is neither possible nor advisable to prepare an agenda *alone*. As part of the preparations for the meeting, we should coordinate with all or at least the important participants in the meeting, give them the opportunity to specify their ideas and wishes for the organization of the agenda and the course of the meeting. The formal rights of motion in certain types of meetings, depending on the legal system, statutes, partnership deeds, etc. remain reserved.

Coordination in setting the agenda and deciding the course of the meeting does not change the fact that, in the end, it is the task of the person chairing the meeting to set the final agenda. Therefore, it is this person's *management decision* to take up certain suggestions and disregard others. For regular meetings it is advisable to set a time by which any ideas and requests should be submitted to the chairperson of the meeting. The agenda must be sent to the participants in accordance with the provisions in the statutes or well in advance to give them time to make their own preparations. These periods of notice must be borne in mind when setting the aforementioned deadline.

A good agenda has *few* items rather than many. The items should be really important, i.e. those that really justify the personal presence of the participants. The principle of concentration is crucial for the effectiveness of meetings. Exceptions are those meetings which deal with the processing of items and formalities agreed upon in advance, for example, dealing with legally stipulated items in the internal relationships of group companies. These meetings can have many items on the agenda, as there is hardly any need for discussion and no decisions are to be taken.

Chairing a Meeting is Hard Work and Requires Discipline

People who chair a meeting are *visible* and *obvious* to everyone. The participants instinctively notice whether or not the chairperson has everything under control. Therefore, this is an opportunity to gain respect, or to lose it, by *management action*. The office or position in the organization held by the person has little to do with it.

Once a person understands what chairing a meeting is all about and what must be kept in mind, the rest is just a matter of *practice*. As with everything else, this must also be practiced. No one can expect to become a passable tennis player without a minimum of training. The same is applicable to chairing a meeting. In the course of time it becomes routine; a person automatically does what is correct, and no longer needs to make a great effort– just as with driving.

Types of Meetings

There are different types of meetings. Some types are well prepared as a matter of course; other types are characterized by a lack of preparation. However, *all* meetings must be well prepared if we are interested in personal and organizational effectiveness.

Large, Formal Meetings

Typical examples here are supervisory board, executive board, advisory board or shareholders' meetings, and annual general meetings. These meetings are usually well prepared, because no one wants to make a fool of himself in front of these bodies. However, this cannot be *taken for granted* even in these types of meetings. The number of inadequately prepared meetings is more than people would like to believe.

Routine Meetings

Regular board meetings, senior management meetings, departmental meetings, or divisional meetings are typical examples. In well-managed companies, these meetings are adequately prepared, but the effectiveness of such meetings can be greatly improved in many cases. For example, people try to deal with *too many* items on the agenda. Frequently, there is an *unsuitable mixing* of points concerning the operative business and points which deal with the future of the company and innovation.

It is advisable to make a clear differentiation between these issues, because they have to be *handled differently* and, above all, the *time* required for each of them *varies*. One option could be, for example, that every second or third management meeting is devoted exclusively or primarily to innovation issues.

Meetings of Working Groups, Cross-Departmental Teams, etc.

Usually *very little* preparation goes into these meetings, even though they are often more important than the first two types of meeting. The task of preparing and chairing most of these meetings is in the hands of group leaders or project managers who have, however, little practice or experience in this area and have also been trained for this role inadequately, if at all. These meetings are *most frequ*ently labeled as *inefficient*.

Small Ad-Hoc Meetings, Discussions between a Boss and Subordinate or between Colleagues

These are also meetings. They are the meetings that are held *most often,* and the preparations for them are the *worst*. In such meetings much of what is discussed is "off the cuff". I believe this is a serious mistake and is one of the *most important* reasons for inefficiency. A manager should not simply allow someone to call and say: *I must speak to you...*, or let people simply barge into the office saying, *... could I quickly ...*

It is quite acceptable to pursue an "open door policy" as a manager; managers must be accessible to their staff. But this should not degenerate into an open *invitation to inefficiency* and a lack of preparation. A formal, written agenda is not required, but a habit should be made of asking. *You want to speak to me? About what? What is the objective? What do we want to achieve with our talk? Approximately how long will we need for this meeting? And how do I prepare for it?* It makes a considerable difference whether the person only wants to tell me something quickly, or whether he requires a decision from me that necessitates a few minutes of preparation on my part, such as quickly reading through the most recent correspondence on the issue and briefly thinking over the alternatives.

With these types of questions we should *urge* our subordinates to *prepare* for the meeting, even if it is short, and to think about what the outcome of the meeting should be.

All subordinates complain in interviews that their bosses do not have enough time for them; and managers complain that they have to devote far too much time to their subordinates. Both are right! People always have and get too little time. The solution to this problem lies not in spending more time but *using the little time we have more profitably*. The key to this is *preparation*.

What many managers overlook time and again is the fact that many meetings with their subordinates take up only a little time. Often just 10, 20, or 30 minutes are spent briefly discussing an issue; then everyone can return to work.

However, there is *one* meeting that must last more than an hour, most probably two, or perhaps the time aspect is best left open. These are meetings that are *not* concerned with an *issue* but with *people*, interpersonal relations, or personal matters. Time *must* be made for such meetings. People take time to open up and explain what is on their mind, to find the right words, and to overcome understandable inhibitions.

A manager usually realizes that he is faced with such a situation when the subordinate *fails* to reply to the question: *Why do you want to speak to me?* The person avoids the question: *I would rather speak to you about it face to face...* The manager must react to this signal. Squeezing in such a talk between two other appointments must be avoided. Usually it is possible to say without too much delay: *Unfortunately I am pressed for time today. Tomorrow I am not going to be in office, and on Thursday the customers from France are coming. But come on Friday. From ten o'clock onwards, we can talk in peace...*

It *is* possible, though *rare*, that such a talk cannot be postponed. Very well then, the talk must be held and other plans rearranged in some way. However, this is not normally the case.

What is essential is that interpersonal problems cannot be dealt with hastily, both in a company and privately. No psychological theories are usually required for their solution, but *time, attention* and *patience* are. Everything else seems cynical and smacks of contempt.

Meetings Should not Degenerate into Social Occasions

The purpose of meetings is to produce results. They are work and not leisure time, pleasure, or fun. Their purpose is *not* for interpersonal relationships, even though they do exert a great influence on them. If I state this in seminars and talks, some of the participants seem to find it a bit too strict; they fear that they will seem too autocratic if they work in this manner. These fears are totally unfounded and only show how little the people concerned know about effective management. We can (and should) apply these things very pleasantly, politely and in a cooperative way, but they *must* be done, if we want to be *effective*.

Many also believe that the social components, the interpersonal relationships are neglected as a result. This is a mistake. These people confuse "work" with "social occasion". Of course, there is nothing wrong with exchanging a few friendly words, chatting, enquiring about someone's health, and discussing the previous weekend's football match before or after the meeting or during the breaks. But these things should not take the place of the *work* that has to be done in the meeting. I believe we would be well-advised to separate the two.

Types of Items on the Agenda

The items to be included in the agenda always depend on the circumstances and the situation. With the agenda items the chairperson is defining what he considers important and unimportant. This is one of the *most important tasks*. People who fail to do this well and who waste the time of the participants with trivialities, are neither *effective* nor are they *respected*. The subordinates attend this "circus meeting", only because they cannot do otherwise and because they are on the payroll of the company. However, they quickly form an opinion about the chairperson. The authority of the management and trust in it is inevitably eroded.

There is no formula for selecting items for the agenda, and, therefore, no general recommendations can be made. The items depend on the situation and the individual case. However, *three* important *types* of items must be properly segregated from one another, and the way to handle them must be considered in advance.

Genuine Standard Items

These are things that must inevitably be dealt with in management meetings *each* and *every time*. In a company these could include incoming orders, capacity utilization, liquidity, and the critical accounting benchmark figures. Every organization has these kind of standard items that must be discussed regularly. Of course, they differ according to the type of organization. They will be different in a company, a hospital, or an administrative agency. They are things that recur regularly.

Long-Running Items

Even these are items that recur *regularly*. On closer examination these are not justified standard items, but matters that recur because they have *not been settled properly and conclusively*, for example, the corporate climate in the development department, complaints from customer X, the personnel issue Y, the reject rate on machine Z.

This should *not* be tolerated for long. Such things must either be placed on the agenda with enough time to conclusively *settle* the matter, or they must be settled in another way. A competent person or, if nothing else, a working group should be appointed to look into it thoroughly and then suggest a solution.

Miscellaneous and any other Business

There are experienced people, well-versed in the dynamics of meetings, who patiently wait until all the items on the agenda have been dealt with, and then right at the end, when everyone is tired, they present those things that they quickly want to push through under "miscellaneous".

This should not be *tolerated*. "Miscellaneous" means miscellaneous, and is therefore usually not of particular importance. Anything other than this should not be allowed by the person chairing the meeting.

If something important has happened between setting the agenda and the meeting itself that must definitely be dealt with, it should be attended to at the beginning of the meeting so that, if possible, the agenda can be partly or completely rearranged in the light of the latest events. This situation can certainly occur in our fast paced world and we must react to it. This is a self-evident fact. Anything else, however, is pure tactics. Tolerating such a thing indicates *weakness in management*.

No Item without Action

In most organizations the actual weak link is the *implementation*. *A lot of work* is done but *little is achieved*.

To a considerable extent this can be attributed to *bad discipline in meetings*. After every item the chairperson should ensure that there is *clarity* on the required *measures* so that the decision, the resolution can also be implemented. Questions that must be asked are: *What needs to be done? Who will be responsible? And when should the report of its completion or the interim report be handed in?*

These points are to be recorded in the minutes, and it is the *task of the chairperson* to ensure the *implementation*. The chairperson must *set a time frame* for the measures decided upon and *organize the resubmission*. Only when the participants know and feel that the chairperson will not forget anything and will also take care to settle the issue, will the *meeting* and the *chairperson* be taken seriously, and this gives rise to *effectiveness*.

A meeting should not come to nothing. When the effort has been made and the time set aside to attend a meeting in order to solve problems and take decisions, there must be subsequent action on whatever is decided. Otherwise the meetings are just reduced to the level of a debating club with no commitments. Of course, it is also possible that events occurring within a few days of the meeting may render the measures decided upon invalid, because they are no longer right or important. Therefore, it is only logical not to implement them. But this is a deliberate decision; it is not a case of simply forgetting the issue or letting it fizzle out.

Striving for Consensus

Consensus is important and that is why efforts must be made to reach a consensus. However, active effort to reach a consensus is something *totally different* from the *propensity for harmony* that can unfortunately be observed in many managers.

The essential points of this topic have already been mentioned in the chapter on decision-making. Therefore, in summary, quick consensus is *always* questionable. Frequently, it is simply the result of a lack of courage on the part of the participants to voice their opinion; or the fact that not enough thought has been given to the problem. Decisions reached by acclamations are always risky. Their implementation is usually hindered. Only then do the real opinions and interests come to the fore.

There is, as has already been discussed in the aforementioned chapter, only *one* way to reach a *sustainable consensus,* and that is through *expressed dissension.* And there is only *one* way to express dissension, and that is *openly.* Anything else is just manipulation. It may perhaps serve personal power or glory, but it will hardly raise the quality of problem solving, much less the ability of an organization to implement.

Are Minutes Required?

Yes, usually they are. Formal meetings require formal minutes, possibly word for word. All other meetings also require minutes, even if these are only a few notes. At any rate, *resolutions, measures, persons responsible,* and *deadlines* must always be recorded. This cannot be dispensed with.

This has nothing to do with bureaucracy, but with effective work. Effective managers do not *rely* on their memory or their colleagues, superiors, and subordinates. *They write things down* for two reasons: firstly, to keep their mind free for other issues, and secondly, to ensure clarity. This is what *makes* them effective.

Meetings without an Agenda

In conclusion, a small tip. There is *one* type of meeting that is worth hold-ing without an agenda and, apparently, without preparation.

There are managers who never have problems with their subordinates, who are kept informed of everything, who never have to deal with surprises relating to their staff and whose subordinates only speak well of them, are full of praise for them, and state in particular that their boss always has time for them. Do these people have a natural talent? Are they geniuses?

No, they only do one thing; they have a meeting with *each of their sub-ordinates once a year, just like that,* an open-ended discussion without an agenda.

In reality, they do have an agenda, but it is in their head, a "hidden agenda", and in reality they also prepare themselves for this meeting. In this "meeting" they discuss the following types of questions with each in-dividual, taking plenty of time over it: *What do you particularly like in this company, department, etc.? What is it that you don't like at all? What do you think we should change? What can I do as your manager that will enable you to work better, more easily and more effectively?*

When the authors of books, instructors, trainers, consultants, and even employees maintain that managers do not spend much time with their subordinates and there is too little communication, this is not strictly true, or, to be more precise, it is only true in a certain respect. Managers are in *constant* touch with their staff, and there is a *lot* of communication, some-times *too much*, but it is always related to the task at hand, the business, problems, and difficulties. Time and, above all, activity and the need to perform all exert their own pressure on these conversations. This scenario is not going to change in any significant way.

However, this communication *very rarely* involves *people* as such, though there is much lip service in this regard. We seldom have *time* to simply listen to the person concerned without looking at our watch, or unless it is related to the present activity.

Good managers take steps to counter precisely this in the way men-tioned above. They know that it is not a lot, but it is certainly better than doing nothing. By adopting this method, they send out a signal to their subordinates that they are sympathetic listeners, that they are interested in what they have to say, and that they, occasionally at least, spare enough time.

This is *not* the standard performance appraisal interview. The atmosphere in such interviews, which is tense for the subordinate at least, is hardly conducive for discussing the questions mentioned above. This conversation is something special; it concerns only the individual subordinates, how they feel in the organization, and their opinions. Personal matters may also be discussed if the subordinate so wishes: *How are things at home? Are the children doing well at school and in their studies? Do you have enough time to pursue your interests and hobbies?*, etc.

As I said, *if* the subordinate so *wishes*; some people do not want to as they make a clear distinction between their work and private life. There is nothing wrong with this, and this preference should be respected. However, subordinates may sometimes want to discuss such issues, and they should be helped in this. During the course of such a conversation the managers can show the subordinates that they, too, are ordinary people with hopes and worries, interests, and desires that are unfortunately often sacrificed for the sake of professional commitments.

How far we want to go is a personal decision. But there is no reason why, as a manager, we should not occasionally open up. In any case, people are not taken in by the "golden boy" act which is a vain attempt to pull wool over their eyes. To repeat, the decision about how far we want to go is to be taken personally in each individual case.

And here is yet another small hint. In order to ensure that this talk really does take place and is not forgotten in the mad rush of day-to-day work and the urgency of pressing business, *good managers place this conversation in their schedule*; otherwise it never takes place.

The Most Important Factor: Implementation and Ongoing Follow-Up

As already mentioned, the measures that are decided on during the discussion of each item on the agenda must, at the minimum, be given a broad outline during the meeting.

Even then there is, unfortunately, no guarantee that the measures will *really* be *implemented*. We must *follow up* the issue and *check*. It is certainly not always easy to *pass* resolutions. But *implementing* them is even *more* difficult.

Following up and checking has *absolutely nothing* to do with a lack of trust in the subordinates and their reliability and abilities, as many people believe. It has more to do with the nature of our organizations, with the frenetic pace of day-to-day business, and the pressure of urgent matters.

If we want to be effective, everything in management must be focused on *action*. Managers are not paid for their *decisions*, as important as they may be. They are paid for the *implementation* of those decisions. Thus, I am not really in favor of "decision-oriented" business administration. I would prefer "implementation-oriented" business administration.

Ongoing follow-up, checking on implementation, and concentrating on completion assume greater importance in a *crisis situation*; the more *speed* matters the more we have to deal with *new subordinates,* who are an unknown and cannot be assessed, the more a decision and the related measures are *unlike* others, and, therefore, we cannot rely on *routine effects*, and the greater the *change* in the decisions and measures as compared to what was previously the case.

Second Tool

Reports

In a meeting it is the spoken word that dominates. The written word is the other side of the coin, and it must be made into a tool if effectiveness is to be achieved. Contrary to common opinion, even electronics and telecommunications are not going to change this fact. For the purpose being discussed here, it is immaterial whether the medium of the written word is paper or an electronic display.

The title of this chapter does not refer only to reports in the narrow sense, but *everything that is written*: the minutes of a meeting, notices, file notes, business letters, proposals. It is the proposal that clearly illustrates what this is all about and what it should be. Most proposals are written from the *point of view of the sender*. The company tells its potential customer how good the company is and all that it can do. However, an effective proposal must be *receiver-oriented*. It should state how the *customers* will benefit if they make a purchase. The only significant exception is direct mails that are written professionally.

Many managers display a strong prejudice against correspondence. This often prevents them from adopting a sensible attitude towards it throughout their professional lives. They miss the chance of making correspondence a tool and a means of improving their effectiveness.

Most consider writing to be tedious, time-consuming, inefficient, slow and outdated. But the opposite is true. To begin with the last adjective, outdated or not, this is not a criterion at all. I cannot emphasize often enough that what counts is *rightness* and *effectiveness*. "Modern" certainly does not always mean "better". Written communication, if properly used, is an extraordinarily efficient and effective type of communication. That it can, as can everything else, be misused and thus lead to bureaucracy does not warrant special mention. However, it is not used often enough in areas where it is far superior to anything else. There was no alternative to writing until well after the Second World War. This changed only after the advent of widespread use of the telephone whose distribution and availability took on significant proportions only after the War, except in the USA. The advantages of the telephone are well known. However, its disadvantage is that it has contributed to sloppy communication which has further deteriorated with the advent of the mobile phone.

At a time when telephone charges were high and its usage was considered more of a luxury in business life, people prepared well for their calls. They knew exactly what they had to say and wanted to say. The conversation was kept brief, and it was concise and precise. With today's much lower charges, communication has not increased, as many believe, but chitchat certainly has. If it were not a daily experience, it would be hard to believe the amount of foolishness, superfluous nonsense and rubbish that people are told over the telephone, *even* in business calls. Wolf Schneider, the former head of the Hamburg School of Journalism, who is well-versed in the professional use of language, rightly said that it is highly probable that more can be derived from a minute of reading than from a minute of listening, unless a text was being read aloud.[45] What could be more important in an information society?

In reality, writing does not require *more* time, it requires *less*. It saves time. Writing, electronically in particular, makes personal presence redundant. However, what is most important is the fact that writing provides the opportunity, and even forces us to reflect.

The Small Step to Effectiveness

Most reports are dispatched or forwarded when they actually need a last, thorough revision. They are considered to be complete when the writers know what they want to say, and they put it on paper. However, at this stage the report is most probably still written from the *point of view of the sender*.

It is at this point that it becomes clear whether the writer is merely an *author* and remains *ineffective*, or whether he steps beyond being an author to being a *manager*. One type of writer ends the document at this

---

45 Wolf Schneider, *Deutsch für Profis*, Hamburg 1986, page 115.

point, and they remain authors. The other asks one crucial question at precisely this point, and this transforms the person from author to manager. The question is: *What effect should this report have on the recipient?* Quite often we will discover that the work is not as complete as it was thought to be, but is actually only *beginning,* or, to express it better, the essential part for and in organizations is now beginning. The report must now be worked on in such a way that it has the best possible chance, as far as it is possible to predict, of triggering the intended effect in the receivers that will *prompt them to action.* The report must be recast to be receiver- and reader-oriented.

Up to this point the writing of a document has been dominated by logic, *accuracy,* or truth. From this point onwards logic must be replaced by rhetoric in the sense of the ancient Greek schools of rhetoric, that is, in the sense of the art of *effectiveness.* This is not primarily about style or a display of brilliant expressions, as "authors", too, can master this skill. However, these factors are not very useful in creating the desired effect. In fact, they frequently result in the opposite of effectiveness, in the sense meant here.

Effectiveness means finding out, as far as possible, who the recipient is and to ascertain what the recipient is most likely to react to. The essential things can only be determined in individual cases, but a few generalizations, or, better still, types of categories can be made.

For example, let us take a report of 40 pages. Who reads 40 pages? Should the report be reduced in size? Or should a summary of the essential points be given in three or four pages to be placed at the beginning of the report for those readers who prefer short reports and leave it to the readers' interest to dictate whether they want to go through the remaining pages? With just this simple method the probability of achieving at least the minimum effect increases substantially.

Is it right, from the point of view of effectiveness, to incorporate tables, figures, statistics, etc. in the text? Or would it be better to place them in an appendix to which reference can be made in the text which is, however, written in such a way that it can be understood even without the paraphernalia of figures?

If we know, for example, that the recipient is a *lawyer,* then we should preferably leave out the figures, graphs and tables and work with text only if this is possible. Lawyers are amongst the few people who have learnt to read in the course of their studies and, above all, to read complicated and long texts. We may, in fact we *should,* use a demanding sentence structure, there can be many subordinate clauses and difficult terminology. Some lawyers only take a text seriously, if it is complicated. Anything less than complicated does not meet their high standards.

However, if the recipient is an *engineer*, the text portion should be reduced, and there should be more graphs and, above all, mathematical curves in systems of coordinates. This is what the eye of an engineer is trained for and what arouses his interest. On the other hand, lawyers should not be overtaxed with systems of coordinates. Such a presentation will deter most of them from looking into the issue. Many of them develop a dislike for mathematics in school; it is one of the reasons why they selected law as a subject.

Engineers, on the other hand, are the modern "illiterates", to exaggerate the case. Most of them can neither read nor write well. I do not mean to be disparaging in any way. They prefer other means of communication: technical drawings and the coordinate system. While the eyes of a lawyer will begin to turn glassy at the sight of a mathematical curve, the eyes of an engineer will turn bright and lively. In their mind's eye they see the formula related to those curves, they will immediately check whether the coordinates have been labeled and correctly at that, while the points of intersection speak volumes to them. On the other hand, most of the text between the diagrams bores them; they do not need it to understand the issue, and it almost sends them to sleep.

A *financial expert* should not be overtaxed with either text or graphs. Tables with as *many figures* as possible should be created for them. The typical financial manager, controller, etc. is a *numbers person*; they have a "digital brain". Some have an almost erotic relationship with numbers and figures; where others just see a graveyard of numbers, elaborate multidimensional images spring up for them. The saying that beauty lies in the eye of the beholder, is never truer than in the case of finance people when they look at numbers, figures, and tables. What is important is that line totals and column totals are always there, and everything is given in percentages in both vertical and horizontal directions. Finance people have the almost uncanny knack of picking at a glance precisely that number that cannot be correct, and they can then become most difficult because they consider it inexcusable that the final check was not carried out with complete thoroughness.

To find out all this information about the recipient and the many other details that are required for putting together a report suitable for the reader is not always easy and occasionally even impossible. However, this cannot be used as an excuse for not obtaining at least the information that is *accessible*.

There are people to whom it does not matter to be understood, and some are even proud of this. I suggest that such bad habits should not be tolerated. These are precisely the reasons why communication has become a problem. However, it is, of course, not possible to make progress in communication when there is a lack of simple, craftsmanlike skills, and, furthermore, when sloppiness and indifference are treated as virtues.

Clarity of Language

Unfortunately, it is often found that even people with rigorous academic training have not mastered the *simplest* of rules for the factual and logical *structure* of a text. They do not seem to be able to structure their text properly; and inevitably one cannot help wondering about the structure in their thoughts.

However, even their linguistic expression as such, the grammar, the choice of words, to say nothing of spelling and punctuation, hardly meet the standards of clarity and precision required in an organization. As I have said elsewhere, much in the modern organization is so abstract that it can no longer be perceived through the senses. Therefore, it is all the more vital to summon the intellect to record and appropriately describe the reality of an organization. *Language* and its competent use are primarily required for this. Clarity, conciseness and accuracy of language are indispensable. However, the mastery of these skills cannot unfortunately be taken for granted even if people are highly educated.

Obviously, modern information technology will change little or nothing in the *basic evil* of frequently lamented deficiencies in communication. The abilities discussed here and their utilization as a tool of personal, organizational and management effectiveness have nothing to do with computers or telecommunications. However, what the computer can do in this context is enforce precision, even if it is only *formal* precision to start with. It is not permissible to put a comma where the computer demands a full stop, in an Internet address, for example. In this respect electronic systems are exceptionally stubborn, and have a salutary, educational effect. At the very least, this brings about a realization that precision is occasionally important.

If this same relentlessness is shown by managers, they are considered to be inhuman, outdated, lacking all social skills, and, therefore, totally unsuitable for a management position. Their subordinates and colleagues would be extremely frustrated. These types of things are not only tolerated in computers, but for some it is precisely this aspect that makes them so fascinating. Even dynamic journalists and creative writers are not annoyed by the fact that they have to use a word processing program that operates according to the rules of the software engineer and not "dynamically" or "creatively". (No chief editor or editor has ever achieved anything comparable.)

An excellent example of the professional use of writing is the way George C. Marshall organized and managed his correspondence and documentation as the US Chief of Staff.[46] The preparation and handling of reports was carefully thought out and followed precise rules. Reporting did not only comprise the American side but all other members of the alliance, due to their combined operations in the war. Thus they had to take into account conditions that would have been labeled "multicultural" nowadays, though the professionalism prevailing now is a far cry from that of those days.

Marshall's personal writings are prime examples of clarity and precision. Nothing less is expected from a high-ranking military officer because this discipline is as well practiced by the higher ranks in the military academies as is the mastery of weapons by the soldiers. The writings of Marshall also show, and in a very impressive light, how he was successful in expressing emotions even in conditions of war – humaneness, warmth, friendship, sympathy in suffering, and empathy.

In principle, similar conventions can also be found, even if not in every detail, in the diplomatic service, the secret services, in the Vatican, and also in the way the British administered the Indian subcontinent in the colonial era. I know that all these examples have their negative side as well and can be easily misunderstood. It is clear to me that there is only a thin dividing

---

46 Larry I. Bland (Editor), *The Papers of George C. Marshall*, three volumes: 1981-1991, and *The War Reports of General of the Army G.C. Marshall, General of the Army H.H. Arnold and Fleet Admiral E.J. King*, Philadelphia/New York 1947.

line between professionalism and effectiveness on one side and kafkaesque bureaucracy on the other, and that the latter has been found time and again in all the aforementioned organizations. However, there is little sense in always focusing on things that do *not* work. No one will dispute the fact that bureaucracy exits; however, there is also administrative professionalism, and we can learn from this.

Particularly in the future this will become significant for organizations that have a high percentage of knowledge workers, are integrated in complex networks, and in which virtual forms of work are important. The rules and the discipline of professional reporting are crucial for the success and failure of all forms of work that have been made possible by modern communications technology.

Bad Practices, Unreasonable Demands and Foolishness

There are a few other peculiarities that should be noted in written communication: the *keyword epidemic*, for example. Its origins date back to the advent of the overhead projector and the transparencies it requires, in themselves an improvement in many respects upon the old slate. However, transparencies have, unfortunately, promoted or in fact almost compelled the presentation of contents to be given in fragments of sentences and keywords. Apart from the fact that terrible jargon has come into fashion, a keyword can have almost unlimited interpretations. As such it has no specific meaning. Hence, it is certain that people will interpret it to suit themselves, and the more tricky, difficult and unpleasant the facts, the more they will be inclined to interpret keywords to please themselves.

Another bad habit is presenting a *graph* for absolutely everything – a diagram, small box, arrows, circles, or whatever it may be. This is justified by the claim that a picture is more expressive than a thousand words. Unfortunately, this is true only in *very rare cases*, and it is almost certainly not true of those "pictures" that are usually used in modern organizations.

Of course, an image *can* have a highly informative value. This is all the more true the more specific it is. Furthermore, it *can* have a high information content for *experts*. The ground plan of a building can be very informative to the trained eye of an architect, the civil engineer, and the statistician. To anyone else, however, whose profession has nothing to do with planning and building, a ground plan means little or nothing, and it is likely to only confuse and put them off. It leads to misinformation rather than information.

Now, there is at least logic in the way ground plans of buildings are drawn. The conventions of design have evolved and been refined and improved upon over the centuries. Each symbol has a specific meaning which is the subject matter of training, and because of this, it tells the trained person at a glance all that he needs to know.

On the other hand, there are no such conventions for the presentation of management and organizational facts. A rudimentary set of presentational rules can probably be found for classical organizational charts that, in any case, say so little about an organization that they conceal more than they inform. The majority of whatever else can be found on presentations in literature is neither logical nor expressive[47], but is often very arbitrary, self-contradictory, and quite often reveals a complete lack of thought.

Not only do such "pictures" not express more than a thousand words, on the contrary, they require lengthy explanations without which they would remain totally unintelligible, and (this has been referred to several times because it is important) they create confusion and are open to all kinds of interpretations. They *create* a communication problem instead of *solving* one.

One last habit that I do not want to leave unmentioned is the replacement of the portrait format by the *landscape format* for written reports. Pages in landscape format, as little text as possible, a stuttering language with the largest possible letters; we have fallen below the level of illustrated books for four-year-olds. How long will a person as a manager put up with the degeneration of communication into baby talk? What will be the effects of this on the company for which they will be held responsible? And what more do the authors of such "writing" believe they can still subject managers to?

This mania started in the consultancy sector. One of the many riddles of modern management is how such rubbish could gain acceptance. There is only one situation in which such things could perhaps still be justified, and that is when the contents of transparencies cannot be read due to distance or the writing being very small, and a hard copy also being required as a

---

47 A notable exception is the diagrams of the English cybernetician Stafford Beer that can serve as a standard for informative drawings.

handout. Otherwise there is no justification for the bad habit of using landscape format.

Landscape format is unsuitable from the point of view of psychological and physical perception. It *impedes* perception instead of facilitating it, as advocates of landscape format never tire of asserting. Well-designed newspapers, magazines and news magazines have already shifted to multi-column setting. Even the line length of a normal A4 size paper is set at the upper limit of what the eye can cover. Therefore, it is with good reason that a book seldom has a format that comes even close to an A4 size.

We can, of course, question whether it is really worth the effort to concern ourselves with such matters which, on their own, seem trivial. Considered in isolation they *are* minor details that can be shrugged off, because the managers have only themselves to blame for putting up with such bad habits. Strangely, these bad habits have spread. Therefore, attention must be drawn to the fact that these are *bad habits*. Documents should facilitate communication and not hamper it. Consequently, we should take this into consideration when drafting and preparing the layout of reports, always assuming that we are interested in effectiveness, or should be.

Third Tool

Job Design and Assignment Control

If objectives are to be effective, the *tasks and jobs* of all employees must be *properly designed*. Therefore, the third tool is job design and, closely related to it, control of the deployment of people, which I have called assignment control here.

A lot of money is spent on product design in the business world, and rightly so. In this case nothing is too expensive, and only the best is good enough. However, only a few companies, let alone other organizations, pay attention to the fact that *jobs* also need a *design*. To be more precise job design is basically limited to *manual* work. Inadequate, badly thought out job design is one of the main sources of demotivation, dissatisfaction, and low productivity of human resources. This is particularly true of areas where the *manual worker* is no longer required but the *knowledge worker* is.

The category of knowledge workers, which is mentioned here once again, shows the *greatest rate of growth by far* in all sectors of the economy (and not only in the service sector), and *knowledge will be the crucial raw material of the future*. This is why job design and assignment control will be of prime importance. Both are either not known at all in most organizations or are underdeveloped. Previously, we could rely on the *job to organize the people* as I have already mentioned in section II. Today, *the people must organize and design the job*.

Six Mistakes in Job Design

Designing jobs is not particularly difficult, if a few rules are observed and a few common mistakes avoided.

First Mistake: Too Small a Job

The biggest and most frequent mistake in job design is the job that is too small. Most *people have tasks that are far too minor*; they are always underdeployed. This mistake is the main reason for frustration and a lack of productivity. Of course, there are people who enjoy their small jobs but they should be removed sooner or later.

Employees who generally finish their work at three o'clock because their job is not big enough have no reason to think about working effectively, their own productivity or the delegation of tasks, and this cannot be held against them either.

Jobs must be *big*; they must *challenge* the people *completely*. In their own interests, people should "stretch" themselves a little to complete the task assigned for the day. This alone leads to the *development* of people, it *calls forth inner abilities* and hidden *capabilities,* and it stimulates thoughts about effective work. This has already been stated in the discussion on the development of people. Job design is the tool for the implementation of this idea.

There is much discussion these days of the reduction of hierarchies, and rightly so. Whether people should be subordinate to others is now a matter of doubt. As a result of this, in well-organized companies it is the *task that controls the employees* and not primarily the manager. In the future, people will not only have to tolerate this, but many will actively seek such situations, the good employees at least.

Therefore, jobs that are too small are the *biggest* mistake in job design because this mistake is *not noticed,* and therefore it *cannot be corrected.* The employees go to waste, and only the best go to their managers to tell them that their work does not keep them fully occupied and that they would like to carry out a bigger task.

Second Mistake: Too Big a Job

It is also possible to commit the opposite mistake of making jobs too big. People *can* be overtaxed, but this is *not so simple*, as already mentioned. Most people accept self-imposed limits far too quickly. The entire history of mankind provides evidence that people are capable of far more than they think possible. No sports record has been held forever; they have all been broken. Time and again, people suddenly surpass themselves and are capable of performances that they never thought they could achieve. And it is evident time and again that *the performance itself and its results are a source of the utmost motivation*. Therefore, the tasks must be made big.

There is, of course, also a limit beyond which a person cannot go. Therefore, a job that is too big is certainly a mistake but, and this is important, it is *easy to recognize and correct*. There are several indications: The employee misses deadlines, he makes mistakes, or he does sloppy work. And then they sooner or later speak to their managers about the overtaxing work. A job that is too small is a "mortal sin"; the too big job is a "pardonable sin".

Third Mistake: The Apparent Job or Non-Job

This mistake will hardly be found in small and medium-sized enterprises, but it is a type of epidemic in *large organizations*. Almost every position that has the designation "assistant" or "coordinator" is a non-job. There are exceptions, but these are rare. Many staff positions are also included in this category. However, these are not apparent jobs or non-jobs, because the people in these positions do not have enough to do – staff members and assistants often work very hard.

The problem is more complex; they are non-jobs, because in these cases we come across a devilish combination of *great influence* with a complete or substantial *lack of responsibility*. Without responsibility a task lacks an essential, defining element. This combination corrupts; it *corrupts* the people who have such jobs, and it *corrupts* the organization. The temptation to exert influence and the associated power is almost irresistible, especially when there is no responsibility attached. This poisons the mentality and morals. All the employees in the organization know, of course, exactly how to interact with these eminences grises, and this again poisons the organization.

Therefore, these jobs must be kept to a minimum. No one should stay more than two or a maximum of three years in such a position. Thereafter, the employee must be assigned a line function with clear responsibility.

Fourth Mistake: The Multi-Person Job

These jobs are such that a person cannot complete, finalize or settle anything *independently*. The person is constantly dependent on cooperation and coordination, always requires half a dozen other colleagues and accordingly many meetings before anything can actually be done. Matrix organizations are particularly susceptible to the proliferation of multi-person jobs. Experience shows that either matrix organizations never function as they are intended to, or they function as intended only with the utmost discipline.

The rule is that it should be possible for *one person* and the person's *organizational unit* to carry out a task. I know that this is difficult to follow, and it cannot be adhered to completely. But this rule sets the right standard, and it clearly contradicts the opinion in vogue that everything must be interrelated. Whatever can be kept separate should remain separate. Improperly understood interrelatedness is the main cause of the increase in complexity. If multi-person jobs are necessary, they should only be entrusted to very *experienced* and *disciplined* people.

Fifth Mistake: Jobs with "a Bit of Everything"

These are jobs that compel people to *dissipate and squander their energy*. Reference to the third principle shows that, in any case, managers are already subject to this menace to such a great extent that it should not be exacerbated through this mistake in job design. This type of job *paralyses* people who may be busy, but do not achieve *any results*. In our complex world of organizations the following rule can perhaps no longer be applied: *one man, one boss*; but this rule can be: *one man, one job – one big job*.

People need to *focus* in order to achieve results. During an operation a heart surgeon concentrates fully, totally, and exclusively on the task; he does not go off to make a quick phone call or attend a meeting. The tasks must be big, and they should force people to concentrate on *one* issue. This is the *easiest* way to get results and for the knowledge worker it is the *only way*.

Sixth Mistake: The Killer Job or the Impossible Job

This refers to positions that sometimes, literally and metaphorically, *kill* a person. This does not happen because a person has too much to do but because the job has such a wide range of *very different* requirements that no ordinary person can hope to meet them all. There are occasionally geniuses who can cope with such jobs, but they are the exceptions. Jobs must be designed in such a way that they can be performed by *ordinary* people, even if they are difficult.

A good indication of this kind of job is when a manager has gone through two or three good and also carefully selected subordinates in one particular position. By the third case at the very latest, the cause of the failure should not be sought in the people; the job should be changed.

Even though I know that this will not be well received in smaller and medium-sized companies which frequently make this mistake, a good example of a killer job is the combination of sales and marketing into a single position. Sales and marketing are two fundamentally *different tasks* that also require such *different capabilities* that they can rarely be found in one person. Selling means persuading people to sign on the dotted line of sales contracts. Marketing, on the other hand, essentially means changing ideas in people's minds. The consequence of such killer jobs is that a person is either excellent at sales, but terrible at marketing; or vice versa, there is brilliant marketing but terrible sales; quite frequently a person is good at *neither* marketing *nor* sales. All three are different but very sure ways of ruining a company. It is only the amount of time it takes for this to happen that varies.

Let us now move away from the subject of mistakes and turn to something positive. Jobs must be big; they must force people to concentrate and focus; they must have inner coherence and should not simply be an aggregate of unrelated activities; they must allow objectives to be achieved; they must be designed for ordinary people who are selected according to their strengths.

Assignment Control

Job design is to a certain extent the *static* aspect of the tool proposed here. However, there is also a *dynamic* part which I will call assignment control.

There is occasionally a question about whether job design and assignment control are two *different* tools. I prefer to cover them together, because a well-designed job is a prerequisite for the proper use of assignment control and vice versa, assignment control is not possible without a job.

Assignment control is virtually unknown in modern organizations. This is one of the main reasons why companies are *weak in implementation*. It is one of the main causes of ineffectiveness and particularly the neglect of human resources or their incorrect deployment. Usually there is no lack of *efficiency*, but there is of *effectiveness*. There is no better definition of efficiency and effectiveness than the statement by Drucker[48]: *Efficiency means doing things right; effectiveness means doing the right things.*

To many people this statement seems to be a nice play on words, and when we use it in a lecture, we can be sure (though it has since become an age-old saying) that we have "got in a gag"; the audience laughs or they at least smile. However, it is of course much, much more than just this. It is *not a play on words*, but a *very great difference*. It is the difference between *success* and *failure*, *effort* and *performance*, *work* and *results*, *right* and *wrong*.

Something can be done with a hundred percent efficiency, but if it is the wrong thing, it is a hundred percent ineffective. The right thing done with twenty percent efficiency is always much more effective than the wrong thing done with one hundred percent efficiency.

This is obvious and to be honest, it is banal. However, it is important, and it must be ensured that an organization's employees understand this perfectly. Therefore, it must be preached tirelessly.

However, this is unfortunately not enough. People listen, nod, and then they forget. Therefore, the *tool of assignment control* must be used; or in other words, assignment control must be *made* into a tool. Two things are necessary for this: *firstly*, knowledge of the difference between job and assignment and *secondly*, active control of the deployment of people.

The Difference between Job and Assignment

The assignment is the *task* in a job that must be given the *highest priority* in the coming period.

A job is always a *set* of tasks that are bundled together from an organizational perspective. A person can assume at a particular time that these tasks are to be carried out for an unlimited period of time (until the job

---

48 He perhaps used it for the first time in *The Practice of Management*, New York 1955, 17th edition 1995.

itself has to be changed). However, these tasks are not linked to any specific *priorities*. Priorities cannot be set *in general terms*; they can only be set according to the *specific* and *current* situation.

As a result of this, the job descriptions of similar jobs are practically the same around the world. The job of a sales manager in the engineering industry in Germany corresponds in essence to that in Japan, the USA, or Italy. And the Russians will have to design this job in the same way if they want to improve their economy. There may be differences in the details but not in the essence.

Most jobs are not only similar at an international level but also share a similarity with jobs in various sectors of the economy. The job of an IT manager in the insurance sector does not differ greatly from that in a bank, a trading company, or a branch of industry. Even in non-profit organizations, public administration, the UN, Red Cross and charities, there are great similarities. The same is true of personnel and financial management, for example, but not accounting, which differs greatly in the different sectors.

Incidentally, *whether* job descriptions are used in an enterprise is immaterial in this context. I am of the opinion that they are required. But the difference between a good and a bad job description is, of course, clear to me, and I also know that there are companies that have achieved nothing but an increase in bureaucracy with the introduction of job descriptions. However, there must be *clarity about the jobs* in one way or another; whether this is accomplished through the contract of employment, (good) job descriptions, or in some other way is irrelevant. Sometimes adequate clarity can be attained simply through practical experience of the job and its routine, or the product and technology, or common sense and experience. Regardless, a lack of clarity about the job or mistakes in job design are a serious organizational weakness in many institutions; they have serious consequences for the functioning of an organization, and they cannot be removed in any way other than with precise job design.

However, we are digressing from the topic. Whether job descriptions are *not* used or jobs are *very* well designed, the distinction between job and assignment is important.

The *job* tells us: A is a trumpeter. But it does not tell you what is being played *this evening*. Is Beethoven or Wagner being played, jazz or folk music? We always need trumpeters, but what and how they should play is completely different. "First trumpeter" is the job; "Mahler's Seventh" is the *assignment*, the specific assignment that takes precedence in the next performance, it is the same for the next week or the next 15, 18, or 24 months.

The post of the Catholic bishop as we know it today was designed and established in the fourteenth century, since then it has hardly changed. However, the concrete tasks today are totally *different* from the tasks of those earlier times; they have been subject to a tremendous historical change. The fact that this does not seem to have been understood particularly well may be one of the reasons for certain difficulties faced by the Catholic Church.

The job of a divisional commander is more or less the same in armies all over the world. However, it makes a great difference whether the task is to set up and train a division, or to lead one into battle, or to rearm and mobilize a defeated and decimated one. The divisional commander is always at the top, but what he has to do specifically, where his priorities lie, *differs* completely depending on the assignment. In each of these examples what is to be done and the requirements a commander must meet are so different that in military organizations, a different person will be entrusted with the command in each case. After centuries of painful experience it is finally clear that it is highly improbable for the same person to have such different abilities. In this respect at least, military organizations, as compared to companies, have much greater flexibility, and, as a result of this, they also have the ability to implement. This is something the business world is somewhat arrogantly ready to acknowledge about military organizations.

In the business world, if the assignment changes and other priorities have to be set, changing or wanting to change the person is the exception rather than the rule. It is all the *more important* to establish absolute clarity about the main task specific to each job depending on the company's current situation.

An example: The job is sales management. Completely different abilities and activities are required, if the assignment for the sales manager is as follows:

1. To sell existing products or reduce the range by 40 percent;
2. To look after existing customers or win back disaffected customers
3. To work with the existing sales force or to radically introduce new blood, because the workforce has too many older people.

Another example: the position is controlling, and it includes all that controllers must normally do. However, the existing controlling system now has to include a debtor result calculation; or the IT infrastructure has to be completely updated; or new and different factors for measuring productivity are to be introduced in which the value-creation chain is to be represented; or activity-based costing is to be established. For the period of reorganization, until some type of routine sets in, totally different abilities and activities are necessary.

These things are immediately clear to some employees, and they act accordingly, because they are talented people. However, most people have to be made *aware* of the priorities and must be specially asked to work *in line* with them and *focus* on them.

This works best in those companies that are commissioned to carry out *projects*, for example, consultancy or engineering firms. Here, the definition of a project and its organization automatically delineates the overall project plan and the associated subjobs clearly and properly. This is the case in well-managed companies of this type, because otherwise work cannot be done properly, and is done as a matter of course and is hardly noticed. Similarly, clarity about working with assignments is also to be found in people with good military training, because management by tasks is one of the most important functional principles of every modern army. However, in all other organizations, this is *not* done as a matter of course. People are inclined to blindly trust that the jobs are clear and that the people in those jobs are aware of their priorities.

It is advisable to specify assignments in *writing*. This is absolutely imperative in difficult and complex cases and particularly when *massive* changes must be brought about *quickly*. This is one of the "secrets" of effective managers.

Assignment Control

The "dissecting" of priorities and the clear and precise definition of assignments is the *first* necessary step for the effectiveness of an organization. But even then the *second* essential step is neglected far too often, and that is the effective *control of the deployment* of people.

Sometimes I carry out the following exercise with participants of a seminar. I ask them to write down the names and activities of their *best* subordinates. The participants usually complete their list very quickly. Why?

They only have to note a *few* names because no one has *many* "best" people. There are three, four or five people. The longest list that I have seen to date had twelve names. However, it soon became apparent in the discussion that the manager concerned had included the names of the second-best and third-best subordinates.

Therefore, the lists are short, and under the column "activity", the *job designation* of the named person is given: such as Müller – marketing, Huber – product development, Meier – controlling. The exercise then continues as follows: *I have obviously not expressed myself clearly. When I said activity, I did not mean what your best people do in general terms but what they are doing now, today, on Wednesday at 4.15 p.m.*

The participants now look at me puzzled and say: *Yes, I have already written that. Müller is in marketing, Huber in product development, and Meier in controlling.*

I then suggest a half-hour break in the seminar and ask the participants to phone up and *find out* what their best people are actually doing at the *present moment*, and as precisely as possible. Sometimes their reactions are ill-natured, but they finally do as I have asked.

In the discussion that follows almost all of them have an embarrassed look on their faces when they realize that their best people are dealing

- with *yesterday* instead of *tomorrow*;
- with *difficulties* instead of *opportunities*;
- with the *interesting* instead of the *important*;
- with *product modification* instead of *product development*;
- with customer *complaints* instead of *acquiring new customers*;
- with *routine* instead of *innovation*.

Then comes the question: *If the best people and their staff are absorbed in the first set of activities, who is dealing with the second?* The answer is clear: *No one!* And thus the enterprise *has* no future; therefore, *nothing* changes as a result, and there is *no* innovation. Their hands are full with managing the *present* –the *future* is left to chance.

Of course, the first category of work does need to be *done*. But should the *best* people be doing it? Could these things not be done by the second-best or third-best? And should not the greatest attention be paid to ensuring that the best subordinates are unburdened by these tasks, even if this is usually difficult, so that they can concentrate all their energy on the really important issues?

The best people constantly allow themselves to get involved in the first category of things precisely, *because* they are the best. Wherever "it's urgent", they step into the breach. Whenever a problem crops up, they get to work and take action. This is usually the reason why they are considered the best. But do they also apply themselves to the *right* issues?

It is here that *assignment control* must be applied. It must be ensured that the priorities are clear with no room for misunderstanding; then it must be ensured that each employee can, as well as possible, concentrate his energy and abilities on this, *undisturbed* and with *undivided attention*. This is particularly applicable to the really good subordinates who tend to deal with everything and help everywhere out of a sense of duty and responsibility.

As positive as this is in principle, there is always the risk of *wasting energy* and *time*. It is the really difficult tasks for which only the best people can be used, which usually require *complete concentration* and quite frequently effort that verges on the impossible. Therefore, effective managers always "cover for them" when they are dealing with really difficult tasks. They relieve them, as far as possible, from the daily routine and everything else so that they can devote themselves totally to the priorities.

In this way these managers also make an excellent contribution to the development of the second-best and third-best employees, and that, too, in accordance with the recommendations of the third section. They, too, now receive bigger and more responsible tasks, those that were previously done by the best employees. In this way all the employees are shown where the priorities lie, and this leads to what most organizations want so passionately – a mutual feeling of obligation and responsibility, *shared commitment*. This is not achieved in the ways that have been given preference since the "discovery" of corporate culture – through pompous programs, ritualistic oaths, or the collectivistic bonds from the Far East – but in a much simpler though more effective manner: through the way people work and manage...

It is the same in a well-adjusted family. If a child has a serious illness, the members of that family will do their best to relieve the mother of her other tasks so that she can devote herself completely to the sick child; when one of the children has to prepare for their examinations, he or she is relieved of all their other duties so that he or she can concentrate completely on the examinations.

Practical Procedure

Assignment control is relatively simple once it is understood and its necessity is realized. It is an exercise that is done along with budgeting and determining objectives at the end of a planning period. This is also the best time to determine the priorities.

1. First, senior management has to deal with the issue of priorities for the *entire organization*. The basics for this are the corporate policy and strategy as well as the assessment of the current situation. The question should be: *What should we focus on in the next planning period in view of our long-term policy and the current situation?* The list of priorities must be short. More than seven plus/minus two things which I have already mentioned in the chapter on objectives should not be tackled simultaneously, unless there are important reasons for doing so. Managers should work with great tenacity towards determining as small a number of focal points as possible.
2. After this, the result must be made known to the next level of management, and usually it is very advantageous to inform a wider circle of employees, in fact all employees in small and medium-sized enterprises, clearly and precisely.
3. With this in mind everyone who is a direct subordinate of members of corporate management teams will be given the task of considering and working out on the basis of his job description (or whatever they have instead of a job description) the focal points of his *own* activities in relation to the company's priorities. This is in preparation for an intensive discussion that every manager will then have with the subordinates (individually or in a group) in which the assignments of the job are to be determined as clearly and precisely as possible. Here, too, the principle of the smallest possible number of focal points per job is applicable.
4. Whether a written record of the result of this discussion in the form of an assignment is required must be decided according to the individual case. I believe that this is particularly necessary for difficult assignments – where there are considerable changes or innovations, where there are deviations from the normal routine and things have to be steered in a new direction. The time frames do not have to correspond to the twelve months of the following financial year; they can be longer or shorter

periods. The time frame must correspond to the duration of the assignment(s).

An example: *Your main task is to win back a third of the customers we have lost due to defects in XY product within the next 18 months. To enable you to concentrate fully on this task, we are postponing the reorganization of the commission system scheduled for this period, and you can also be represented by Mr. Meier in the project group for this period.*

A sales manager's assignment could be something like this. The sales manager will then *base* his or her specific annual objectives on this assignment.

5. If an assignment is particularly difficult for an employee, if they must concentrate on two, three or four focal points instead of one despite all efforts to reduce them, and the less they can be freed from other duties, the more important the last step becomes – the actual *"control"* element in assignment control. At regular intervals, certainly no longer than every six to eight weeks, the manager should *check on* these people and *verify* whether they are *really* working on their priorities. Otherwise the managers will discover after some time that, except in the case of very professional people, the compulsions of day-to-day business have supplanted the priorities, the urgent has overtaken the important, and routine has killed innovation.

Under no circumstances should we rely on reports and the actual versus target performance comparisons, which are prepared as a matter of routine. This is one of those cases that can only be controlled through *personal supervision*. What is important here is the personal presence of the manager, talking to the subordinates, the signal that the manager is aware that they are working on a difficult task and that everything possible will be done to help them. This opportunity will also be used to constantly remind subordinates of the importance of their tasks within the framework of the whole and in this way give them all the necessary task-related, human and moral support.

Some Additional Remarks

1. A misconception can result from the requirement that the assignments should be *clear and precise*. Some take this to mean "as detailed as pos-

sible". However, this is not what I mean. An assignment can be *clear and precise* even if the details *cannot* be supplied, as they are not yet known. For example: *Your main priority for the next eight months is to explore the Indian market for our business segment X. Your investigation should serve as the foundation for drawing up a strategy for India at a later date.* This could be an assignment for a marketing employee.

For an *experienced* marketing expert this assignment is clear and precise, even though it is not detailed. What they should investigate is not stated or stipulated in detail; this can certainly be left to the discretion of a *competent* marketing employee. However, when dealing with a *less experienced* employee, it is necessary to go into detail, and the assignment should then contain the specific points that need to be investigated.

2. Some managers ask me if assignments are not the same as objectives. This may be the case sometimes. However, I have repeatedly had the experience that there is a tendency to discuss the objectives far *too quickly*, and the important step of determining the assignment is left out. In such a case the foundation that should be laid for meaningful determination of objectives is lacking.

Of course, there are jobs and situations in which this is not important. We can then turn to the objectives *directly*. This is particularly true of routine jobs and, above all, for those jobs in which the product and technology is clearly structured (often even the objectives are not required here).

I would particularly recommend the clear formulation of assignments in the following cases.
a) When an employee has a *new* job in the company. Most people tend to continue in the same mindset of their old jobs.
b) When we are dealing with *innovations* and *changes*. These always require a step into unknown "territory", and old habits are a great handicap in this.
c) When a *new* person is employed. Even if we are dealing with experienced people, we do not really know them, and they do not yet know the company. Therefore, clarity in the main tasks is particularly important.
d) When dealing with *young* and *inexperienced* employees. Experienced people may not present any problems, but clarity and precision are particularly important for inexperienced people. The precise formu-

lation of the assignment shortens the training and probationary period required for new and inexperienced employees.

In these cases it is important to define assignments *of a shorter duration* so that the people can *quickly* show how they work. After two or three assignments, a person can be assessed fairly well; the way they work and behave as well as their strengths will be known.

3. Some managers complain that their subordinates cannot set any priorities. It is usually found that it is the managers themselves who fail to adequately train and encourage their subordinates to analyze the priorities and consider them. Therefore, these are mistakes made in the management, development, and training of subordinates.

Sometimes it is simply a case of employees being *incompetent* in their field. These people should be removed gradually. Young and inexperienced people cannot be expected to have the ability to determine priorities. *They must learn it.* For experienced and competent people, however, the identification of priorities is usually not a problem.

Of cource, it is possible that a manager may have *different* priorities in mind even from those of experienced people. *This must be discussed thoroughly.* Such discussions are usually valuable discussions which result in progress for the individual and the company. All the participants in such a discussion develop a better and deeper understanding of the business.

The application of assignment control leads to an astonishing improvement in the organization's *ability to implement*, which usually becomes noticeable immediately. Suddenly there are *visible* results, and the employees *experience success*, even if this success has demanded great effort. Neglecting this practice, on the other hand, always causes even employees with the best intentions to get stuck in the quagmires of routine and habit. Therefore, at the end of a period there are *results* in the first case whereas in the second, *only work* has been done. In the first case there is *effectiveness*; in the second there is *efficiency* at best.

Fourth Tool

Personal Working Methods

Personal working methods are extremely important for managers. Hardly anything else affects their effectiveness so *directly* and so *comprehensively*. And more than anything else, it is a manager's working methods that determine their results and success. Therefore, a careless attitude should not be adopted towards our own working methods or those of our subordinates. We cannot be too vigilant, or too patronizing, or too cooperative in correcting the working methods of our subordinates when they reveal deficiencies, even though this is usually somewhat irksome and at times even embarrassing for both parties.

Boring Perhaps, but Extremely Important

Admittedly, this topic is not very exciting; it is simply *important*. It becomes exciting when the effectiveness of people with a well thought out working method is compared to the effectiveness of those that pay this subject scant attention.

The differences are tremendous, and not only with regard to professional success. The effect of a methodical, efficient working method can affect a person's private life, too. I maintain that almost all the frequently discussed adverse effects of work and professional pressure such as stress, the frenetic pace, damage to health, and many familiar complaints can be traced to defects in working methods. A lot of hard work does not make people ill very easily. They just become tired. They fall ill due to inefficient, meaningless, and unsuccessful work.

I, therefore, advise people to pay the *maximum* attention to their personal working methods, even if they do not feel challenged *intellectually*.

Despite the importance that should be attached to good professional training, adequate intelligence, experience, and other attributes, abilities and talents, all of these are *worthless* without appropriate working methods. They remain unfulfilled potential.

Many reject methodical and systematic work, because they believe it to be incompatible with *creative* work. I have already touched on this point in the principle of concentration. This is a widespread but completely *incorrect* opinion. The opposite is true. It is precisely the creative people, at least those who are *successful*, who have very well-developed, systematic work methods. Only in the case of pseudo-creative people do creativity and chaotic work go hand in hand.

"The everyday life of most people who accomplish great things is drudgery", writes Wolf Schneider in his highly recommended book *Die Sieger*[49], which is about great and famous people, and focuses in particular on what helped them to achieve greatness and fame. He proves convincingly, with the help of concrete examples ranging from Leonardo to Thomas Mann, from Kant and Balzac to Franz Schubert and Paul Klee, that all worked very methodically, apart from a few exceptions. Their working methods were, and this is important, usually very *different* but they all *had* a method. None of them worked without a *system* and *discipline*.

Systematic and methodical work is the *key* to the utilization of talents, to translating abilities into results and success. Therefore, the question of whether a person has learnt to work systematically must be an important *selection criterion* for managers. Unfortunately, it is rarely mentioned in any list of criteria.

It is equally mystifying that no importance is attached to personal working methods in academic courses and other forms of training. Most people are left to their own devices and are, therefore, not very good in this area when they start their professional career; in fact, apart from a few people with natural talent, the vast majority are *bad* to *dreadful*.

I was no exception, even though my studies in economics had contained many elements of systematic work. At any rate, stenography and typewriting were compulsory subjects for several years, even though they were not very popular, and a minimum of systematic work was required to ensure that the condensed tabular statement of balance sheet figures in bookkeeping corresponded to the calculations, otherwise they never worked

---

49 Wolf Schneider, *Die Sieger*, Hamburg 1992, page 175 and chapter 17.

out. However, I hardly paid attention to, nor had any interest in these things either then or later at university and even years afterwards.

These days, working methods have almost become a hobby. Why? For the same reasons that most people begin to show an interest in them sooner or later: *As a result of hard and bitter experience.* Twice I found myself in situations in which I finally had to tell myself: Either you fail in your *task,* or your *family* breaks up, or *you* will be ruined or…? Is there a *fourth* possibility? Yes; *or you change the way you work!* To my shame I must admit that *one* such experience was not enough for me. I needed *another.*

Today, I am interested in *everything* that has to do with working methods. I never miss an opportunity to discuss this topic with managers and other people who have achieved something in their lives, and also to observe them while they work whenever possible. And even though I am only able to implement part of this, I have been able to learn a tremendous amount from it.

In comparison, I was able to learn, even though this may sound paradoxical, only a little from books or seminars on work techniques, which I read or attended for some time with great hopes and expectations. This baffled me for a long time. Not that these books and seminars were bad as such and in the usual sense, even though bad ones are also available. The problem was something else. They were simply not *suitable*; they were *not relevant.* At first, I could not explain this. Only in the course of time was I able to realize why this was so.

Fundamental Principles of Effective Working Methods

Working Methods Are Personal and Individual

The main reason for the irrelevance of many books and seminars on the topic of "working methods" is that the *wrong thing is generalized* or it is generalized in the *wrong* way. This is the conclusion I have drawn from my observation of a large number of managers at all levels and in many industries.

A working method is something that is extremely *individual.* Not without reason do we talk about *"personal"* working methods. No two people work in the same way, even if each person works very methodically and systematically. Thus there are very *different* methods and systems. Therein lies one of the key problems of most seminars on working methods. They teach *one* method for *everyone*. Their starting point is the assumption that one and same method is suitable for everyone or at least a large number of people and situations. Consequently, the content of the seminar is not methodical work as such but involves teaching a very specific system that claims to be *generally applicable*. This is a grave error.

The demand for methodical work itself can be generalized for those who are interested in effectiveness, and the problems that need to be solved by working methods can also be generalized, as I will explain. On the other hand, the individual methods and techniques and their combinations *cannot* be generalized. All effective people work methodically; but they all have their *own* method and their own individual combination of methods and techniques.

Working Methods Depend on the Overall Conditions and Circumstances

Apart from a person's own idiosyncrasies, the "best" working method in each case depends on a set of circumstances and existing conditions that are determined by the *situation* in which a person is. These are, for example:

1. The *person's occupation*: Field work in sales has a different logic and requirements for working methods than conventional office work; the management of a manufacturing plant is different from the management of a research institute; marketing requires different methods of work from accounting.
2. *The position within the organization*: Whether a manager has subordinates or not, and whether they are many or few makes a considerable difference; whether the manager is in the upper, middle or lower levels of an organization also makes a difference.
3. *Age*: At the age of 47 no one works in the same way as he did when he was 27, and this is not only due to differences in age and position. The tempo and rhythm of work changes with age; the physical and psychological conditions are different.
4. *The travel component*: A person whose job entails a lot of traveling requires a different method from someone who spends most of his time working in the office at his desk.

5. *Infrastructure*: A person who has a secretary can and must work in a way that is different from one who does not. People who have secretaries working for them exclusively work differently from those who have to share a secretary with others; a person who has a pool of secretaries and possibly even assistants requires yet another method.

6. *The organization*: The matrix organization places entirely different requirements on the method, system, and discipline of working than those of a functional organization; the enthusiasm for networked organizations that are so highly praised at present wanes quickly when we think of the almost superhuman discipline they require, if they are to function to any degree.

7. *The boss*: Every boss is different. People who have a chaotic person for a boss really have only two options – they can become chaotic themselves and will perhaps never achieve any results, or they are so disciplined that they can channel their manager's chaos in the right direction. On the other hand, if a person has a manager who works systematically and precisely, he can and will have to work in a totally different way.

8. *The industry*: Work is done differently in an airline and in a fashion house; in an insurance company a different working method is adopted from that in a food processing company, a publishing house or a television station.

Furthermore, and above all, working methods depend on *past* managers and *habits acquired along the way*. Therefore, as managers who value effectiveness we must at some point in time ask the question: *Do I wish to hang on to what I have learnt from my old boss and habits I've acquired along the way?*

Consequently, it is senseless to recommend or teach only *one* and the *same* working method to everyone, given the various types of situation. This only leads to inefficiency; in this way working methods are not an aid, but become a personal straitjacket and choke performance capability.

Regular Review and Adaptation

Unfortunately, it is not enough to have a personal working method. The *right* method is required for each individual *situation*. It is also possible to be *inefficient* in a very systematic manner. There are quite a few people who make themselves systematically ineffective, because they obstinately continue with a method that has long outlived its relevance in a situation that has clearly *changed*. Therefore, every working method must be reviewed from time to time, especially on certain occasions, and it must be adapted or even changed radically, even if most people find this difficult to do.

At any rate, working methods must be reviewed:

1. Approximately every Three Years

There is much talk everywhere about change and dynamics, and rightly so. The practical consequence is that approximately every three years, or five years at the most, there will be different requirements, even in a job that remains the same itself. Therefore, the way we work must be analyzed at regular intervals and thoroughly re-examined. This does not require a lot of time. One or two rainy days at weekends will generally suffice. It requires more discipline and no slackening of our interest in personal effectiveness.

2. When Taking on a New Task

A new task *usually* requires a *changed* method of working. This is so obvious that it hardly seems worth mentioning. Even so, there are so many mistakes that are made here that I want to draw particular attention to it. Usually, employees are prepared for a new task from the point of view of *expertise* but their method of working is seldom given any attention.

3. With every Promotion

This point is closely related to the previous one. A *higher* position usually involves *new* tasks. However, what most people who have just been promoted do not pay attention to is one of the most important and frequent reasons for failure in the new position. The maxim should be: *Whatever led to the promotion is usually more of a handicap than a help.* Accordingly, it can be assumed with a great degree of certainty that the previous methods of working cannot be continued in the new position.

4. When We Get a New Boss

Most bosses will, often very eloquently, talk about flexibility and adaptability, new behavior, and new forms of cooperation. By this, they always mean "the others". However, one thing is certain. If I get a new manager, I must change *my* method of working; they will not change *theirs* or at the most only to a limited extent, despite all the lip service.

5. Generally for every Major Change in our Situation

It makes a great difference whether it is "business as usual" in the company, or the company is going through a crisis, whether it is expanding or scaling down. The situation changes when we have new subordinates and new colleagues.

The maxim of regularly reviewing our personal working methods and adapting to changed circumstances also pertains to our *private life* which we must *integrate* into our working methods under all circumstances. Working methods should differ depending on whether a person is single or has a partner, whether a person has children or not, and it makes a considerable difference, if the children are very young, adolescent or adult. I have known managers to keep two different diaries, one for official appointments and one for their private ones. It should be obvious that this method cannot run smoothly for very long.

Each of the situations described here requires renewed thought and a review of our personal working methods and usually major adjustments in the way we work. However, we are suitably compensated for the effort involved. The objective of continuously improving and optimizing our working methods is not, as is frequently assumed, to work more and harder, even though not many people are spared from this these days. The objective is not to be a "workaholic". On the contrary: *Don't work harder; work smarter* must be our objective.

Of course, one of the results of optimized working methods is *also* that *more* can be achieved, *bigger* tasks can be taken on and handled *better*. Hardly anyone can be successful and get to the top of his profession without the willingness and the ability to carry out more and bigger tasks. That will perhaps always be necessary. On the other hand, what is *not* necessary is to make ourselves ill because of this, to sacrifice family life and do without the more pleasant side of life.

My suggestion, and it is not made from the comfort of my study but is the result of over 20 years of personal experience as well as observation and analysis of countless managers, is to approach personal working methods with a relaxed but sporting attitude. Any type of tension or compulsion is as much a disadvantage here as it is in sport and training. However, a focus on achievement is as important here as it is there. The guiding formula should be: *Let's see what we can achieve.* People should *experiment* with themselves and their methods and *try out* new things. Whatever doesn't work can be discontinued; anything that helps can be incorporated. Along with the successes that are sure to materialize quickly will come pleasure in that success and the desire to experiment a little more.

The *motives* for improving our working methods are not very important. One person may do it to have a better career, another to gain more freedom. *Why* we do it is far less important than the fact that it *is* done. The reasons for people's behavior, their motives, and motivation are always unknown. What is important is the *result*.

In the next section I will be covering those areas or problematic fields for which a special method must be adopted, if a person wants to be effective; these are fields that require certain rules and a certain system. The type of system and method selected by each person can, will and must be different. This is the only way to avoid the mistake of *unacceptable generalization,* which is so detrimental to personal working methods. *What* we can control through our working methods can be generalized; *how* the method should look, on the other hand, is very *personal*.

The Basic Areas

In this section I shall cover what, for want of a better expression, I will call the *basic areas* of personal working methods. It deals with those problematic fields that are to be found in *every* management position. All managers must bring these problems under control if they want to be effective. They must define their attitude towards these problems and develop a method for solving them. I will not be going into the details of alternative possibilities; they are generally obvious in individual cases.

Utilization of Time

Everyone has the same amount of time available, not in their lifetime but *each day*. However, when the way people make use of their time is observed, *enormous* differences are apparent. An awareness of time forms and develops in people in different ways. Many people are hardly aware at all of the importance of time. Others, rather less, are far too aware. Most people have a very *vague* relationship with time. Only a few have ever systematically thought about time and its characteristics. Unfortunately, nature has not given us a *time organ*, and our *sense of time* is usually very unreliable.

On the topic of "time" I always ask participants in a seminar the following question: *How many hours are there in a year?* Less than 1 percent give the correct answer quickly and spontaneously, without thinking it over and having to calculate. I believe that every manager should be able to answer this question immediately.

A normal year – not a leap year – has 8,760 hours. Is this a lot? Is this a little? That depends on how we use these hours. Everyone requires approximately eight hours of sleep each day. The remaining *5,800 hours* are actually available to a person to be used.

The path to effectiveness begins with the question: *How do I want to use my 5,800 conscious hours each year?* Everyone has to answer this *themselves*, but answer it they *must*. Otherwise they do not manage but are managed; otherwise they cannot be effective but will allow themselves to be driven and will drift through life.

Of course, effectiveness does not in any way mean *working* 5,800 hours a year. As I have already mentioned, I am not thinking about "workaholics", precisely because others considered me to be one for some time, and they may have been right. The opposite: *Do less in order to achieve more,* would be a notable motto.

We should consciously and deliberately *decide* on how to use our time. How much of it do we want to or have to devote to our *profession*, how much to our *family*, how much is to be reserved for *ourselves*, how much time should we keep free for *interests* and *recharging our batteries*, etc. People who do not systematically consider these questions and do not make any decisions run the risk of being driven by circumstances and or wasting their time.

The instrument for the best possible utilization of time is an *agenda*, a diary. Managers should begin organizing it *well in advance*. Far too many managers wait far too long to do this. It is worthwhile to define the most important basic values two or three years in advance. I am not talking about rigid planning here but a rough *structuring* of our schedule, even if our intentions cannot be kept. There will always be something that is unforeseen and urgent, and managers will always have to or want to change their priorities. This is fine or, to be more precise, it is an unavoidable part of the reality of a manager's life. However, this does not lessen the necessity of organizing our time with the help of an agenda.

Therefore, I particularly advocate a *long-term* perspective because most people who have a lot of demands on their time due to their job *cannot* change anything in the *short term* anyway. For the majority of managers, numerous appointments have already been made well in advance for the coming year. These are the inevitable results of existing professional duties. Therefore, if a manager wants to make a fundamental change, there will be a long response time in any case. However, if there is no attempt to make a *definite start* with the change at some point in time, *nothing* will change. People who cannot control their time and use the little time that they have in an effective manner will never be genuine managers. Improving our utilization of time begins with the question: *What should I stop doing?* This concept is mentioned in the chapter on objectives and just a reference to it will therefore suffice here.

Processing Inputs

The stream of things that land on a manager's desk, or increasingly on his computer these days, never stops. From what we can observe it keeps increasing. Everything that is submitted to managers, which they are confronted with every hour of every day, is what I generally call *input*, regardless of whether it is necessary or superfluous, interesting or uninteresting, important or unimportant, and irrespective of the format – whether it is on paper or in bits and bytes.

Therefore, every manager needs what I call an *input processing system* – some method of coping with this flood. Some managers always succeed in having a clear desk. On the desks of others, the majority, there reigns more or less complete chaos: organized and disorganized stacks, correspondence, reports, memos, files, written records, notes, newspapers and magazines, books, etc. Many not only have an overflowing desk but every other flat surface in the office is also full to overflowing, and quite a few even make use of the floor.

This should not happen! I would certainly not like to postulate some primitive correlation according to the motto *a clear desk = effectiveness*. This, of course, does not hold true. There are people whose surroundings are very orderly but even so they do not achieve anything, and there are others who, despite the chaos around them, are very effective. Whatever the case may be, we have to process the hourly, daily or weekly input. A good secretary, who understands how to create order out of chaos, at least temporarily, is of great help here. However, not everyone has a secretary and certainly not a good one.

A useful input processing system begins with a few simple questions: *What do I have to deal with myself? What do I have to want to get others to do? What can be done later or needs time and, therefore, has to be dealt with later?* These questions, or rather the answers to them, contain the skill of delegating and distinguishing between importance and urgency.

Working with Different Means of Communication: Telephone, Fax, E-Mail

The fact that communications *technology* has made great advances hardly needs to be mentioned. However, whether *communication* itself has become better is a matter of some doubt; in my opinion it has clearly *deteriorated*. The strongest indication for this is the fact that, in practically every company, these days even in the small ones, difficulties in communication top the list of problems. However, *technology* cannot be blamed for this because it is now available in even the smallest companies and organizations. Communication technology cannot, of course, replace communication. The technology is only an instrument and, as such, is only effective when it is used properly.

Amongst all the different means of communication the *telephone* still occupies the top position, even though it is far from being the optimum means for all purposes. Fax and e-mail have their own advantages for a few important things. And then there is still the good old letter...

Despite or perhaps precisely because of all the other electronic innovations, the telephone will remain important to most managers. As much as it is a blessing and it increases efficiency, people can also let themselves be terrorized by it, especially the mobile phone. Therefore, managers must make a conscious decision to use the telephone sensibly, otherwise they can become its slave.

Most people call *spontaneously*, either when the thought enters their heads or when they get the idea from some external factor, impulsively and instinctively. This is *usually wrong*. Even though everyone, as I always emphasize, should seek and define his own attitudes to the basic areas of his working methods and thus also the way he deals with the telephone, spontaneous and instinctive calling is not usually a good working method.

People are not only spontaneous and instinctive in using the telephone themselves. They also *let* others call them, or they pick up their telephone at all times, irrespective of whatever they are busy with at that moment. Even though I admit that there are positions and situations in which nothing else will do, in which we must simply learn to live with it, this is not a good working method in general either.

Following three very simple rules can usually bring about clear changes and improvements in our working methods. *Firstly*, before reaching for the phone, we should question whether there are *other* means of communication that will allow us to achieve the purpose better. *Secondly*, if the telephone is really the best means, then the telephone conversation should be *prepared*, otherwise it can easily degenerate into a time-consuming chat and mere gossip. *Thirdly*, we should not distribute the calls we make throughout the day, but, if possible, *set aside blocks* of time for them.

Even though the telephone will retain its importance and perhaps even gain in significance, its disadvantage is that it leads to a lack of precision and long-windedness.

This disadvantage can be eliminated almost completely through fax, e-mail, and letters. Even people who spend a long time on the telephone always express themselves concisely when they write, and we are usually more precise in the written form than in the verbal.

Preparing Documents

Managers not only need to read quite a lot, they also have to write a lot. This will not change to any great extent even in the future. Therefore, we require efficient techniques for preparing documents as an element of our working method. It should be noted here, too, that this is regardless of whether it is then printed on paper or is presented electronically.

Therefore, we need to think about the attitude we want to adopt towards *dictating machines* and *word processing*. There are still far too many managers who laboriously write their notes in longhand and then give these usually illegible hand-written notes to their secretaries to type, and only after several edited drafts is something useful finally produced. In view of the technical advances made in this field this Stone Age method can only be justified in very rare cases.

I am not in favor of higher-level managers in particular typing their correspondence *themselves*. It has been observed that even average secretaries are usually *much* quicker than the best "self-typers". A manager should acquire at least a sound mastery of dictating machines. The dictating machine *increases* productivity, and it does not require the physical presence of the manager in the office. Another variation is dictation that the secretary types in immediately at the computer keyboard. This is sometimes *more practical*, because it can be corrected directly on the screen. However, this is *much slower* than the dictating machine. The only thing that prevents many managers from using a dictating machine is the fact that some *practice* is required and dictating complex texts needs *preparation*. Even if voice-sensitive machines become available in the near future, there will be no change in these rules of effectiveness; on the contrary, they will become even more important.

Ongoing Issues and Appointments

Every manager would be well advised to set up a *perfect* system for keeping appointments and dealing with ongoing issues. How they do it or get it done, if they have a secretary, is of secondary importance. There are several good options. However, there can be no doubt that one of the *fastest* and above all, *surest* ways to lose respect, credibility, and effectiveness is carelessness in dealing with appointments and ongoing issues. A "watertight" *resubmission* system is required. Everything that passes across the manager's desk and has even the slightest importance must be stored in this system.

We must be able to say, with a clear conscience: *I do not forget anything. Follow-up* and *follow-through* must be organized. Deficiencies in this area are the most *important* cause of companies' *weakness in implementation*. All too often and with greater frequency these days the reasons for this weakness in implementation are thought to lie in some unknown aspects of *corporate culture,* and then attempts are made to remove this using appropriate measures. In reality, there are only two reasons for a weakness in implementation: *Firstly*, we take on too much that is, above all, far too diverse; and *secondly*, the follow-through is not organized.

The Memory System

A big problem for many, and for a rapidly growing number of managers in particular, is the question of how they can sensibly organize the great *variety* of *different types of issues* that they inevitably have to deal with. At a superficial level this has to do with *storage*. In reality, however, it is much more. It is the difference between *storage* and memory. Storage is *passive*, memory is *active*. The skill lies not in filing something but in *finding something again* when it is needed, often years after it has been filed away, and in exactly the context in which it is needed *then,* which is usually totally *different* from the one at the time it was filed.

It is only in very simple management positions that this problem does not occur. For *higher*-level managers and all *knowledge workers* the solution to this problem is crucial for their professionalism and effectiveness. The term "knowledge management" comes to mind in this context; however, I cannot help but notice that at present only a few people who write on this subject really understand the problem.

In this context the possibilities offered by modern electronics are referred to far too quickly and automatically. The computer does indeed have its advantages but it does not provide the solution as such. Above all, electronic equipment does not solve the *essential* part of the problem, and that is the *definition of contexts*. These must still be defined by a person, even when electronic equipment is being used.

Making Processes a Part of the Routine – in Praise of the Checklist

In the last few years "routine" has become a word that is seldom used with any pleasure. The focus was, and remains, on innovation, change and flexibility. *Routine* and *making something routine* seem to be *incompatible* with these and are therefore rejected. As important as innovation and flexibility are, and I do not wish to dispute their importance, routine has its own value. Therefore, we must be careful not to throw the baby out with the bath water. Routine is important for *productivity* and *functional certainty*. Both are important for every organization, even if the focus has to *temporarily* be placed on flexibility and innovation in many cases.

Routine, and thus efficiency and productivity, too, are not a problem where something has to be done very often such as on an hourly, daily, or weekly basis. Here the routine sets in *automatically*. The issue becomes problematic when something has to be done *repeatedly* but at *longer* time intervals. In such cases no routine can set in.

Usually these types of processes, even if they are *infrequent*, must be carried out with great *professionalism when* they do need to be carried out. Examples here are the typical two or three fairs or exhibitions, in which the company has to participate, the obligatory festivities once a year at Christmas, the general meeting once a year, the three to five board meetings, etc. None of these events occur often enough for their organization to become routine. However, each is important enough to be organized with the greatest of professionalism, that is, *as a matter of routine*.

The most important instrument for bringing such things under control is the *checklist*. Whether we like it or not, it is an invaluable aid for precisely this purpose. International air traffic would have collapsed long ago had it not been for checklists. They help in making all that can be made routine in a process into an effective routine.

Managers must think carefully about where and how they use their checklists. They may not need a great many nor even very complicated ones. However, these lists will help a manager to remain in command of even the types of situations described here, to manage these processes *confidently* and usually without *stress*. And above all, they will help the manager to cope with many, greater and more complex tasks than would be possible without the checklists. This can be crucial for entrepreneurial success and for the manager's career.

A System for Maintaining Relationships

What makes managers valuable? What are their assets? Strictly speaking, only two things: their *experience* and the *relationships* they build in the course of their lives.

As anyone with any experience will tell you, relationships need to be constantly maintained, cultivated, and nurtured. Relationships cannot simply be revived when we need them if they have been neglected for years. No one is so stupid that he would not notice this, especially not those who are valuable contacts. Perhaps they would do the favor but they certainly notice the intention and are most often a little put out.

A manager who is interested in professional and personal effectiveness, and especially those who wish to get to the top, must develop a system for maintaining relationships. Here again the same thing is applicable: How this is done is not as important as the fact that it is done. There are many ways of doing this.

We need not go as far as one chairman of a large bank who had an entire office, not just one secretary, meticulously documenting all his contacts. He gave instructions to record anything that had even the slightest importance. He knew the hobbies of the people who were important to him; he knew which wine they appreciated and the flowers their wives liked, he knew their interests. He never missed an opportunity to do people a favor, to be of service to them, or do something to make them happy. The continuous, intensive cultivation of his contacts was important to him, and they were very useful to him.

As mentioned earlier, there is no need to be quite so systematic. The fact that contacts are important and must be maintained is almost too obvious to be mentioned. I have always found that most managers agree when I speak to them about it but, unfortunately, they do not do it.

Use of the Secretary

So far I have mentioned the secretary only in passing. The eight basic areas of working methods must be regulated and brought under control methodically, irrespective of whether we have a secretary or not. But, of course, the availability or non-availability of the services of a good secretary makes an *enormous* difference to the type of solution or working method.

The demise of the secretary is prophesized with great regularity in view of the advances made in technology. I do not believe this will happen in the foreseeable future.

Certain categories of manager who previously had secretaries as a matter of course no longer have nor will have secretaries in the future; this is the reality. These are managers who never were managers in reality but *executives* disguised as managers. They should deal with their administration and correspondence themselves. Other categories of managers, the *genuine* managers, have to depend even more on their secretaries than ever before. In such cases there is often a completely misguided effort to save costs.

The *job profile* of the so-called secretary has changed to a great extent. She still does the typing, looks after the filing, and attends to visitors, etc., but that is not her main task. *Firstly*, she *manages* the manager. *Secondly*, if used properly – as an assistant – she *enhances* the performance, reach and influence of a manager. However, a manager must learn to use the secretary *properly*.

Far too many people hardly bother to do this. They simply take it for granted that it can be done. In my experience this is a *serious* mistake. In my 20 years of work as a management consultant, I have come across only a few managers who have mastered this by themselves. Almost all have had to learn. And I have not met many who are accomplished at it. Most do not exploit the vast potential of their secretaries, and this is completely incomprehensible when we think of the possible benefits and the costs of a good secretary.

The things that have been covered in this chapter should not be left to chance. As I said at the beginning, they are the basic methods for effective work. Effectiveness begins here or is lost.

I am only too aware that these are not wonderful and exciting topics; they have no academic credibility and are almost never systematically taught and learnt. Rather they are passed on as customs are, by word of mouth and by learning from other people. Usually managers gradually improve their competence in these fields by *trial and error*, by simply trying out all sorts of things. The objective can be achieved in this way, too, but it is a longer and *more laborious* route. That is why great potential remains unrealized in every organization. And the origins of many so-called conflicts, communication problems, difficulties in interpersonal relationships, etc. can be traced to deficiencies in working methods.

I suggest that readers who make personnel-related decisions, handling the selection of personnel and recruitment, should keep *professionalism in working methods* in mind along with other criteria. Of course people cannot be employed *on the basis of* their working methods, but those who do *not* have a working method, who play down and neglect these things should not be employed. Working methods are certainly not responsible for *success*. But a lack of or deficiencies in working methods are quite often the cause of *failure*.

Fifth Tool

The Budget and Budgeting

One of the most demanding tools for a manager is the budget. Competent application of the budget sometimes requires a special knowledge of business administration terms, facts, and interrelationships. Unfortunately, even some of those with a degree in business administration are incapable of preparing a budget. The experts in this field are naturally those that have a degree in financial management and accounting. However, practical mastery of the budget and budgeting system can hardly be expected from people with other focuses such as organization, personnel management, marketing, IT and others. Nor can it be expected from people with a technical or scientific education, or from lawyers.

Therefore, many managers are only too happy to hand over what could be their most important tool to others. This is certainly the case in companies. However, it is much worse in organizations outside the business world where people really have difficulties with this tool.

In some of these organizations, the employees seem to have a fundamentally unbalanced relationship with numbers which is detrimental to the effectiveness and the credibility of their organizations. Quite frequently, particularly in institutions in the field of culture as well as non-profit organizations, a certain form of arrogance can be observed; the employees are proud of not understanding anything about the mundane financial side of their activities. In these organizations a meaningful, transparent budget that guides activities, a system and order to the figures, and a well functioning accounting system are misunderstood as signs of an antisocial or materialistic nature that is hostile to art and culture.

The result of this absurd attitude, almost without exception, is that organizations in which the employees think in this way cannot fulfill their purpose in the long term, as noble as that purpose may be. Even when they receive substantial funds, they suffer from financial constraints; they lose their friends and benefactors because they lose credibility, and quite frequently they sink into a quagmire of scandals, because such an attitude is an open invitation to misuse, fraud and corruption. Neat budgets and a proper budgeting system are much *more important* for non-commercial organizations than they are for companies.

This chapter is based on the observations of Peter Drucker, among others. These observations have proved to be right time and again in my experience. Drucker is one of the very few, if not the only one, who recognized the budget as a *management* tool and not as an instrument of financial and personnel management (which it also is, of course).[50] Unfortunately, there is hardly any useful information on the budgets and budgeting systems in management literature. It is to be found almost exclusively in the specialist literature of finance and accounting or controlling. This may be one of the main reasons why so few understand anything about it, let alone are proficient in it. In the fields of marketing, research and development, personnel management and even in non-commercial sectors hardly anyone has a need to read specialist literature on financial management, or to consult accounting texts. Therefore, in the following chapters I will be restricting myself to those aspects that should be familiar to every manager. Specialists would, of course, want to go far beyond this.

One of the Best Instruments of Effective Management, if Properly Applied

The budget and budgeting process should *not* be considered exclusive instruments of the *finance department* and the *controllers*. They should be seen as one of the most important *tools* of the manager, that is, of *every* manager.

The budget must be established and used as a *tool* particularly by those managers who have to manage *units responsible for results*, irrespective of what their designation may be: profit centers, cost centers, market centers, divisions, areas of activity, subsidiaries, etc. There are a number of reasons for this.

---

50 Peter F. Drucker, *Management*, New York 1974, fifth edition, London 1994, page 412 and following pages.

1. The budget is the best tool for *experienced* managers, because they can organize all their planning and work "around" it. It is the best tool for *inexperienced* managers, or managers who have assumed charge of a *new post*, to get to know the company and their area of responsibility.

   There is no better way for people to familiarize themselves with the nature of a business and its interrelationships and "legalities" and to get to know about them in depth than by *preparing the budget* for the business concerned *from scratch*. Unfortunately, this method is completely ignored in most companies when new employees are being shown the ropes. The reasons for this are not clear to me. As important as all the other things that trainees learn in their training may be, it is only when they prepare a budget, and their budget proposal is sent back for revision two or three times (because they are not usually right in the beginning) that we can count on them having gained some real understanding in this area.

2. It is the best instrument for *productive deployment* of *key resources*, particularly *people*; the budget is basically the only tool to make resources productive *at all*.

3. It is the best tool for *planning in advance* the *coordination* of all the activities for a particular area and the company as a whole. If the interaction of the parts with the greater whole is flawed, it is often interpreted as an *organizational problem*, and people start to reorganize. *In reality*, however, there is seldom an organizational problem. It is better and simpler to use the budget as a means of coordination than to change an entire organization.

4. The budget is the best instrument for *integrating the staff* of one area of activity, including its manager, into the organization. In general, integration is often a topic of discussion; it is seen as a corporate culture issue. The employees should identify with the company, it should be one "big family" etc.; however, so far only a few companies have thought of using the budget and budgeting as a means of integration.

5. The budget is the only and also the best tool for knowing how and when plans need to be *revised*, what discrepancies can be corrected and, more importantly, the way in which the *circumstances* and *assumptions* on which the budget was based have changed.

6. Finally, and this is rarely understood by psychologists, the budget provides an important foundation for effective and good communication. There is little sense in holding courses on communication when the *sub-*

ject matter of communication is not clear. However, the budget, its implications and consequences are certainly important enough to be the subject matter of communication. *This* is what employees should know about, talk about, and it should be the focus of their work.

These points should be reason enough to take the budget and its preparation seriously and not leave it to the controllers alone. Nothing is taken away from the controllers, this hardly needs to be mentioned, so there is still a lot for them to do. In actual fact, this enhances their work. The more actively the managers handle the budget, the better their work is understood, and it is that much more respected.

From Data to Information

There is no lack of *data* in organizations these days. Rather, we have too much of it. *Information*, on the other hand, is always in short supply, and it cannot be assumed with any certainty that all managers will know how to derive information from data. Though the budget alone cannot solve this problem, it is one of several ways of getting closer to a solution.

The facts explained below should actually be self-explanatory. However, experience has repeatedly shown that explanations are required. The following information relates to the preparation, implementation, and control of the budget.

Information is always Based on Differences

Gregory Bateson[51] defines information as related to the element of difference. He says: "Information is a difference that makes a difference". It is this difference that is significant and has meaning.

Therefore, a budget must always show *comparisons* and *differences* in its most important items, and this should not only be the case at the stage of budgetary control but at the actual preparation stage. What is to be compared with what depends on the specific case and must be de-

---

51 Gregory Bateson, *Steps to an Ecology of Mind*, New York 1972, passim.

fined in relation to this. Essentially, it is always *comparisons with previous periods*, with other comparable *parts of the company*, with *results*, with *benchmarks* and *other budget items* that are important, particularly when *structural* changes are made during the process of budgeting (e.g. increase in external borrowing and simultaneous reduction of internal funding, or the use of high-quality raw material instead of inferior material).

Differences Should Be Explained, Preferably in Writing

Usually it is not simply a case of *more* consumption or expenditure, but something being used in *a different* way. The range of goods or the combination of materials has changed; qualities and prices, batch sizes and batches, the customers' order structure and ordering pattern have changed; a non-profit organization's projects have changed. This must be identified and explained. Figures and numbers are not objective variables, even though they seem to be, and are frequently accepted as such. They *require interpretation*, and there is usually wide scope for interpretation. Therefore, explanations and comments are important.

Positive Deviations Are to Be Analyzed as much as the Negative

The fact that negative deviations are investigated in detail is obvious. As a result of total concentration on these, the *positive* deviations are usually forgotten. *Where have we worked better than expected and budgeted – and why?* This is a question that is asked far too seldom. *Positive deviations* are the first and usually very reliable signs that there exists a unique *opportunity* or a *strength* that had not previously been noticed. These things remain undiscovered if a special effort is not made in this regard. Therefore, it should be demanded of the controllers that they specially identify not just the negative deviations but also the positive ones in preparation for the meetings. Wherever positive deviations are discovered, it is usually worthwhile increasing the expenditure and effort because a more than proportional result can usually be anticipated. The budget is the tool for controlling this allocation process, as it is called in the business world.

Every Budget Must Contain Structural Information

This is meant in relation to the *percentages* of the budget items in relation to one another as well as in relation to time and changes. The important items should be expressed as *index numbers*, and the base of each should be clearly specified.

In order to provide the correct picture, a comparison with previous periods is not enough. The best way to compare time is with the help of *moving averages* over a period of 36 or 48 months, for example. Moving averages and the trends that can be derived from them provide the essential information for analyzing those trends and for forecasting. These moving averages distil a *pattern* from the data, and these patterns provide the information, as we know from the research done in perceptive psychology and brain physiology.

Moving averages are, of course, only one of several options for finding patterns. There are others whose application, however, occasionally requires specialist knowledge.

Budgeting Ratios

Apart from the absolute budget items (such as revenues and expenditures), we should also include a few *selected ratios*.[52]

Even though this depends to a great extent on the specific case – a small company certainly differs from a large one, and a manufacturing company is considerably different from a service company – there are a few ratios that must be considered in every case. These ratios are primarily related to those areas that I referred to as standard target fields in section III in the discussion on objectives, and which I would like to mention again here.

- *Market position* and everything related to it: customer benefits, quality, market share, etc.;
- *Innovation performance*: time to market, success rate, milestones;
- *Productivity*: total factor productivity and its individual components such as the productivity of money, physical resources, work, time and knowledge;

---

52 See Hans Siegwart, *Kennzahlen für die Unternehmungsführung*, Bern/Stuttgart/ Vienna, fifth edition 1998.

- *Human resources*: fluctuations, absentee figures, etc.;
- *Liquidity* and *cash flow;*
- *Profitability* beginning with the rate of return on capital before interest and taxes, which can then be differentiated, refined and arranged.

Extended ratio systems can be developed for all of these areas, the details of which are the territory of specialists. However, every manager should know the basics.

Special Tips

The Budget Is a "to-do" Tool

The basis of and the key to an effective budget is always the question: *What results do we want to achieve in our important fields of activity?* A budget should not be an extrapolation of the past. Where the past is simply extrapolated, the enterprise gets into difficulties sooner or later. The budget is and must be a *declaration of intent.*

The budget is a means of making everything crystal clear, a means in which everything is brought together and summarized: long-term plans and intentions, strategy, creativity and innovation, clearing out extraneous things from the company, re-allocation of resources, etc. And everything must be guided by the question: *What needs to be done now, i.e. in the coming period, to implement these intentions?*

Money Variables Are a "Shorthand" for Quantitative Variables

A budget is usually formulated in *monetary* terms. It is expressed in *money.* This creates widespread misconceptions.

Monetary variables should be seen only as a type of *"shorthand"* for *real* variables, for the *quantitative* variables. Thus, a correction of monetary variables does not result in any change, if there is no quantitative change.

Cost Control Is a Consequence, not the Purpose of the Budget

A good budget requires thorough, careful and conscientious *consideration* of the expected and desired results, and the means and measures necessitated by them.

If the budget is viewed *only* as an instrument of cost *control*, it is unlikely to be effective. Most employees will find it irrelevant and bureaucratic, and it will degenerate into a straitjacket. Its more important functions are the consideration of the *origin* of costs, the *cause* of costs and the *breakdown* of expenditure and, as already mentioned, control of the utilization of resources and thus an organization's priorities.

Zero-Based Budgeting – Selective

In order to eliminate naïve and dangerous extrapolation and force a conscientious consideration of all activities, it is necessary from time to time to prepare the budget for an area of activity *from scratch*, free from all previous constraints, habits, and conditions.

This is time-consuming and difficult, but very rewarding. Therefore, zero-based budgeting should always be done *selectively*, not for *all* activities every year, but for *every* activity at longer time intervals. Above all, the really critical activities that are crucial for success should be repeatedly budgeted in this way.

Life Cycle Budgeting – Breaking Free from the Straitjacket of the Calendar or Financial Year

A budget usually covers a period of twelve months, and this is necessary and right in principle. However, *not all* operations can be compressed into twelve-month periods. If an attempt is made to do so, there is a risk of severing the natural and logical interrelationships. A *rolling* budget over several periods can be an improvement on a fixed twelve-month period, but no matter how it is done, *artificial* and largely *arbitrary* demarcations of periods will have to be made in every case.

The main reason for massive cost overruns is not simply a lack of discipline, gross extravagance, a lack of control or carelessness; it is *not taking the follow-up costs* of a project *into consideration*. This is why people suddenly find themselves in a quagmire of constraints. When we decide on something, we must later accept the consequences. This is one of the main reasons that the approval of budgets by supervisory and executive boards is, essentially, frequently irrelevant. We no longer have a *say* in the matter, but are compelled to place the seal of approval on all subsequent measures.

The best example of *incorrect* budgeting is the former practice of the US Ministry of Defense, which is typical of all areas of governmental administration and also many other organizations. For the procurement of a new weapons system only the costs of the first year were included in the budget. However, by doing so, only the costs of the *start-up* were recorded, and no one was clear about the follow-up costs. It was only under McNamara[53] that life cycle budgeting was introduced. Today, the *total costs of the life cycle* of a weapons system are budgeted, including maintenance and service, spare parts, training, operating personnel, and scrapping the system.[54]

Of course, mistakes can be made in this because the budget must be based on many assumptions. However, it forces us to deliberate in a different and more practical way on all the related aspects than does budgeting for only the next twelve months in each case.

In general, we should always be guided by the following premise: The really substantial costs are not caused by things that *fail*, but by those that are *successful*. They create high follow-up costs. Therefore, we must be particularly prepared for the *follow-up costs of successes*. Ruin can indeed be brought about by failures. However, the really tragic cases are those of companies that experience success, but cannot afford the *costs of this success*.

Two Budgets Are Required – an Operating Budget and an Innovation Budget

Closely related to the above, it has been found time and again that *two different* budgets are actually required. These should serve two totally dif-

---

53 See Deborah Shapley, *Promise and Power. The Life and Times of Robert McNamara*, Boston 1993.
54 See also Hans Siegwart, *Kennzahlen für die Unternehmungsführung*, Bern/Stuttgart/Vienna, fifth edition 1998.

ferent purposes and differ accordingly in the degree of difficulty of preparing them.

a) The *first*, standard budget is the *operating budget*. This budget covers the *existing, current* business, the things that are known and are *familiar*. In this case, though we should not simply extrapolate, the past and present figures are good and at least partly reliable reference points. The key question for this budget is: *What are the minimum resources required to continue to run the business successfully?* In this case the entire classical way of thinking in business administration is appropriate and right.

b) The *second* budget, which is unfortunately only prepared in very progressive companies, is the *opportunities budget*, the budget for new things, the *innovations*.

In this case there can be no focus on figures based on experience, because there is no experience of the new. As this budget is also burdened with many major uncertainties, it should not be combined with the other budget. *Firstly*, it would weaken the operating budget, and *secondly*, the uncertain aspects of the opportunities would be *obscured*.

Two questions must be asked in the opportunities budget. *Firstly, are we using resources for the right opportunity, chance, innovation? Secondly, if so, what are the maximum resources the opportunity requires for us to really seize it and ensure a resounding success?*

"*Too little, too late and split between too many different sectors*" is the main reason for the failure of so many well-meaning and in essence totally relevant public programs, and the same is also applicable to programs in the business world.

The key to the success of new projects is, in a figurative sense, the maxim of General Guderian of the German Tank Corps in the Second World War: "*Don't do it by half measures*", that is to say total concentration on a *few* things and implementation of those things with *total* commitment.

Critical Items Budget

Careful and conscientious budgeting will always face one problem: the sheer number of different items that have to be taken into account and considered. Therefore, it is worthwhile asking the following question: *What are the 10 to 20 percent really important items? Which budget items, when we really have them under control, will exert an influence on the others?*

In a normal company it makes little sense to budget the postal or telephone charges in detail. In a mail-order business, however, it is one of the important budget items in terms of amount as well as of use. The utilization of space is important in only a few companies. However, it is a crucial item for a supermarket chain.

The critical items budget was introduced in 1920 at General Motors under the management of Alfred Sloan, and it was perfected in the Pentagon in the sixties. It was found that out of the millions of budget items only a few hundred were really important.

Incidentally, this is also the foundation of the sensible application of management by exceptions, which is hardly heard of these days, though this does not mean that it is any less useful.

Budgeting Names

However the budget is prepared in the end, and whatever form it may finally take, only *people*, and this means *individuals*, can actually do the work. Despite all the lip service paid to people being the most important resource, this fact is usually ignored. The amount of money to be spent on the people, the staff *costs*, are budgeted, but the staff *performance* is not.

In the final analysis there is only *one* resource that can produce a *performance* and that is people. As has been the case throughout this book, what is meant here is not people in general but *individuals*.

A budget is not effective if a name is not attached to it, and to each budget item, if possible. This is the *name* of the *person responsible. Whose job is it, what are the results expected, and what is his responsibility?* This is the key question here.

The most important instrument for this is the assignment, which I have covered in this section. Therefore, what should be allocated using the budget are not primarily costs but the *strengths of individuals*. It is the only way to ensure that things are also *done,* and above all, that they are done *well.*

Indispensable: the Worst Case Budget

Finally, I can do no more than strongly recommend that a *worst case budget* also be prepared *always and under all circumstances*.

There are three reasons for this.

a) *Firstly*, nothing is certain in business; there will always be surprises, and no prognosis is truly reliable. Countless cases of insolvency could have been avoided had people thought about the worst case scenario in enough time and made all the necessary provisions for such an occurrence.

   We should not let ourselves be persuaded by anyone that this is pessimism and, therefore, is misplaced in a company. This is nothing more than conscientious management and the essence of genuine leadership. *Leadership is calmness under stress.* However, only people who have a lot of experience with stress-related situations can remain calm, people who can at least imagine the situation, because they have given the issue thorough consideration and have made all the necessary provisions.

b) The *second* reason for this is that only by preparing a worst case budget is it possible to *ascertain* the areas and ways in which the company is flexible, where it can react if it has to. There is a great deal of talk about flexibility, and rightly so. But only a few people make the effort to properly identify the areas where flexibility is possible, and how it can be incorporated into the company, if necessary. This requires *consideration* of all business activities. The best means to do this is the worst case budget.

   What is to be viewed as the worst case differs from case to case. One possible procedure is simple and rough but very effective. *How would our company be affected, if we had to make do with 30 percent less sales?* This is occasionally considered to be very far-fetched. How could something like that be possible? In the nineties many people had to learn that this was possible, whether it was as a result of the state of the economy or advances made in technical and scientific fields.

c) The *third* reason for the worst case budget is that it is the best method of *thoroughly* reviewing the business and its internal workings. This is understood far better *after* such an exercise than it was *before*.

Clear Documentation

In most companies and their constituent areas the complete budget will ultimately consist of *one* or *a few* pages. This is fine, but only if the underlying assumptions, considerations, and terms are *clearly* and *precisely documented*. Otherwise, meaningful budgetary control is simply not possible. If these things are not documented, the things people had in mind while preparing the budget are forgotten within a few weeks. The consequence of this is that the budget is interpreted in vastly different ways, and blame is shifted and excuses are made; clarity of thought no longer dominates but rhetorical brilliance does, and those who show the greatest imagination in inventing excuses emerge victorious.

The company and its culture soon adopt a *defensive attitude*; everyone knows exactly what will *not* work and *why*. There will be an atmosphere of bitterness, cynicism, and lethargy; people feel they have not been treated correctly. The standard response is big corporate culture projects; people babble pompously about "learning organizations", seeking the cure in all manners of charlatanism and send people on the psychological trip.

Frequently, though not always, the problem can be solved much more simply and in a better way: People have only failed to use craftsmanlike professionalism, thoroughness, and prudence in the budgeting process. They have failed to *manage effectively*.

Sixth Tool

Performance Appraisal

Many managers seem to have trouble using the tool of performance appraisal. They reject it and find it useless. They go through the periodical (usually annual) ritual, because it is demanded of them. But they do not support it, and therefore, they dispose of this irksome duty with a minimum of time and thought. Even a good amount of well-meaning training is of little help here.

If we get to the root of the matter, however, it is not the performance appraisal as such that managers reject but the performance appraisal *systems*; it is the accursed bureaucracy that is invented and developed by appraisal specialists and personnel experts and permitted by top managers. As soon as we differentiate between performance as such and the application of tedious procedures, it is usually found that a majority of managers consider performance appraisal to be important. Where is the problem?

The usual systems are the exact *opposite* of what managers require for their questions on performance and those giving the performance. This becomes apparent as soon as we find out how performance appraisal systems were developed. They were essentially developed in clinical psychology, by doctors. What interests a doctor, and, therefore, what is the objective of their questions? Their objective is to discover a person's illness, whatever is troubling them, their *weaknesses* and deficiencies. The objective of medical treatment is to cure the patient. Therefore, from the beginning, the relationship between the doctor and the patient is geared towards a *termination*, an end. For me the doctor's job is to establish as soon as possible what is wrong with me, and heal me just as quickly. He is someone whom I do not, hopefully, have to meet ever again, at least not in his capacity as a doctor, because he has cured me completely.

However, the situation for managers is the exact *opposite*. The manager must pay attention to a person's *strengths,* and the manager's relationship with his subordinates must be designed for *permanence* and *continuity*. I do not need to justify why attention should be focused on strengths after all that I have already said on the subject. That the relationship is to be designed for continuity is obvious. Nothing could be simpler than to dissect somebody so completely in a performance review that he can no longer look me in the eye and definitely cannot work with me ever again. Anyone can do that. But this does not help anyone; not the person being assessed, nor the supervisor, nor the company.

Therefore, it is easy to see that the adoption of appraisal systems from the clinical field that are based on a doctor's questions is completely inappropriate and damaging in management.

No Standard Criteria

The formulation of questions in the clinical setting primarily results in the application of standard assessment criteria. Once a disease is known and researched, symptoms of diseases can be described by a set of criteria that are equally applicable in all cases. Measles, influenza, scarlet fever, etc. occur in people in remarkably the same way. That is why the processing of a list of symptoms, the description of the symptoms with the greatest possible precision, and, if possible, their quantification represents a great advance in medicine. In a further development the quantitative manifestations of each criterion are then determined, and if the values are within the normal range the person is healthy, otherwise he is ill. Basically, every medical test today is designed according to the same pattern, as can be seen from the simple example of a blood test.

As useful as this procedure is for medicine, and perhaps also for other areas, it is useless, even destructive in management. As I have emphasized time and again in this book, barring certain exceptions that I will discuss, what matters in management is *not* the aspects that can be standardized but the particular features of a certain *task* and the characteristics of the *individual*.

Typical lists of standard requirements include characteristics and abilities such as: interaction with people, ability to handle stress, decision-making ability, creativity, innovativeness, and team spirit. These or similar criteria can be found in almost every organization, and for reasons that I have explained in section I, they culminate in the description of an ideal type of manager. In the best of cases these lists are attempts to answer the question on the abilities required from managers *in general, by and large,* or *typically*. Even in this form they are unusable and misleading.

The application of these lists in performance appraisal leads to an absurd situation that is instinctively rejected by managers with common sense, and rightly so. Situations arise in which innovativeness has to be assessed where it is not necessary, but on the contrary, could possibly be damaging; in which they also have to comment on someone's "decision-making ability", when the person has never or seldom made decisions, let alone important decisions. Why should we assess "interaction with people" if the job has little to do with people – in which case this is not a crucial factor in the person's successful performance ?

Now I am not, of course, against requirements as such. I am only against those that, regardless of whether it is intentional, depict an ideal type, an all-around genius.

Basically, the pitfalls of requirement profiles can be easily avoided. All we have to do is be specific instead of being abstract. The correct question is not: *What requirements should managers meet in general?*, but: *What is required for this very special, specific position in this specific company and in this specific situation?*

Perhaps a few elements can be generalized to the extent that they could be important in a greater number of situations. In sports, for example, conditioning and strength is always important. But this is the limit of generalization and commonality. What type of conditioning and what type of strength are being referred to here? The hundred-meter sprint requires a different type of conditioning from that of the marathon, and the training for both these disciplines is so totally different that they are mutually exclusive. The strength of a weight lifter is different from that of a high jumper.

It is possible to state quite precisely the requirements to be met and thus the training required for performance in each individual discipline. However, when everything is combined, added up and generalized, all of it becomes useless again.

Of course, a ski racer must be able to ski. But taken by itself this means nothing. Only when we are faced with the question of whether we are dealing with a downhill racer or a slalom expert, do we attain a useful degree of specification. However, it is really only useful in the particular individual case. Thus, it is certainly possible that a downhill racer can compensate for his or her lower body weight as compared to his or her competitors through appropriate training in racing techniques. At this level things become useful and practical.

Thus, we can to some extent determine the requirements for the hundred-meter runner, the high jumper, and the discus thrower. However, this is hardly possible for an athlete in general or for a manager. Even if it were, it would be so general and vague that we could do nothing with it. People may say, what about the decathlete? There are good decathletes, but they are as rare as "genius" managers.

No Standard Profile

The use of standard criteria practically necessitates the designing of *standard profiles*, which generally fall within the neutral area, within the *average range*.

The reasons for this are clear. *Firstly*, the manager does not want to harm the subordinate. Performance appraisal is rendered particularly difficult in view of the fact that it always has an effect on income in one way or another. If things that are irrelevant to the subordinate are to be assessed, the subordinate should not have to suffer for it. *Secondly*, a manager will not want to create any difficulties, either with the person appraised or his own manager to whom he will have to submit the appraisal. If a manager assesses a person as *bad* in some way, he has to justify this and, what is more, he will also face problems with the person concerned. If a manager assesses the subordinate as *good*, he has to be prepared for wage demands and requests for promotion by the subordinate. The manager must not only justify the subordinate's good appraisal to his own boss, but also possibly explain why the department is not performing better when it has *such* good people in it. Therefore, whatever managers do, performance reviews can create difficulties. And it is precisely this that they want to avoid, with a non-committal, neutral appraisal.

Despite all that has been spent on setting up performance appraisal systems and associated training, the system produces something that *no one* wanted, namely *meaningless* appraisals, and so we learn that we "have a lot average people in our organization". This insight could have been gained in a much cheaper and simpler way.

A Better Method

What is really required? Certainly not information on the degree to which mediocrity exists. It is more important to find out the *particular strengths of the individuals* in the organization. As has already been mentioned in the topic on developing people, strengths can be recognized most reliably by studying a person's *previous* performance. This is the true purpose of performance appraisal. It can and should be the basis for many things, such as promotion decisions. Once the managers in an organization understand this, and they are allowed to identify this precisely, all resistance to and rejection of performance appraisal usually vanishes, because this knowledge is extremely relevant to managers. Therefore, the tool of performance appraisal must be designed accordingly.

The best instrument for this is literally a blank sheet of paper, without any knick-knacks, aids, tips, instructions, small print, and footnotes on which the manager has to write down an assessment of the performance and the person giving it. The empty page forces the manager to *think* about the person being assessed, whereas ticking off criteria in a list and filling in a profile form hinder this, in fact they lead to mechanical superficiality.

In the practical application of this procedure managers will initially often have to account for how little they know about the people being assessed; how little they have been in contact with these people throughout the year, even though they are these people's supervisor; how superficial their contact has been and that they know virtually nothing about the people "behind" these human resources.

The outcome of a performance appraisal must comprise several things. *Firstly*, the performance *as such* must be assessed independent of the person. Performance cannot exist in a vacuum; it is only relative to previously fixed objectives, otherwise we are just talking about work; it must be possible to refer to the objectives at this stage, as they have been discussed in section III.

Secondly, we should know the person's individual, specific strengths and weaknesses. At the risk of repeating myself, I emphasize, *individual* and *specific*. *What can this person do or not do particularly well? How have I reached this conclusion and how do I justify this? Are there latent strengths that should be examined in more detail? And how should the tasks be structured to strengthen or refute these suppositions?* These are the types of questions that must be conscientiously asked and answered.

Here, lists and profiles are of little help, because they conceal the essential things instead of leading to them. It is only by using this procedure that performance appraisal can be made a tool.

Apart from the fact that the purpose and objective of performance appraisal must be clearly understood, proper judgment is required for the appraisal of performance and those giving it. It is exactly this that people want to supplant by formalizing performance appraisal, and it is precisely this that renders performance appraisal "anemic" and reduces it to a formal ritual.

Judgment can be trained and sharpened. I have already referred to this in the chapter on supervision. It cannot be expected to be highly developed in young people. Judgments require experience, as I have explained in depth.

Judgment can be developed and taught. This applies to the appraisal of people as well as the assessment of other areas. To a certain extent we can learn to judge music or painting; we can learn to assess the risk of avalanches in the mountains and storms at sea, and, similarly, doctors can improve their judgment when it comes to diagnosis.

It has become fashionable to dispute this fact both explicitly and implicitly; attempts to develop systems and procedures that seek to replace judgment with pseudo-quantification amount to nothing else but this. There are various reasons for this. These include an incorrect understanding of science or political ideology, a misunderstanding of humanity coupled with well-meaning intentions, and sheer stupidity. As diverse as the reasons may be, the result is always the same: apparent precision, apparent objectivity, irrelevance of content, and the replacement of responsibility with formal rituals.

Where Is Standardization, Allied to Caution, Appropriate?

Standardization is acceptable and appropriate when there are a large number of similar cases, when essentially the same task is to be carried out by several or many people, such as in a sales force in the insurance industry, or sales staff in similar supermarket or department stores, etc. However, these are not managers. Examples in the field of management are branch office managers in a supermarket chain for the same type of branches, or branch managers in banks and other similar institutions.

It is here that standard assessment logic, with its standardized lists of requirements, is most likely to be useful. However, I have my reservations, even in these cases. Time and again, it is found that no two people carry out their tasks in the *same* way. This is precisely what is astonishing and important, and it is always overlooked. Even for tasks that are the same or similar to a great extent, people perform and get results in different ways, and as soon as we make the application of their individual methods difficult by making them use the same assessment criteria, their performance *deteriorates*, because their use of their personal strengths is restricted. *Firstly*, this is harmful for the company, and *secondly*, it is inhuman. There is absolutely no reason for this type of procedure.

The wide variety of behavior that produces results can be observed particularly well among *successful* salespersons, regardless of the industry. Some achieve their results by using their expert knowledge, others use charm and humor, yet others are particularly good at maintaining their long-term contacts; then there is a fourth category of salespersons for whom the root of their success is not clear. Though this can be particularly well *observed* in sales, it is *valid* for all job-related and management tasks.

How Do the Experts Do It?

There are people who, to all appearances, have an excellent understanding of people, because of their success in their personnel-related decisions. The assumption is that these people have a special "perspective" or a special flair for people.

However, if we get to the root of the matter as much as we can, something totally different emerges. These people approach the appraisal of people with whom they work with *particular care*. The aid that they use is not a "highly developed" appraisal system, but a "little black book" in which they record everything that they notice and consider worth noting. They do not do this *once* a year just before the performance appraisal but *continuously*, every time something catches their attention.

If we investigate further, we find that they repeatedly ask themselves, with great care and conscientiousness, the question of what it is that *really* matters in a particular task. They have a clear understanding of what I have called assignment. They know that, in order to find the right placement for someone what matters is a person's strengths; their weaknesses need be known only in so far as they provide information on where a person should not be deployed. These managers are not interested in generalizations, but in the individuality of the specific people.

The content of their notes is, among other things, what are known as "critical incidents". Considered in isolation, these are small, meaningless incidents that escape the attention of inexperienced people and remain unnoticed; however, in context and for experienced people, they are critical incidents that provide information on what a person is really like. How do people behave when they think they are unobserved; when they have had one drink too many; towards their staff and colleagues, particularly women, if the person is a man, on a company outing; how do they react to double entendres; and how do they behave in situations in which there is an opportunity to display truth, honesty, decency, openness, and integrity?

I am indebted to my colleague at the University of Economics in Vienna, the industrial psychologist Linda Pelzman[55], for telling me about an old rule that was used by Hungarian businessmen to assess potential business acquaintances. Firstly, you should see him when he is drunk – then he will not hold back the truth. Secondly, you should share an inheritance with him – there he will not hold back his greed. Thirdly, you should be imprisoned with him – then you will know whether he loses his head and lets other people down. In normal circumstances we would rarely get the opportunity to experience all these situations, but the rule illustrates what is meant.

Proven judges of human nature are not knowledgeable about people due to an ability to see something "at a glance"; they do not have a special ability to empathize nor an ability to assess through some secret antennae a person's charisma (whatever that may be) and personality (also a very ambiguous term), as is repeatedly asserted in the relevant pseudo-scientific, senseless, and even naïve literature. What they do have is acute powers of observation, learnt over many years and continuously sharpened and analyzed.

---

55 The methodical use of critical incidents is described in detail by Pelzman in her essay "Was nicht im Personalakt stehen darf. Critical Incidents: Informationsquelle für verborgene Risiken", [What cannot be in the personnel file. Critical incidents: source of information for hidden risks] St. Gallen 1999.

And what about Those Who Do not Want to Be Assessed?

No discussion on performance appraisal is complete without the question of whether appraisal is legitimate in the first place and what sort of attitude is to be adopted towards the school of thought that is fundamentally opposed to the appraisal of performance?

There are, of course, people who do *not* want to be assessed. How are they to be dealt with? In my opinion the answer is very simple, even though it is sometimes not easily accepted, or may even be totally disregarded. *All true performers want to know where they stand.* Anyone who does not want to know has a reason for this, and it is usually a reason that no organization will find positive or tolerable. Apart from temporary ignorance that can be addressed through clarification, the only reason that appears repeatedly is *poor performance.* This can involve resistance to performance or even pronounced hostility to performance based partly on arguments that appear to be scientifically presented, but are often outrageous ideology. Resistance to performance appraisal can also be due to incompetence and even sheer laziness.

Good people want to know how they stand performance-wise, whether their performance is improving or deteriorating. This is why athletes train and musicians and all other artists practice. It is perhaps *understandable* that people with poor performance will be reluctant to face reality and would rather not know anything about it, but this is unacceptable in an organization. Whatever people think in private is their personal affair.

One of the causes of the resistance to performance appraisal that is apparently justified scientifically is the dispute about awarding grades at school. I do not want to infringe on what is a specialist's territory. However, one thing is clear. People who cannot get used to the facts that success and failure are two sides of the same coin, that achieving and failing to achieve objectives are a part of life, and that there are ways to improve performance, will always face difficulties in society and in their organizations. Whether they can be best helped to gain these experiences through grades or in some other way is a subject for experts. At any rate, the difference between performance and non-performance, between good, better, and poor performance should be so clearly identified and expressed that it cannot be misunderstood. Unmistakable failure should also be experienced. The principle of positive thinking covered in section II or that of focusing on strengths is not to be interpreted to mean that poor performance is no longer possible, because it has been explained away, glossed over, and eliminated using rhetoric. This would have a crippling effect on people and their performance capabilities.

The right people want to know where they stand; and only such people can be used in organizations. I think I also voiced the opinion that most children and students want to perform. They are not perhaps, as was once claimed by teachers in a discussion on awarding grades, "greedy" for *grades* but many of them are certainly "greedy" for *achievement*, the achievement that can be recognized. Doing without performance appraisal and excessive egalitarianism are, irrespective of the reasons, the opposite of humanity and solidarity because this robs people of the opportunity to become effective and successful.

Systematic Waste Disposal

Organisms have systems that dispose of their waste – kidneys, intestines, skin, etc. Each individual cell has a mechanism for waste disposal. Without systematic, continuous detoxification, survival is impossible.[56]

Largely Unknown, but Important

Something analogous is applicable in and to organizations. Therefore, I suggest making the concept of systematic waste disposal the seventh tool. A *process of eliminating everything that is old, passed down, and superfluous* should be set up in every institution. We could say: *Get rid of the rubbish!*

The concept[57] can easily be developed into a method and makes the crucial difference between unwieldy and lean, inefficient and efficient, slow and fast, lazy and dynamic organizations.

As mentioned in other parts of this book, people and organizations are inclined to do too much, too much that is different, and too much that is useless. We carry too much dead weight around. People, and in the figurative sense also organizations, are "creatures of habit" – "hamsters". They lug everything around and collect it out of sheer habit, because they have not developed an "organ" that systematically frees them from waste and toxins.

---

56 Manfred Reitz, "Zelluläre Müllabfuhr", *Pharm. Ind.* 59, No. 3 (1997) page 70 and following page.

57 The author of this idea, as with so many others that are of real use in management, outlasting all fads, is Peter Drucker.

From the Concept to the Method

The method is as simple as the idea itself. It consists of regularly asking the question: *Of all that we are doing today, what would we not start to do if we were not already doing it?*

This question may be awkwardly formulated but it is *extremely effective*. It should be noted that the question is not: *What should we not have started with back then?* Though this question sounds similar, asking it, however, is futile. It deals with the *past*, whereas the first question is directed towards the *future*. It may be interesting to think about the past but it is, in this context at least, of little use. *What would we not start if we were not already in the middle of it? What, therefore, should we eliminate? What should we simply stop and put an end to?* These are the questions that will lead to action for a different and better future.

The importance of this method can be most clearly illustrated when contrasted with the *usual* behavior of people and organizations. Apart from everything that is already being done, something *new* is added every year, because of the desire to be modern, to be innovative, because we do not want to miss anything, etc. However, this is the surest way to "suffocate in our own rubbish". Dynamic organizations deliberately and systematically turn this behavior around and ask the question: *What should we get rid of? What should we stop doing?*

According to reports, the systematic and resolute application of this question was what transformed General Electric from an unwieldy, sluggish and bureaucratic colossus into one of the best managed, most dynamic and profitable companies in the world.[58] At the center of the turnaround that General Electric experienced in the eighties was the decision made at the start of that decade to abandon those sectors in which the company was not at least second in the market. Some of the divisions could be eliminated with the stroke of a pen while, in the case of others it took more than ten years before these divisions could be cast off, because delivery commitments and warranty obligations had to be met, spare parts had to last, and loyal customers could not be left in the lurch. However, even though it took

---

58 According to what is known, the resolute application began with Jack Welch, who assumed charge of General Electric at that time. This achievement by Welch should be rated higher than the achievement for which he became famous ten years later, maximizing shareholder value.

a long time to achieve this objective in each division, if the decision had not been made in the early eighties, the company would still be active in those profit-draining areas today with all the associated consequences and burdens on the organization and above all, its earning power.

Anything that is possible for large companies should be that much easier for small and medium-sized companies to accomplish, if they apply this method in a systematic and well thought out way.

The question: *What would we no longer start with...* should be asked approximately every three years with regard to products, markets, customers, and technologies. And it should be asked for everything else that is done in an organization *once a year*: for all administrative procedures, computer systems and programs, forms in use, lists compiled, reports prepared, and meetings held, in fact for everything that is done out of habit and no longer produces results.

Most of these things *were* useful and made sense at the time when they were introduced. That is why the question: *What should we not have started (then)?* does not lead to the objective. *At the time* when something was introduced, there were reasons for doing so, the issue was considered thoroughly, and there were no better alternatives. However, nothing *loses value* as quickly as administrative procedures and management programs, and, at the same time, nothing becomes a well-loved habit so quickly and resists elimination so tenaciously as these.

In areas characterized by fastmoving developments it does not, of course, hurt to examine products, markets, customers, and technologies every year instead of every three years. The time intervals should be selected according to our judgment and the nature of the business. However, we should not wait longer than three years in any field to check what is still relevant and what has, in the meantime, become rubbish and dead weight.

This question should not only be applied to the enterprise as a whole, but it should be a standard *tool for every manager* to be used in their departments as well as for their personal benefit.

It would be best to reserve *one whole day each year* to discuss this question with the most important employees, and this day should indeed be reserved for *just this issue* with no other items on the agenda.

When this question is put to subordinates, some of them may be at a loss at first. They are used to being asked: *What else should we do?* The question has never been: *What should we stop doing?* Therefore, if there is a lack of clarity or some reserve in the beginning, we should insist on an answer to the question and briefly explain the reasons for the question. We will soon find a list of things that are nominated for disposal by the subordinates (especially the good ones). Long lists are made in the discussion. However, this step should not be followed with the question: *Should we or should we not eliminate these things?*, but rather: *How quickly can we get rid of them?*

As mentioned earlier, some items can be sent for "waste disposal" as soon as the decision is made; in other cases it may take years before this is possible. However, a start has at least been made, and things are moving on the right track; above all, we have steered the thinking of our subordinates in a totally different direction. We are heading for *detoxification* of the organization, towards freedom from the dead weight and habits that have been handed down.

Key to Wide-Ranging Consequences

Systematic waste disposal is the *key to at least three wide-ranging consequences. Firstly*, really effective *lean management* and the right type of *business process redesign*; *secondly*, effective *management of change* and *innovation*; and *thirdly*, effective analysis of the *essential nature* of an institution, definition of the fundamental business or organizational purpose – the *business mission*.

Properly understood, lean management and business process redesign do not mean: *How do we make everything we are doing today better, cheaper, more economical and faster?* It means starting with the question: *What should we stop doing?* In the age of computers and telecommunications, almost everything can be made "better, cheaper, and faster". To do something faster or make it 50 percent more economical is indeed a great step forward, but it is still a hundred percent wrong, if it should not be made *at all*. The real pioneers in this field have known this from the start; however, it has seldom been practiced. Far too many people are smitten by the new technologies and, therefore, find it extremely fascinating to re-engineer and make lean even those processes that should be completely *abandoned*.

Effective management of change and correct innovation management are unthinkable without ridding the organization of dead weight. Unfortunately, many think of even these tasks as something to be done in *addition* to all the existing tasks. This approach is essentially wrong. It causes existing tasks to become even more firmly entrenched, and the new task has to be done in addition to them. Large-scale programs and rituals based on the idea of an organization being capable of change, learning, and innovation have been introduced, but these waste the employees' time and keep them from the really important work. Everything is given a scientific twist, and a new type of bureaucracy is formed. Though it may indeed be a *new* form of bureaucracy, it is nonetheless bureaucracy, instead of which a simple question of "waste disposal" could be asked.

Nothing leads to such rapid and radical change as the question: *What should we stop doing? Stop doing the wrong things!* This is the best way to change an organization, and it is also the way that encounters least resistance. It is only too clear that people will resist, openly or covertly, if they have to do additional and new work. To *stop* doing something is, on the other hand, far more acceptable except to those that may fear for their jobs. If this is one of the consequences of systematic "waste disposal", this measure must be prepared with particular care and then implemented just as quickly.

However, the most important thing is that the question on detoxification almost always leads to the *real core of the matter*, to the question: *Why do we do anything at all? What is the purpose of this administrative process, this meeting, this form, etc.?* In doing this, we inevitably come to the basic purpose of an organization.

Companies, though this applies to all types of organizations, are not established for the purpose of setting up a particularly modern accounting system, highly developed personnel management, computer-enabled administration, or brilliant employment opportunities. They are formed to *satisfy customers;* they develop, manufacture and sell products and services, heal the sick, help drug addicts overcome their habits, or prevent the destruction of the environment. Accounting, the IT division, the personnel department, administration, intellectually stimulating jobs, etc. are the *consequences* (and usually not especially economic consequences) of the actual purpose of an organization.

However, these things unfortunately tend to become an *end in themselves* and develop *a life of their own.* All the support functions that are required as consequences of the main purpose of an organization have an inherent tendency to dominate, and, therefore, these things and the way in which they are handled must be repeatedly questioned in the light of the organization's main purpose.

Only in this way can an organization be compelled to become and remain dynamic, fast and productive, and only in this way is it possible to create a culture of utility maximization, of elimination of parasitic ways of thinking and behavior, and of concentration on what is really essential.

The Path to Personal Effectiveness

The method of systematic waste disposal is, at the same time, the easiest and fastest way in which managers and their subordinates can achieve personal effectiveness. I have mentioned this in passing several times, and I will repeat it once again. Effective managers set aside one day each year to consider thoroughly and conscientiously the question: *What should I stop doing – because it has outlived its use, because I have outgrown it, because I want to develop in another direction, because there are other and better methods, because there is something more important to do, because I am older now and must set other priorities, etc.?*

They then begin to systematically work on these things. They change the allocation of time in their schedule; they utilize their time in a different way; they begin to restructure their field of activities – *they throw out the dead weight.* And thus, they create space for the new things which they need if they are to succeed. This also involves the utilization of resources being *re-routed* from less productive to more productive purposes. This is a never-ending task; it must be tackled over and over again.

At the same time, these managers urge their *subordinates* to apply the same methods. Particularly when they agree upon objectives with their subordinates, they are not satisfied with only a list of goals for the coming year. They demand another list, *too,* which mentions all the things that are to be *disposed of,* to be *stopped* in the coming year.

Truly brilliant musicians have learnt to follow a simple rule that has the same effect. When they include a new piece in their repertoire, they eliminate an existing one. They know that no one, even if he is extremely talented, can play too many different pieces really brilliantly and like a virtuoso. Of course, they can play many different pieces with *a moderate degree of competence,* but *only a few* can be played at the *highest level.*

What if We Cannot Eliminate...?

Perhaps everything on the "rubbish list" cannot be completely disposed of. In such cases there are other ways to handle things according to their degree of importance to the organization and their real contribution. Perhaps the solution does not always lie in "complete disposal"; sometimes an item can be "outsourced" or "refocused". Perhaps a decision can be reached to do something with just the minimum of expense until elimination is possible at a later date. Or something may have to be positioned in a totally different way.

The *simplest* but also the *worst* way is to continue with things as they are. This creates *lethargy* and *inertia*.

On the other hand, disposing of what is outdated and throwing out the dead weight leads to the *revitalization* and *self-renewal* of an organization. It is a detoxification and self-cleansing process from the inside out, a fundamental principle in the living world. Anyone who makes this into a working method will never have to do an analysis of overhead, or an elaborate change program, and they will hardly ever have a problem with corporate culture.

A Tip in Conclusion

Because this tool cannot be used every day, it is easily overlooked and forgotten.

Therefore, effective managers fall back on a *little trick* that ensures *implementation*: In their schedules they enter the date on which they wish to use this tool with or without their subordinates. Even if they have to postpone the date, they do not let it disappear altogether from their schedule.

Once more, it should be clear that this is not about changing people by making unusual requirements of them. *Being* dynamic, capable of learning, innovative, vital, etc., and *thinking* in this way would be wonderful, but difficult. On the other hand, following a practice, using a tool once a year is quite easy. No one needs to change. One must merely adhere to a date.

Summary

Touchstone of Professionalism

The mainstay of an organization's competence is its mastery of the tools discussed here. These form the touchstone of the *craftsmanlike* side of a manager's professionalism.

The tools and their professional utilization build the bridges between efficiency and effectiveness. Principles and tasks determine what the "right things" are; the tools are the requirement for "doing them correctly".

Will computers bring about a change in their importance? Yes and no. The existing effects of information technology have brought about far *fewer* changes in the work of managers than was generally predicted 30 to 40 years ago. According to the prognosis, a veritable revolution should have taken place.

This did not happen or at least only to a marginal extent. IT has brought about a far greater change in the way of *job-related tasks* are carried out. A revolution can indeed be observed in this area. Without IT, a company's functions would not be possible today – neither research and development nor construction, design, production, logistics, and marketing. The administration of practically every organization cannot be managed without computers, and their use has, in some ways, completely changed the way these tasks are carried out.

This is not the case for management tasks. Managers who can handle computers competently are not necessarily more effective than others. If they are, it is not, because they use a computer, but because they have understood quickly and thoroughly that a computerized organization requires better, more precise, and more professional management. The information, service, and knowledge society that is emerging from the foundation of technology, science, and education cannot tolerate any dilettantism in management.

Without a mastery of these tools there can be no productivity or profitability, useful teamwork or innovation, change management or utilization of opportunities. Professionalism in the use of management tools is the lever that allows increasingly bigger, more difficult, and more complex tasks to be carried out. It is the only way in which stress can be kept under control despite continuously increasing strain.

However, what is more important is the fact that, in the unanimous opinion of experts, people require a certain amount of stress to remain healthy; there is such a thing as positive stress, eustress as it is called by the stress researcher Hans Selye. Mastery of the "craft" is one of the requirements for experiencing positive stress. Whether we have to or want to perform without the necessary equipment, we experience stress in the negative sense – distress, torture. However, anyone who can nonchalantly answer the oft-asked question: *Are you under stress?*, with: *Stress? I have a lot to do but I am not under stress....* is always a person with great professionalism, someone who "masters his or her craft". I believe this mastery is one of the most important bases for self-assurance and personal sovereignty. As I mentioned in the principle of focusing on results, it is a source of pleasure, not in work but in personal effectiveness. We undertake to do something, or there is a task to be done, and we do it, because we can.

Herein lies what could be called the actual secret of those managers who can cope with tasks that often appear to be superhuman, and still manage to remain human themselves.

Postscript

From an Art to a Profession

With this book I have attempted to erase several prevalent misconceptions, errors, and erroneous theories. One of the reasons for their stubborn persistence is that there is, *in principle*, a great lack of clarity about the nature of management. What is management? Is it an art? Is it a science?

My suggestion that management be considered a *profession* is, as I can determine on many occasions, taken as anything other than natural. It is hardly ever accepted without resistance. Reactions are very different and range from rejection to skepticism to positive surprise in the sense of "finally, someone is saying it". Therefore, at the end of this book, I wish to address a few fundamental issues related to our understanding of management for readers who are interested.

In my opinion, the best way to do this is to consider management a *practice*, a *discipline*, comparable to the professions of doctors or engineers. What counts is not whether the theory is right or wrong but rather the success of the action. It is not the diagnosis but the healing of the patient that makes a good doctor. The fact that this depends on the accuracy of the diagnosis does not have to be emphasized. The important thing is that just understanding and explaining is not enough. Application and action are an inextricable part of all professions. This differentiates them decisively from science. Managers are not paid for the accuracy of their analyses, but the results of their actions.

In section I I have made a distinction between management as a profession and management as a vocation and as an amateur activity. However, it seems necessary to me to define the boundaries of management as a *practical discipline*, and at the same time to relate it to the understanding of *management as an art, as a science,* or *as common sense.*

What I call management here must previously have been something like an art, an art of action: the art of an entrepreneur or the art of becoming rich or powerfull, or, in general terms, being successful. There have always been people who have mastered an art in this sense, and there always will be in the future. However, they are isolated phenomena. Through their behavior they reveal the *opportunities*, but they *alone* cannot change the world. This can only happen, if they can be *copied*.

To a considerable extent progress has been made in exactly the way I have suggested here by making a profession out of an art in the general sense of the word. To be more precise, by making what can be *taught* and *learnt* in an art accessible to a larger number of people, mainly through training. Though this is not possible in all fields, it has been the case in medicine and architecture, for example.

This does not make an art any less important or unique. It will probably always be the sole domain of the arts and artists to conquer new horizons and set new standards. In this way they are often the trendsetters for the *direction* of progress. Progress *itself*, its *implementation*, has been possible, however, only when an art could be turned into something that many people were capable of practicing – a profession.

The transformation of an art into a profession is not automatic. There are resistance, obstacles, and also dead-ends. I would like to highlight three of them.

Firstly, it can often be observed that there is opposition to the attempt itself. People want to keep an art an art and save it from *becoming mundane*, quite frequently with missionary zeal. It is astonishing how often we come across the opinion that management is, and must remain a question of special talents and characteristics that the average mortal does not have, and can never hope to; management is something that cannot be learnt, a person has to be born to it. Management still has the aura of the secretive and unattainable.

The idea of a vocation, of being the chosen one, is accepted with open arms. Contributing to this notion is a flood of relevant literature. Even people at the top, whose curricula vitae clearly prove that they learnt everything that helped them in their careers, tend to attach a degree of mysticism to the path to the top. Some seem to be positively ashamed of the fact that they had to learn so much in a hard and painful way, though this is in fact proof of achievement. There is nothing special about a *genius* gaining prominence through great achievements. The genius has done nothing other than use what God or the genetic code has given him by chance. However, it is certainly remarkable when people without special talent achieve something in their lives which they can attribute to their *own efforts*.

The *second* inappropriate development is the attempt to make a science out of an art which not all fields are suited to. Incorrect understanding of scientific nature or, to be more precise, the tendency to want to *convert something into a science* cannot be overlooked in management. Of course, I have no objection to science; in fact it is urgently needed in management. However, a distinction must be made between good and bad science, and attempting to make something into a science belongs to the latter category.

As a consequence of the general belief in science, even pseudo-science is accepted. Management seems to be particularly susceptible to this. The desire to use scientific knowledge is remarkably disproportionate to what people in general understand about science. Even among well-educated people there are only a few who have been educated in the theory of science, even though this field has achieved a high level of development in the last few decades. It would be useful if a majority of managers were better able to evaluate cure-alls under the label of science. A lack of knowledge in this area is one of the reasons why charlatanism and pseudo-scientific rubbish have gained a foothold in management.

I do *not* consider management itself to be a science but rather, as mentioned, a *practice*, although these days it has become a practice that is almost impossible to pursue without the support of science. The parallels to medicine are obvious here. The medical profession is a practice that is unthinkable without academic training and the knowledge of numerous sciences. Yet doctors are not scientists despite their education having had a great deal to do with science and the fact that they also apply science. The same is true in the case of management. Even the director of a scientific institution, or a laboratory, or a research institution in the business world, in fact the dean of a university, too, are not scientists in their capacity *as managers* though they can certainly be active in the field of science.

The objectives of science and management are completely *different*. If we lose sight of this fact, we can be neither good scientists nor good managers. Science is focused on *knowledge*, management on *benefits*. Science is focused on *truth*; management on *effectiveness*. Science strives for *universality*; the manager, however, deals with the *individual case*. The manager's objective is not the *acquisition* of knowledge but its *use*; not the *discovery*, but its *application*. Theory asks: *Is it true?*, while management asks: *Does it work?*

I believe that an awareness of these differences would make it relatively easy to resolve many well-known problems and misconceptions with regard to the relationship between theory and practice and hence between scientists and managers. Above all, it is only from this practical point of view that it is possible to determine the contribution management should expect from science.

The nature of management as a practice also defines something that creates great difficulties for many scientists, namely how to communicate with management if they want to be heard and understood. The reverse is also true. With this understanding the irrelevant developments usually become apparent very quickly, such as the remodeling of the mathematical and physical chaos theory that soon led to chaos management, as a result of which an important scientific theory became a harmful fad. It is the same with the term "synergy", derived from physics, which became not only impractical but also harmful due to its unmodified application.

What role does so-called *common sense* play in management? Practitioners justifiably consider common sense important, though many do this in a way that devalues what they want to uphold. In order to *increase the value* of common sense, they *devalue* theory and science, which is not necessary or justified.

This is unnecessary, because common sense is by no means an alternative to science. As is proven in modern scientific theory, the two are more closely connected than scientists would like to believe. A well-expressed justification for this is to be found, for example, in the writings of one of the most important philosophers of the twentieth century, Karl Popper. He never got tired of emphasizing that good science was common sense. He always said it was Common Sense – *Writ Large*. What he was talking about was not just *any* common sense but *critical* common sense. Not everything that enters a person's mind at a certain point in time, even if the person is very experienced and successful, is *sensible* common sense.

Common sense is an indispensable element of good management, and its value, if we want to rank it, is probably higher than that of science. However, what is most important is that *common sense is not enough*. It has its limits; it is not sufficient on its own. This is what many "full-blooded practitioners" are always happy to overlook. There are issues and problems in management, not only in large companies, which cannot be resolved by common sense *alone*, even if it is very "healthy". These issues include not only those of technology, but to an increasing extent they are issues of entrepreneurial strategy, organizational structure, accounting systems, logistics, IT, and production. However, there are also other problems related to the consequences of the organization society that can no longer be resolved without science.

I am making the suggestion that management be considered a profession in order to invoke professionalism as it is expressed through diligence, conscientiousness, and thoroughness, that is, the responsibility of the professional. Management takes on the nature of a *discipline*, a *"clinical"* practice by virtue of the fact that it is the meeting point of art, science, and common sense. It is a rational practice that not only carries out the tasks assigned to it, but can also justify its actions. Management must be committed to this; only then is social, political, and moral legitimacy possible. This view of management that I referred to as the constitutional approach at the beginning of the book is, in my opinion, the only way in which people and organizations can perform at their best in a responsible way.

Appendix

Synopsis

I have refrained from using graphics in this book. As I said in section IV with regard to reports as a management tool, it is simply not true that a picture is worth more than a thousand words, as the proverb goes. This is only applicable for those pictures that existed, when this proverb came into existence. However, they were not the abstract diagrams that are found in specialist literature today.

It certainly does not apply to the diagrams in management literature, which are not only abstract, but usually completely meaningless, illogical, and arbitrary despite being easy to create on a computer and generally very impressive in appearance. Apart from a few exceptions, they are completely superfluous. Quite frequently they seem to be fulfilling the sole purpose of at least outwardly giving the appearance of a "book", as far as the scope and volume is concerned, to what would otherwise remain a consumptive brochure.

I am not against working with graphics and visualization in principle. I have worked a lot with diagrams in some publications, perhaps not always with a sufficient level of discrimination. These days, I am rather skeptical when someone works with too many graphics, be it in a book or a lecture, and I scrutinize them properly to verify whether they really impart information and fulfill a real purpose.

The following diagram may, with all the reservations just expressed, be useful in so far as it can, at the end of the book, facilitate recollection of all the book's most important elements in context and perhaps also provide help in remembering them.

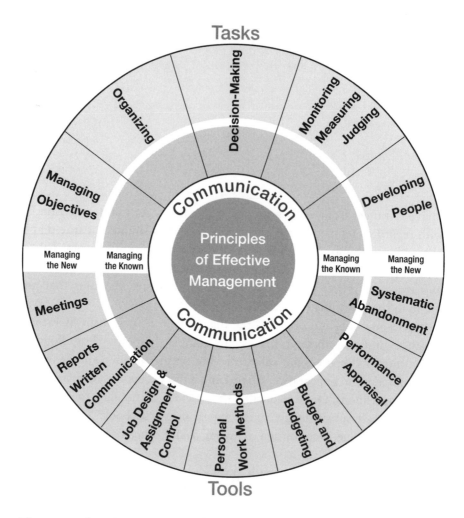

The *principles* of effective management form the innermost circle influencing everything else. In the top half of the circle are the *tasks*, while the bottom half consists of the *tools*. Through this depiction I wish to express the fact that the principles, as described, determine how tasks are carried out and tools are used. They have no meaning and no effect, if they exist in isolation, or are printed in glossy brochures, and are occasionally declared in an upbeat manner. They must guide the type and quality of managers' working methods.

Around the circle of principles are two other concentric circles that form three different rings. In the innermost ring is *communication*, corresponding to the thoughts at the end of section III, not as a task or as a tool, but as a medium through which managers do their work. The middle ring is for the *operational* and the outermost for the *innovative* work of managers. I commented on these at the same point. Managing innovations, new things, and the future is not fundamentally different from managing operations, familiar things, and the present. They are different fields of the application of management. In both cases the same tasks need to be carried out and the same tools need to be used; it is only the conditions of application that differ in their degree of difficulty.

Literature

Bateson, Gregory, *Steps to an Ecology of Mind*, New York 1972.

Bland, Larry I. (ed.), *The War Reports of General of the Army G. C. Marshall, General of the Army H. H. Arnold, and Fleet Admiral E. I. King*, Philadelphia/New York 1947.

Bland, Larry I. (ed.), *The Papers of George C. Marshall*, 3 vols. 1981-1991.

Cray, Ed, *General of the Army. George C. Marshall – Soldier and Statesman*, New York 2000.

Drucker, Peter F., *"The Effective Decision"*, in: *Harvard Business Review*, Jan./Feb. 1967.

– *Adventures of a Bystander*, New York 1978, 2nd ed. 1994.

– *Management*, New York 1974, 5th ed. 1994.

– *The Age of Discontinuity*, London 1969, 2nd ed. 1994.

– *The Effective Executive*, New York 1966.

– *The Practice of Management*, New York 1955, 17th ed. 1995.

– *Zaungast der Zeit*, Düsseldorf/Vienna 1979.

Eccles, John C., *Die Evolution des Gehirns – die Erschaffung des Selbst*, Munich 1989, 3rd ed. 1994.

Frankl, Viktor; *Der Mensch vor der Frage nach dem Sinn*, Munich/Zurich, 3rd ed. 1982.

Gomez, Peter/Malik, Fredmund/Oeller, Karl-Heinz, *Systemmethodik: Grundlagen einer Methodik zur Erforschung und Gestaltung komplexer soziotechnischer Systeme*, 2 vols., Bern/Stuttgart 1975.

Gross, Johannes, *Von Geschichte umgeben. Festschrift für Joachim Fest*, Berlin 1986.

Hayek, Friedrich August von, *Die Verfassung der Freiheit*, Tübingen 1971.

– *Law, Legislation and Liberty*, London 1973-1979.

IMD Lausanne/LBS London/The Wharton School of the University of Pennsylvania (ed.), *Mastering Management – Das MBA-Buch*, 1997.

Kouzes, James M. and Posner, Barry Z., "The Credibility Factor: What Followers Expect From Their Leaders", in: *Management Review*, Jan. 1990.

Lindemann, Hannes, *Allein über den Ozean*, Berlin 1993.

Malik, Fredmund, *Strategie des Managements komplexer Systeme*, Bern/Stuttgart/Vienna 1984, 5th enlarged ed. 1996.

– *Wirksame Unternehmensaufsicht. Corporate Governance in Umbruchszeiten*, 2nd ed., Frankfurt am Main 1999.

Miller, George A., "The Magical Number Seven Plus/Minus Two", in: *Psychological Review*, No. 63, 1956.

Otte, Max, *Amerika fur Geschäftsleute*, Frankfurt am Main 1998.

Pelzman, Linda, *Was nicht im Personalakt stehen darf. Critical Incidents: Informationsquelle für verborgene Risiken*, St. Gallen 1999.

Peters, Thomas J. and Waterman, Robert H. Jr., *In Search of Excellence*, New York 1982.

Piaget, Jean, *Einführung in die genetische Erkenntnistheorie*, Frankfurt am Main 1973.

Popper, Karl R. and Eccles, John CL., *The Self and its Brain*, New York 1977.

Popper, Karl R., *Conjectures and Refutation*, London 1963, 4th ed. 1972.

Puryear, Edgar F. Jr., *Nineteen Stars. A Study in Military Character and Leadership*, Washington, DC 1971.

Radlinger, Lorenz/Iser, Walter/Zittermann, Hubert, *Bergsporttraining*, Munich 1983.

Reitz, Manfred, "Zellulare Müllabfuhr", in: *Pharm. Ind. 59*, 1997.

Schaffelhuber, Stefan, *Inner Coaching*, Frankfurt/Berlin 1993.

Schneider, Wolf, *Deutsch für Profis*, Hamburg 1986.

– *Die Sieger. Wodurch Genies, Phantasten und Verbrecher berühmt geworden sind*, Hamburg 1992.

Schultz, I. H., *Das autogene Training*, New York 1932, 18th ed. 1987.

Searle, John, *Minds, Brains and Science*, Cambridge 1984.

Shapley, Deborah, *Promise and Power. The Life and Times of Robert McNamara*, Boston 1993.

Sherwood, Robert E., *Roosevelt and Hopkins. An Intimate History*, New York 1948.

Siegwart, Hans, *Kennzahlen für die Unternehmensführung*, Bern/Stuttgart/Vienna, 5th ed. 1998.

Stemme, Fritz and Reinhardt, Karl-Walter, *Supertraining*, Düsseldorf 1988, 3rd ed. 1990.

Tuchmann, Barbara, *Die Torheit der Regierenden*, Frankfurt am Main, 3rd ed. 1984.

Watzlawick, Paul; *Gebrauchsanweisung für Amerika*, Munich/Zurich 1978, 7th ed. 1984.

Zand, Dale E., *Wissen, Führen, Überzeugen*, Heidelberg 1983.

Zimmer, Dieter E., *Die Elektrifizierung der Sprache*, Munich 1997.

– *Tiefenschwindel*, Hamburg 1986.

Index